SECOND EDITION

Victoria Nabors

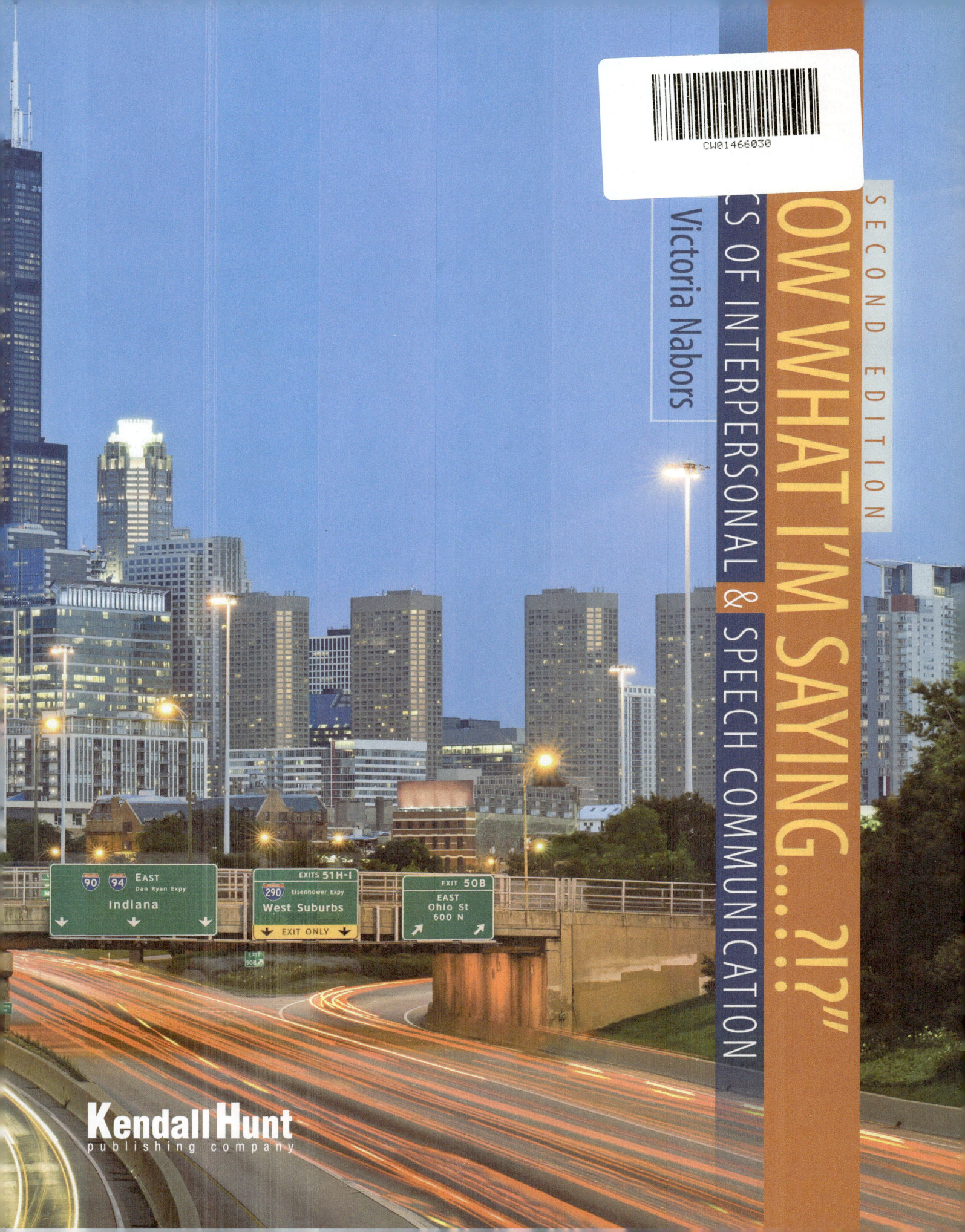

OW WHAT I'M SAYING...?!?"

CS OF INTERPERSONAL & SPEECH COMMUNICATION

Kendall Hunt
publishing company

Cover image © Shutterstock, Inc.

Kendall Hunt
publishing company

www.kendallhunt.com
Send all inquiries to:
4050 Westmark Drive
Dubuque, IA 52004-1840

Copyright © 2015 by Victoria Nabors

ISBN 978-1-4652-7703-9

Printed in the United States of America

Contents

Note to students from the author

This textbook/workbook was designed with you in mind. As you flip through the pages, you will notice that this is not your typical collage textbook. It was developed from student feedback combined with years of studying the learning preferences of Millennial and Generation X learners. The layout of this text shifts the paradigm (Google it - LOL) of how learning content is organized in textbooks. Internet access is integrated into most lessons as the technological era that we live in creates exciting and engaging avenues from which to research, learn, explore, and grow.

If you use this communication textbook/workbook the way in which it was designed, you will quickly discover its hands-on approach that supports your development from one lesson to the next. Each chapter includes brief lessons followed by an example of the lesson and a comprehension practice question. The purpose of the comprehension questions is to help you apply each newly learned skill to real life experiences. It is important that you respond to these questions after reading each assigned section to be prepared for class discussion. Because humans are unique, everyone will bring different experiences to the conversation that makes learning more personal and interesting. You will also find homework assignments in many chapters that ask you to think critically about a prompt and respond in writing to it.

The prompts in Part One require you to view television programs and YouTube video clips to identify examples of human communication behaviors in action. Part Two introduces public speaking and provides students with a step-by-step building process towards the first speech presentation. Part Three is divided into two appendixes that include tear out assignments, grading rubrics, and other learning activities, everything you need be successful in this course. The perforated format is designed to make it easy to tear out the homework, speech assignments and outlines.

I hope you enjoy using this textbook/workbook to improve your overall communication skills.

Sincerely,
Victoria Nabors
Professor of Human Communication Studies

Do you know your learning style?

Have you ever studied by using your learning style?

Have you ever spent a whole weekend studying for an exam but still earned a low grade? There's a possible explanation for that frustrating outcome; you probably didn't study by using strategies that reflect how you learn. Most people can tell you how they learn; visual, auditory, or touch - but that's about it. Wise students are intentional about how they approach new skills; they organize their study material in a way that reflects their learning style.

It just makes sense - "Work smarter, not harder!"

There are three primary ways that we learn: auditory (listening), visual (watching/seeing), and tactile (hands-on). Knowing your preferred learning style can help you:
- understand how you learn best
- identify study strategies that are helpful when studying for exams
- study more efficiently and effectively in a way that saves wasted time.
- enjoy greater academic success in your courses

There are many types of learning style assessments that you can take to get a clearer understanding of you personal learning style. Most people have a primary and a secondary learning style. The easiest way to discover your learning style is to take a learning style quiz. You can Google *"learning style quiz,"* or, go to one of the following websites to complete a learning style survey. Select one that is best for you.

1. Education planner (you will answer twenty questions)
   http://www.educationplanner.org/students/self-assessments/learning-styles-quiz.shtml
2. VARK a guide to learning style (a more in-depth survey requires more time)
   http://www.vark-learn.com/english/page.asp?p=questionnaire

## PART 1

Interpersonal Communication and You

Introduction to Interpersonal Communication

This chapter will answer the following questions:

WHAT *are the benefits of improving your communication behaviors?*

WHY *is human communication important?*

WHAT *is communication?*

HOW *messages are sent and received?*

VOCABULARY BUILDERS: *Blithesome*, adjective
Light hearted; merry; cheerful
"I will remain blithesome throughout my stressful college years."
Fortuitous, adjective
Happening by chance, good luck
"If it had not been for our fortuitous meeting, I would have never gotten my nerve to approach you."

Communication is a skill that you can learn. It's like riding a bicycle or typing. If you're willing to work at it, you can rapidly improve the quality of every part of your life.

—Brian Tracy

Just about everything we desire in life must be communicated through verbal or nonverbal means. Unfortunately, sharing our thoughts and feelings accurately is not easy because people create meaning through their personal experiences. Since no two people are the same, or share the same experiences, the meaning of a message will be misunderstood quite often. Think about it. How often have you had to repeat something you said to a friend because they didn't understand? It happens more often then you might think. Acquiring effective communication skills can help strengthen your ability to be understood, and avoid these frustrating situations.

Listening is directly related to human communication because we must listen effectively to understand and respond. At times a message that we receive will not require us to respond; while other times the message asks us to do something. The truth is that most people are poor listeners because listening is an active process which requires us to make sense of what we hear. Listening skills will be discussed further in Chapter Three. Chapter One presents a basic introduction to interpersonal communication studies and explain the importance of communication to human survival.

Benefits of Improving Communication Behaviors

Question: Do you believe that you have excellent or moderate communication & listening skills? Not sure! Consider the following questions.

1. How often are your communicated intentions misunderstood?
2. How many times have you found yourself in situations where you just couldn't find the right words to express what you are feeling?
3. How many times did you think you were listening to someone, only to find that you hadn't heard a word they said?

The answers to these questions are probably, *"quite often*!"
The truth is that most people are poor communicators because they lack skills.

Studying human communication is essential. Why? Because strategic and concise communication helps us satisfy basic and higher level desires. In learning how to translate feelings into thoughts, and thoughts into appropriate verbal expressions can greatly improve your ability to be understood. Strategic listening skill must also accompany communication endeavors as they work together to achieve desired results. It is through effective listening that we are able to comprehend meaning and respond appropriately. Still, know that comprehending messages sent by others will always present some form of challenge. Studies show that we will misunderstand others or will be misunderstood almost 90% of the time. When you live in a diverse country like the United States, assigning meaning to messages from others can be a matter of perception. As such, acquiring effective communication and listening skills are critical assets to have as you set out to achieve various goals. Whether studying with classmates or interviewing for a job, your ability to express yourself in meaningful ways will result in personal fulfillment. This textbook will is designed to assist in the development of key communication and listening skills.

It is helpful to begin by reflecting on your current communication behaviors. Think about interactions you've had with people where mutual understanding came easy, and other times where miscommunication occurred often. Different types of interactions play a critical role in how miscommunication occurs. For example, it's rare when your close friends misunderstand the intentions of your messages because they've learned how you think. However, this outcome is not the same when talking to general acquaintances, certain family members, classmates, or strangers. Sometimes you may have trouble finding the right words to express your thoughts and feelings. Other times you find that you struggle to respond appropriately because you don't understand what they're asking you.

To measure your growth over the course of this semester, you must identify three areas of weaknesses that you will focus on strengthening.

Levels of Communication

YOUR COMMUNICATION SKILLS INVENTORY
Use full sentences to list three communication skills that you are most interested in improving.

1. _____

   _____

2. _____

   _____

3. _____

   _____

Communication occurs on different levels as shown in the table below.

Intrapersonal Communication This form takes place within a single person, often for the purpose of clarifying ideas or analyzing a situation. Another goal of intrapersonal communication is to reflect upon or appreciate something. Also known as "self-talk," intrapersonal communication involves talking to oneself; internally or externally.	
Interpersonal Communication This form of communication involves two individuals engaging in conversation. This form of communication is also known as a "dyad." Interpersonal communication is often identified as interpersonal interactions	
Group Communication This form of communication involves up to eight individuals who usually form to solve problems, plan events, or socialize. Group communication may also involve interpersonal interactions between the participants.	
Public/Mass Communication This form of communication commonly known as public speaking where one individual addresses listeners. When a speech is broadcast through television, radio, or Internet platforms it is considered mass communication.	
Electronic/Mediated Communication This form of communication has quickly evolved as a result of advance Internet technologies. Computers, laptops, tablets, and smartphones are quite busy today hosting conversations via Facebook, text messaging, Skype, email, and other Internet supported applications that allow for real time communication.	

SHARE YOUR UNDERSTANDING!

Read the five scenarios below to identify and explain the level of communication.

1. You and three friends have gathered outside of a nightclub for a night of fun. One friend pulls you aside and asked if you would loan him some money because he didn't have a chance to cash his check.

   Answer: _____

   Explain your answer: _____

   _____

2. Ron and his assigned project partner are at their workstations in a biology class. The lab assignment is to dissect an animal. The teacher informs the class that the mystery animal is a baby pig. Ron is not afraid of dissecting animals, but he never considered that the animal would be a baby pig. Ron thinks about Otis, his family's little pot belly pig, and become concerned. "Can I do it?" he wonders.

   Answer: _____

   Explain your answer: _____

   _____

3. Your just received a text message from your sister asking you to pick her up from work later that night. You respond, "Sure! "Identify the level of communication in this scenario.

   Answer: _____

   Explain your answer: _____

   _____

4. A large group of college students have gathered in the student union of their college campus to listen to the presidential state of the union address on a large screen television provided by the college. Identify the level of communication in this scenario.

   Answer: _____

   Explain your answer: _____

   _____

5. Neighbors who live in a community that has experienced ongoing flooding in their homes have gathered in front of their alderman's office to confront her about the problem. After a half hour of yelling for her to come out and respond to their concerns she emerges and begins to address her constituents.

   Answer: _____

   Explain your answer: _____

   _____

Why Human Communication is Important

Communication is a human need

Through interpersonal interaction, people are able to satisfy four basic survival needs: *physical*, *identity*, *social*, and *practical goals*. Let's look at each of these important human survival needs satisfied through communication.

We satisfy physical needs

Think of this "need" as the link between human interaction and physical well-being. Human touch and interactions are important and necessary to maintain health. We are highly social creatures unlike certain animals that are wired to live isolated lives. People who are isolated from others because of unexpected circumstances such as rejection or loss risk becoming emotionally and physically ill. As listed below, studies have identified many health problems that result from extended periods of forced isolation.

1. A 1997 study by medical researcher Sheldon Cohen suggests that socially isolated people are four times more susceptible to catch a common cold than people who have active social lives.

2. People who are isolated from others are two to three times more likely to die prematurely than those who have strong relationships.

3. Research shows that divorced men, younger than seventy, die from certain diseases at a higher rate than married men.

4. Divorce people are at much higher risks of developing cancer than their married counterparts.

5. The likelihood of death increases when a close relative dies.

Self-isolation is not the same as forced isolation. At times, we feel a need to self-isolate for reflection, mental health, or personal reasons. This type of isolation is considered healthy because the person will eventually end their self-isolation. The bottom line is that people are able to satisfy their physical needs when they have close relationships with family or a circle of friends. People need human touch, such as a hug or a pat on the back; and, require meaningful interpersonal interactions with others because humans are social in nature.

Close Friendships / Romantic Relationships

Belonging and feeling connected

"In everyone's life, at some time, our inner fire goes out. It is then burst into flame by an encounter with another human being. We should all be thankful for those people who rekindle the inner spirit."

—*Albert Schweitzer*

SHARE YOUR EXPERIENCE

Provide one example of how your physical needs are satisfied through interactions with others.

_____

_____

_____

_____

We satisfy identity needs

"Who am I?" We learn who we are through feedback from others. For example, it is quite amusing to watch an infant discover her or his fingers or toes. Over time, they understand that these strange things connected to their body are called arms and legs because someone communicated this to them. Babies learn more about their identity as they interact with parents, grandparents, siblings, or caretakers. Such information learned includes their name, gender, and personality characteristics. As the child grows older, she or he will begin to accept commonly used labels (names) that parents, siblings, or grandparents use to define their characteristics or behaviors: adorable, mischievous, smart, dependable, disobedient, leader, easy-going, or helpful. Without communication from others we would not know who we are. As we grow, our identity is further shaped by this type feedback and impacts how we think and speak.

What labels (names) were used to describe or define your behaviors as a child that you eventually accepted as true? Example: Your older sister always called you goofy. Eventually, you began to believe you were goofy. As an adult your behaviors reflected one of being "silly."

Identify your labels:

_____

_____

_____

_____

_____

Who Are U?

Another way that identity forms is through social interactions with people that we feel a special connection to. These interactions can *change* or *confirm* parts of our identity.

- **CHANGE:** At times, we mirror certain behaviors of people that we feel connected to. For example: Your good friend always uses the word, "Really!" to express displeasure or disbelief. Over time, you pick up that expression and unconsciously begin to use it. Another way that social interaction can change identity occurs when you feel a close connection to another person. You find yourself wearing similar attire, colors, or even hairstyles. This action can be conscious or unconscious. When people feel a close connection, they tend to mirror one another.

- **CONFIRM:** Interpersonal interactions with like minded people can help to validate your feelings, ideas and uniqueness. Confirmation occurs when parties support each other's unique views, ways of behaving, or supports each other's ideas or aspirations. People normally generate towards others who are like them because having that type of support affirms their identity.

We satisfy social needs

> *"One of the most beautiful qualities of true friendship is to understand and to be understood."*
>
> —*Lcius Annaeus Seneca*

Because humans are social creatures, we also have social needs that we seek to fulfill through friendships building. Ongoing studies have shown that humans are healthier when they are accepted socially. The truth, however, is that fulfilling social needs can be one of the most stressful challenges or amazing accomplishments that we'll experience because getting to know a person intimately takes time and patience. Still, most of us manage to attract a like-minded person or circle of circle of friends to fulfill social needs. Below are several ways that we achieve this goal.

- Pleasure—having a good time with people in a way that releases "feel good" hormones.
- Affection—caring for others and being cared for when in need.
- Inclusion—feeling included in activities and having someone to talk to who understands you.
- Escape—delaying a task until later to have time for socialization.
- Relaxation—taking time to unwind and relax with others.
- Control—taking charge of a situation to reach a goal.
- Competition—challenging others to a competitive game or sport

SHARE YOUR EXPERIENCE

How do you satisfy your social needs?

_____

_____

_____

_____

We satisfy practical goals

The fourth basic human need that is satisfied through communication is "practical goals," which is achieved when you get others to do what you want them to do – compliance. For example, during a job interview, your practical goal is to get the interviewer to agree that you are the best person for the job. The outcome of getting the job is a paycheck that allows you to be self-sufficient and not have to depend on others. Here are some additional examples of practical goals that are satisfied through communication.

- A trip to the barber or beauty shop: You use descriptive communication to explain how you want your hair cut or styled to avoid a horrible outcome. The practical goal in this scenario is to get the barber or stylist to comprehend and apply.

- In a public speaking class: You've worked hard on your first major speech and are preparing to present it to your class. The practical goal in this scenario is to be heard.

Without communication we would not be able to satisfy our practical goal of gaining compliance from others.

Three methods of communication are used to satisfy practical goals:

Informative communication is sharing knowledge and understanding with others, but does not go as far as telling the listeners what to do or think.

- *Practical Goal:* To convince others to listen to information you wish to share with them.

Persuasive communication occurs when we attempt to change, reinforce, or modify another person's beliefs or actions.

- *Practical Goal:* To get others to stop doing or thinking something, or to start doing or thinking something.

Entertainment communication occurs when we desire to share good feelings, celebrate an event, or pay tribute to the achievements of others.

- *Practical Goal:* To transfer our feeling good-will, happiness, inspiration, or pleasure to the audience.

Abraham Maslow's Hierarchy of Human Needs

Abraham Maslow, an American psychologist felt that human communication satisfied more than the four basic needs as previously discussed. Maslow developed a pyramid-shaped model that builds upon the four basic human needs that we just investigated; you will notice some over-lapping areas between the lower level basic needs and Maslow's higher level needs. He ranks human needs satisfied through communication from lower level needs at the base of the triangle to higher level at the peak. When people fulfill a level of need, they feel comfortable moving up to the next level of needs to fulfill them. The following is a description of needs that are fulfilled at each level of the pyramid beginning at the bottom.

- **Physiological needs** are our most basic human needs required to survive: air, water, food, shelter, and rest. Once these needs are met, we feel comfortable looking to the next level of needs.
- **Safety needs** refers to feeling protected from harms. Safety measures include law enforcement, regulations that prevent air and water pollution, and food contamination. Once we feel secure we search for friendships.
- **Social needs** reflect a human desire to feel loved and accepted by others, and to feel connected to social groups outside of the family unit.
- **Self-esteem** needs are satisfied when we feel good about who we are; we have self-respect. People need to achieve self-respect and know that they are respected by others. When we feel good about ourselves, we feel prepared to fulfill personal goals.
- **Self-actualization** refers to personal growth and potential. Humans have a desire to know that they have achieved their goals and enjoy self-fulfillment. Self-actualization goals are not the same for everyone. Some individuals may desire a simple job with earnings that pays the bills and provides a little extra for entertainment. While others seek careers that require an advanced degree or training. Examples: Artist may feel that they've reached this level when they sell one of their pieces of art for a decent price. And others, when they meet and marry the person of their dreams or become parents. Self-actualization may occur several times in a person's life as they seek out and reach for new goals.

ABRAHAM MASLOW'S
Pyramid of Self-Actualization

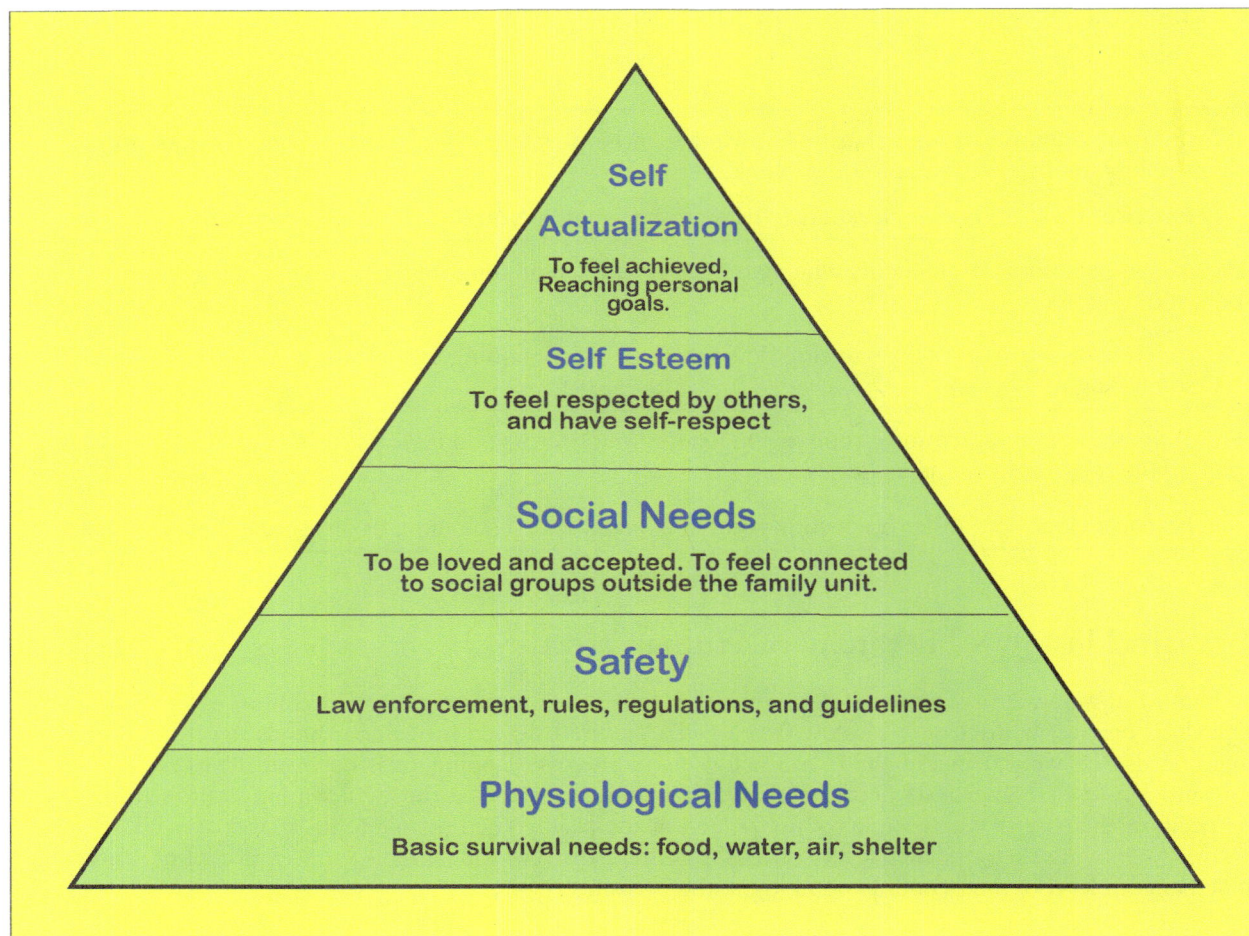

Self Actualization
To feel achieved, Reaching personal goals.

Self Esteem
To feel respected by others, and have self-respect

Social Needs
To be loved and accepted. To feel connected to social groups outside the family unit.

Safety
Law enforcement, rules, regulations, and guidelines

Physiological Needs
Basic survival needs: food, water, air, shelter

SHARE YOUR UNDERSTANDING

Self- actualization goals are different for everybody. For some, college graduation that leads to a prized career is required in order to feel achieved. For others, living up to one's potential can simply mean graduating from high school, getting a job, a spouse, an apartment, and big screen television.

Have you reached a level of self-actualization to date? Explain. What achievement are you seeking to met to feel fully actualized?

_____

_____

_____

_____

_____

_____

_____

_____

_____

_____

_____

_____

_____

_____

_____

_____

_____

_____

_____

_____

_____

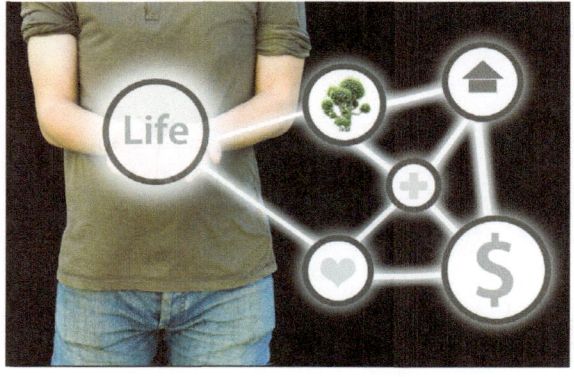

HOMEWORK!

This assignment involves viewing your favorite television programs to **identify three examples** of how the characters satisfy basic needs as learned in this section. Once you identify a television program, describe the shows and the characters that you will focus on. Next, select interpersonal interactions between the characters that provides clear example of how they use communication to satisfy their needs. Concepts that you should focus on to complete this assignment are: physical, identity, social needs, and practical goals, as well as Maslow's Hierarchy of Human Needs model.

You may be asked to share this response with a peer, on in a small group, before submitting for a grade.

NAME: _____   DATE: _____

Televised Show: _____

Brief Description of Show: _____

Characters: _____

Example #1:

Describe clearly what communication need is satisfied in the interactions between the parties in this scene and how?

_____

_____

_____

_____

_____

_____

_____

_____

_____

_____

_____

_____

_____

Example #2:

Describe clearly what communication need is satisfied in the interactions between the parties in this scene and how?

_____

_____

_____

_____

_____

_____

_____

_____

_____

_____

_____

_____

Example #3:

Describe clearly what communication need is satisfied in the interactions between the parties in this scene and how?

_____

_____

_____

_____

_____

_____

_____

_____

_____

_____

_____

_____

What is Communication?

Now that we understand how important communication is to human survival, let's define human communication. Scholars have come up with over 127 definitions that describe human communication. Although each varies to some degree, all include two words "process" and "product." Therefore, a basic definition of human communication suggests that it is *"an ongoing **process** of sending and receiving verbal and non-verbal messages that leads to a desired **product** (meaning)."* Verbal message are messages composed of words understood by others. Non-verbal messages include body-movement, facial expressions, gestures, and vocal sounds.

Communication is a Process and a Product

Dictionary definitions define a process and product as the following:

- A *process* is a series of actions that produce something or that lead to a particular result.
- A *product* is the end result of a process.

Example 1:

- **The process** required to earn a college degree begins by applying to a college. The next steps are registering for classes and completing each class with a grade of seventy percent or higher. Steps in this process are repeated each semester until enough credits have been earned to meet graduation requirements.
- **The end product** of this journey is graduation.

A process involves ongoing actions that must be taken to achieve a final product!

Now that you have a better understanding of a process that leads to a product, let's apply this concept to human communication, which is the process of sending and receiving messages that create meaning. The end product of sending and receiving messages must be mutual understanding. If the communicators do not achieve an agreed understanding of the messages, then communication has not occurred.

Communication Example 2:

- **The process:** Two friends engage in a conversation.
  Jalen: Let's to go to the beach, it's hot. Grab your trunks!
  Martin: Yup, it is a scorcher ... makes my head hurt ... feel like crap. (*Martin doesn't want to go.*)
  Jalen: No prob! Pop a few of those pain relievers and you'll be good as new.
  Martin: Well, my gas tank and my pockets empty. (*Martin really doesn't want to go*)
  Jalen: You don't need money, it's the beach! I have to run home to get my swim trunks. I'll be right back, you can drive!
  Martin: But!
- **There is no end product.** Martin's vague responses and Jalen's partial listening has prevented them from achieving an agreed upon understanding (the product).

In other words: *Just because you direct a message to someone doesn't mean you've communicated with that person. There cannot be a product without mutual understanding.*

How Messages are Sent and Received
Transactional Communication Elements Model

A transaction is an exchange of something such as services or money. Therefore, communication between two or more parties is seen as a transaction where messages are sent and received in a cyclical pattern. The communication elements model below is used to provide a visual image of how messages are created, sent, received, and misunderstood.

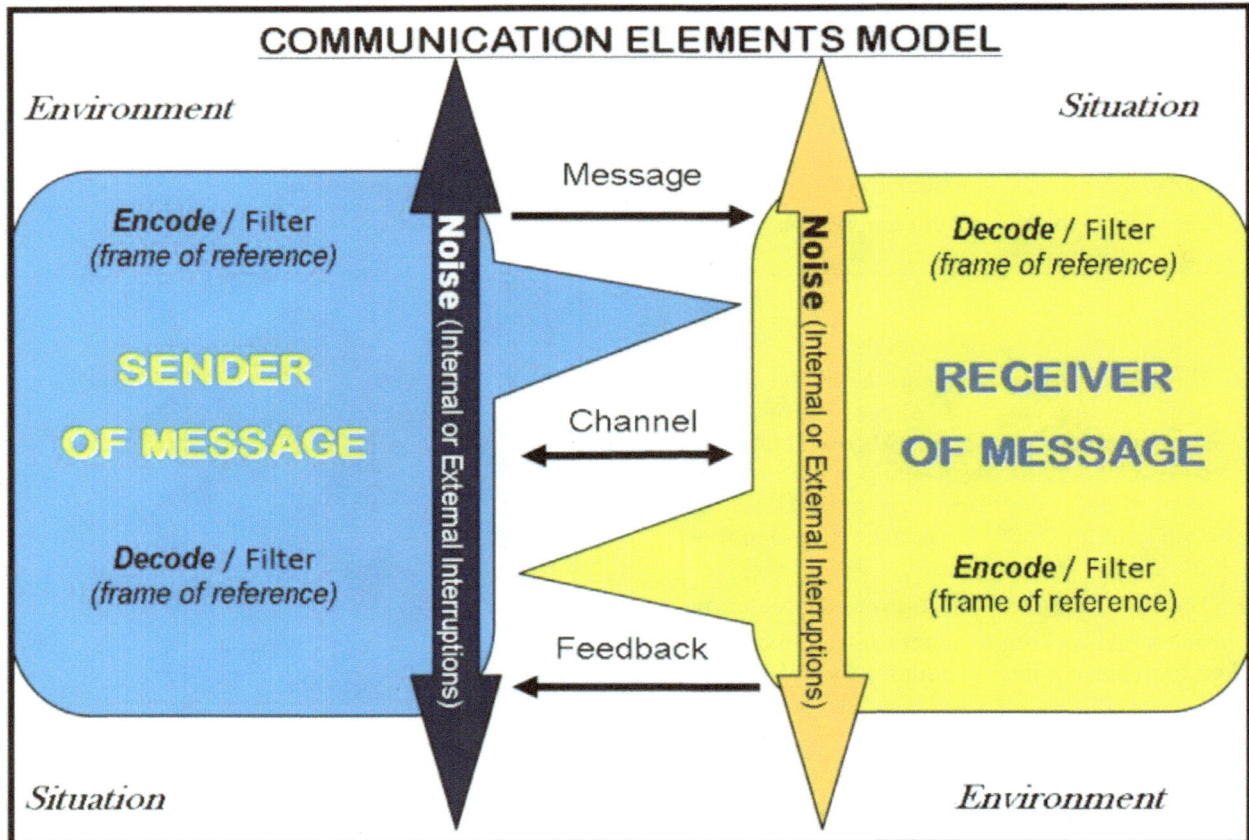

COMMUNICATION ELEMENTS MODEL

Environment   *Situation*

Encode / Filter
(frame of reference)

Message

Decode / Filter
(frame of reference)

Noise (Internal or External Interruptions)

Noise (Internal or External Interruptions)

SENDER OF MESSAGE

Channel

RECEIVER OF MESSAGE

Decode / Filter
(frame of reference)

Encode / Filter
(frame of reference)

Feedback

Situation   *Environment*

The eleven elements of the communication elements model

1. **Encode:** the process of translate ones feelings and thoughts into a message composed of agreed upon symbols and cues that create meaning. Symbols are words or numbers. Cues are non-verbal expressions such as vocal tone or facial expressions that combined with the symbols create meaning.

2. **Decode:** the process of receiving and interpreting the meaning of a message in order to respond with feedback.

3. **Feedback:** consists of verbal and nonverbal responses encoded by the receiver of the message sent to the sender or the message.

4. **Sender of Message:** the person who initiates the message by encoding feelings into thoughts that are transmitted to one or more receivers.

5. **Receiver of Message** is the person decoding the message in order to provide feedback.

6. **Message:** is the encoded thoughts and feels of a communicator sent to a receiver.
   consists of feelings and thoughts that are translated into meaningful symbols before being sent to a receiver.

7. **Noise:** anything that interferes with the accurate receipt of a message. There are two types of noise: *internal* and *external*. External noise occurs outside of you. Examples can be street noise or someone coughing. Internal noise occurs on two levels: *psychological* and *physiological*. Psychological distractions occur when personal thoughts such as fear, excitement, or confusion interfere with encoding or decoding a message. Physiological noise is biological distractions such as hunger, illness, or fatigue that might challenge your ability to think clearly. All interfere with the accuracy of encoding or decoding messages.

8. **Channel:** refers to the method in which a message is transmitted, such as face-to-face, email, phone call, text message, or Skype.

9. **Environment:** is the location where communication occurs; such as, a classroom or park.

10. **Situation:** refers to the specific reason for the communication. Examples are a student/teacher conference, or friends chatting about an assignment.

11. **Frame of Reference:** is composed of a person's life experiences, values, beliefs, and traditions. The frame of reference works as a filter that messages travel through as they are sent or received. When a speaker encodes a message and prepares to send it for example, that message will first filter through their frame of reference as it travels to the receiver. This means the message may be altered to some degree when it travels through the frame of reference. Seepage often occurs because the message picks up hidden emotions or concerns that the communicator does not wish to express. At that point, two message are sent; a verbal and an unintended non-verbal. An example of this can be understood by looking at a hypothetical situation where a sender intentionally encodes a polite message that does not reveal his true annoyance. But, as the message travels through his frame of reference, his annoyance is leaked by the tone of his voice (the non-verbal message). This example shows how two messages are sent when we communicate with others; the encoded message and the frame of reference.

    The frame of reference can also make communication more or less complicated in interpersonal interactions. As shown below, when the two parties share some degree of over-lap in their frames of reference communication will be easier. On the other hand, when two parties do not share any overlapping areas in their experiences, values, or beliefs (frame of reference), communication and understanding will be complicated.

Frame of Reference With Over-lapping areas: Communicators A & B

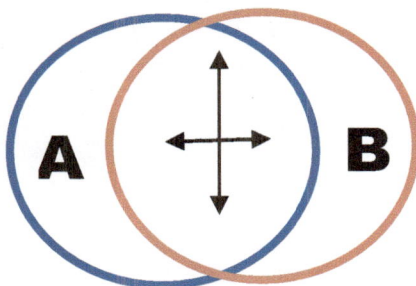

Frame of Reference No Over-lapping areas: Communicators A & B

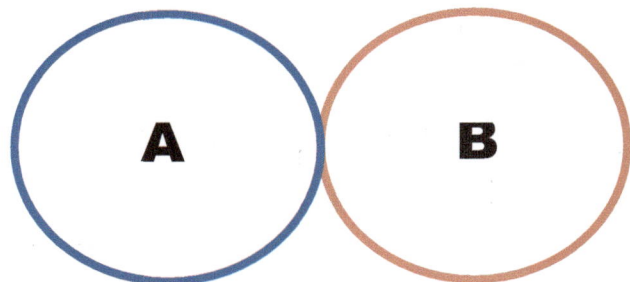

SHARE YOUR UNDERSTANDING

To better understand how the frame of reference works in interpersonal interactions, compare you frame of reference to a person you feel close to. How much over-lapping exists between the two, and how does this affect communication between the two of you?

_____

_____

_____

_____

_____

_____

_____

_____

YOUR CHAPTER NOTES

Use this section to jot down notes from this chapter that will assist with the homework assignments that follow. Your notes will also assist when studying for the chapter quiz.

_____

_____

_____

_____

_____

_____

_____

_____

NAME: _____ DATE: _____ PAGE: _____

_____

_____

_____

_____

_____

_____

_____

_____

_____

_____

Summary

In this chapter, we learned how communication serves as a vital bridge to survival. Because humans are social creatures, we thrive on interpersonal interactions with others achieving a healthy level of well-being. Through such interactions, we are able to satisfy physical needs, identity needs, social needs, and practical goals. Communication occurs on five levels: intrapersonal self-talk, interpersonal dyads, public, small groups, and electronic/ mediated. From birth, feedback from others that we respect or feel connected to helps shape our identity, which impacts how we think and communicate. Feedback from others is the only way we learn who we are.

Abraham Maslow's hierarchy of human needs is a model that builds upon the four basic human needs. His pyramid-shaped model provides us with a visual image of how humans set out to fulfill higher level needs after we achieve comfort satisfying lower level ones. The pyramid moves upwards from the base beginning with: physiological needs, safety needs, social interactions, self-esteem needs, and self-actualization. The Transactional Communication Model provides us with a visual map that shows how messages are sent, received, and distorted. Studying human communication and improving listening skills is important because each provides students with skills from which to express their thoughts and feelings concisely without being misunderstood.

Key Terms

Physical Needs

Identity Needs

Social Needs

Practical Goals

Hierarchy of Human Needs

Process and Product

Intrapersonal Communication

Interpersonal Communication

Group Communication

Public/Mass Communication

Electronic/Mediated Communication

Receiver

Encode

Decode

Feedback

Message

Noise

Channel

Environment/Situations

Frame of Reference

Looking In: Understanding Your Communication Style

VOCABULARY BUILDERS: *Cognizant*, adjective
To be aware of something
"My tutor was cognizant of my fatigue and suggested that we stop."
Equivocate, verb
To be intentionally ambiguous or unclear
"The politician was known to equivocate if asked about gay marriage."

## CHAPTER 2

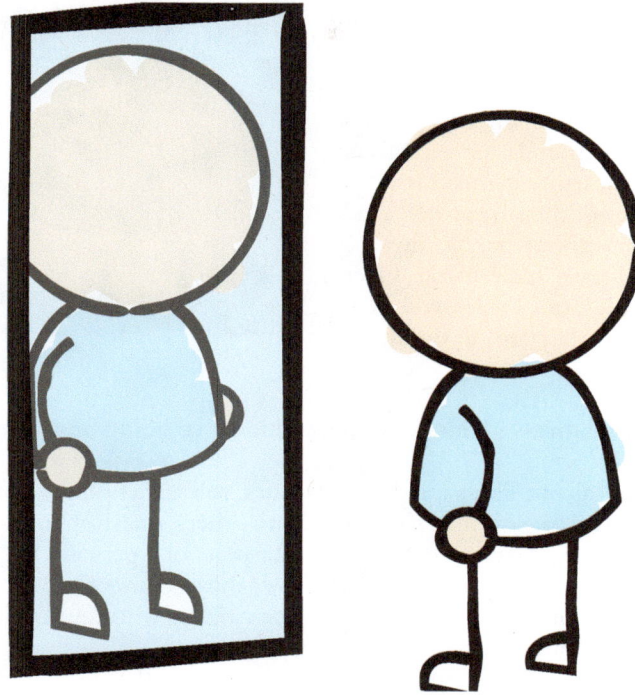

The Looking Glass Effect

"Who Am I?" - "Am I Who Others Say I Am?"

Communication Shapes Personality

"Words! What power they hold. Once they have rooted in your psyche, it is difficult to escape them.
Words can shape the future of a child and destroy the existence of an adult.
Words are powerful. Be careful how you use them because once you have pronounced them,
you cannot remove the scar they leave behind."

—Vashti Quiroz-Vega

Words created you. Feedback from others is the only way that we can satisfy our identify need. When you were born, you were a cute cuddly infant with no notion of anything. You didn't know your gender. You didn't understand the concept of food! You didn't know what pizza, hamburgers, or barbecue was. You were simply an adorable newborn who drooled and smiled when someone played with you, cried when you were hungry, and created lots of messy diapers.

Communication Shapes Personality

The Self-Concept

From birth the young discovers many new aspects about themselves as family, friends, or caretakers interact with them. They learn that those strange things attached to the sides of their head are called ears. The baby also learns about hands, fingers, and feet. They especially learn their name. Over the first 25 years, feedback from others will help the youngster discover who they are; in doing so, the self-concept is born.

The self-concept is a relatively stable set of perceptions we hold about ourselves.

The self-concept is our talents, likes, and dislikes, values, roles, friendliness, and other important characteristics that define who we are. As we continue to interact with others, questions such as, "Who am I?" are answered more in-depth. The self-concept develops over the first 25 years of a person's life before it locks in and becomes resistant to change. An example can be seen in people over thirty years of age who still think, act, or behave the way they did when they were in their twenties, or senior citizens who refuse to embrace new technology that makes it easier to get things done.

Change can be frightening. People in general resist anything that asks them to change their thinking or behaviors because of fear of the unknown. The only way the self-concept can change is through a life altering event; such as loss or going to college. College students are challenged to become deeper reflective thinkers, and are challenged to think outside of "the box." This can be categorized as life altering for college students, because it forces them to change how they think and understand the world around them.

Our self-concept directly influences the way we communicate. Take a look at some identifiable aspects of a teenage boy's self-concept below. He learned these characteristics about himself from feedback as he grew.

I'm a boy	I'm funny	I'm mischievous	I'm asthmatic	I'm 14-years old
I'm outgoing	I'm tall	I'm a math student	I'm a grandson	I'm an athlete
I'm in 8th grade	I'm a son	I'm a brother	I'm cute	I'm a nephew

SHARE YOUR UNDERSTANDING

Can you identify ten important parts of your self-concept as illustrated above?

The Self-Concept & Self-Esteem

Self-esteem describes how you feel – emotionally – about each part of your self-concept.

Self-esteem develops from messages that are consistent or that come from individuals you value, such as parents, teachers, or authority figures. These individuals are known as "respected others." Some messages that you receive from respected others are positive, "ego boosting" messages which influence a high level of self-esteem; while other messages that are negative become "ego busting" messages which lowers self-esteem. Such messages can be verbal or nonverbal.

- **Example – ego boosting message:** *"You make me proud!"*
- **Example – ego busting message:** *"You're a trouble-maker who is always causing problems!"*

Look at the two examples below to understand how self-esteem assigns value to each part of the self-concept.

My Self-Concept	I'm a daughter	I'm a dancer	I'm talkative	I'm smart
If High Self-Esteem	I'm the oldest daughter.	I learn dance routines with ease, and my classmates always ask for my help.	People want to talk to me because I always have something interesting to say.	I'm smarter than all my friends!
If Low Self-Esteem	But, I'm not the favorite daughter.	I love dancing, but I can't dance as well as the other students in my class.	My opinions and thoughts don't matter because people always find a way to silence me when I'm talking.	Mom says I'm smart with school work; but I don't have common sense.

SHARE YOUR EXPERIENCE

Select four parts of your self-concept from the list you created on the previous page. Next, describe your level of self-esteem as related to each part of your identify that you list. Identify only one self-esteem level for each of the four parts of your self-concept.

Your self-concept				
High self-esteem				
Low self-esteem				

Three other factors contributed to shaping your self-esteem: reflected appraisals, social comparisons, and the Self-fulfilling prophesy of expectations.

1: Reflective Appraisal	Example
We see ourselves through the eyes of people that we respect or who have authority over our lives such as, parents, bosses, police, coaches, clergy, significant others, or teachers. When these individuals praise or reject parts of our self-concept it impacts our self-esteem in positive or negative ways. Know that not all negative messages will be accepted; but the many are accepted as true when communicated by respected others. People with high self-esteem are generally more confident, practice self-love, and are optimistic.	Marcus overhears his basketball coach talking about him to the assistant coaches, *"Marcus has so much potential! It's a shame he doesn't put forth more effort. He's tall and I'd like to play him more often."* The coach's opinion (appraisal) is projected (reflected) onto Marcus; he accepts the comment as true because he respects his coach. As a result, Marcus starts to work harder during practice and eventually earns a starting spot on his team.

Confidence	Self-Love	Optimistic

If you received positive reflected appraisals when you were young, you probably have healthy self-esteem. On the other hand, if the appraisals were negative, your self-esteem will most likely be low. Another way that self-esteem develops is when we measure our talents and characteristics against others through a process of social comparison.

2: Social Comparison	Example
We interact in a variety of social situations where we find ourselves comparing our personality characteristics and achievements to peers, classmates, co-workers, and individuals of the same gender or culture. Comparing ourselves to others who we feel are similar to us in some way, impacts how we feel about ourselves and affects our self-esteem (self-worth).	The easiest examples can be observed in teenager and young adult behaviors as they strive to mimic the style and behaviors of popular recording artists such as: Rihanna, Miley Cyrus, Shakira, Pitbull and a variety of other hip hop artists. Closer to home, we may compare our achievements to a high school friend who went straight through college; landed an amazing job; purchased a new car; had a huge wedding; and is now in the process of closing on a dream home. You, on the other hand, never went to college; work a minimum wage job; and live in a studio apartment. A comparison of your achievements to those of your friend can have a damaging impact on your self-esteem.

Comparing yourself to others socially can have a positive or negative impact on self-esteem, which in turn affects the self-concept. If you recall, positive self-esteem is one of the survival needs listed on Abraham Maslow's pyramid of human needs. The important connection here is to understand that the way a person communicates is a direct reflection of their self-esteem. A person's perception of people and the world around them is also a direct reflection of their self-esteem. The self-fulfilling prophesy discussed next also shapes self-esteem.

3. Self-Fulfilling Prophesy of Expectations	Examples of Expectation Types
Self-Imposed Expectations Self-fulfilling prophesies has a powerful impact on one's personality. It can determine how you see yourself today, and influence your future behaviors. This occurs when your expectations of an event make it more likely to become a reality. Self-imposed expectations develops from our self-talk, and can prophesy negative or positive outcomes. Ego boosting or busting messages factor in how a person imposes expectation upon themselves. Examples are discussed in the column to the right.	**1. Example: Self-imposed expectations** • **Negative self-imposed expectation:** Your cell phone does not charge properly overnight, which causes your alarm to shut off. Now, you're running late for school or work. Then, in your haste, you burn your toast. Your day starts out bad, so you proclaim, *"This is a bad sign, it's going to be a bad day."* And guess what? You have a bad day because you spoke the prophesy into existence. • **Positive self-imposed expectation:** You spent the previous evening preparing for a job interview. As you enter the interviewer's office you greet the person, take a seat, and silently proclaim that you will get the job – and, you do!
Expectations Imposed by Others Self-fulfilling prophesies can also be imposed upon you by other people. This occurs when respected others communicate expectations they have of you. Expectations imposed upon you by others can affect self-esteem in positive or negative ways. Read the two examples in the next columns for a better understanding.	**2. Example: Expectations imposed by others** • Your father is teaching you how to ride a bike. You fall several times and beg him to let you quit; but, he insists that you keep trying. He gives you a motivational chat about being brave and never giving up. Your father chants, "You can do it" several times before leaving you to practice alone. Eventually, after more failed attempts you finally get it – you're riding down the street smiling from ear-to-ear. In this situation, the father imposed his expectations about bravery and determination upon his child. • A fourth grader has struggled with pre-algebra since the beginning of the school year. Her teacher matched her with a tutor to no avail, the student still couldn't figure out how to work the problems. Finally, the teacher gives up and tells the student that she will never learn how to do algebra, and that she will have to repeat the fourth grade. The next year, the young girl doesn't try because of the ego-busting self-imposed expectation that her previous teacher placed upon her.

YOUR CHAPTER NOTES

Use this section to jot down notes from this chapter that will assist with the homework assignments that follow. Your notes will also assist when studying for the chapter quiz.

_____

_____

_____

_____

_____

_____

_____

_____

_____

_____

_____

_____

_____

_____

_____

_____

_____

_____

_____

_____

_____

_____

_____

HOMEWORK!

This assignment involves personal self-reflection. Take some time to think about all of the positive and negative messages that shaped your self-esteem, also: reflective appraisal, social comparison, expectations. Reflect on the following questions before writing your response: "Who am I?" "Am I who I think I am, or am I who others say I am?" This reflection should be a written snapshot of you! Explain in detail how communication with others shaped the person you are today. Lastly, explain how your self-concept / self-esteem affect how you communicate with others today.

NAME: _____   DATE: _____

_____

_____

_____

_____

_____

_____

_____

_____

_____

_____

_____

_____

_____

_____

_____

_____

_____

_____

_____

_____

_____

_____

Managed identities

People are very protective over parts of their self-concept that may be rejected by others. Because we seek to satisfy social needs through communication, people manage a wide variety of socially acceptable identities in different environments. There are two categories of identities that we manage daily; a private-self and a public-self. To better understand this, consider how differently people behave when alone in a room; such as the bathroom. Whether they're singing in the mirror, bursting a pimple, or cleaning your nose; do you think this person would change what they were doing if someone was watching? Of course they would! This is the private-self; it is the person you believe yourself to be in honest moments of reflection. In public places we conceal behaviors we think are unacceptable and create more socially acceptable behaviors in order to be accepted. Another reason that we adjust our identities in social settings is to influence how people view us.

Look at the list below and consider how you would adjust your communication and behaviors when interacting in the situations below to create a desired image.

- When chatting with an elderly neighbor.
- When coaching a group of eight year olds.
- When discussing a job with a senior co-worker.
- When asking a stranger for directions.
- When studying for an exam with a study group.
- When talking to your parents, grandparents, aunts/uncles, children, boss, or instructor.
- When interviewing for a job.
- When speaking to a person from a different ethnic group.
- When speaking to a service person: postal worker, cable technician, store clerk, etc.
- When speaking to a police officer.
- When speaking to a clergy person (pastor, minister, or Rabi)

In public speaking, students must learn how to manage an identity of confidence and competence. The strategy is to see the podium as a stage in order to create a different "you" – the public-self. Many prominent performers have shared how they manage identities during performance by creating an alter-ego to combat stage fright. Beyonce Knowles, for example, created an alter ego identity that allows her to give the audience what they want; Sasha Fierce. Perhaps you have name for your presenting public-self; in any case, everyone participates in identity management to satisfy their physical, social, and practical goal needs.

The Self Concept & Perception

The self-concept and perception are intertwined because the self-concept shapes perception. Perception is defined as the way we understand people and the world around us. And, the self-concept is defined as a relatively stable set of perception that we hold about ourselves. Notice how the word perception appears in both definitions; there is a connection. How you look at the world depends on what you think about yourself; and, what you think about yourself influences how you understand the world. For example, if a person has high self-esteem (self-concept), their perception of people and occurrences around them will be optimistic. On the other hand, if the person's self-esteem (self-concept) is low, they will perceive people or experiences negatively.

Perceptual Constructs

People categorize their personal experiences by creating little boxes of meaning called constructs. Organizing daily experiences into categories helps us group and understand certain human behaviors and events as they occur. *Constructs* can be seen as statements that suggest, *'If "A" is in effect, 'then it must mean "B"* is occurring.' Let's simplify this statement. "If" you encounter a person wearing a law enforcement uniform, "then" that person must be a law enforcement officer. Without perceptual constructs we would have no way of understanding behaviors and events.

Faulty Perception

Perception becomes faulty because people forget, generalize, or distort details that they observe. Distortions involve twisting or bending information out of shape. One reason that people *distort* information is to make interactions support their existing beliefs and values. Another reason why people distort information is they can only observe small parts of their environment at a time. The result is that people miss critical detail and fill in the blank areas with what they know or believe to create meaning. Faulty perception also occurs when people *generalize* events that are observed a few times, and conclude that what was true in the past will prove true in the future. *Deletions* are the final type of faulty perception. At times people erase, blot out, or cancel information that contradicts their beliefs. In other words, the information does not rank high in importance to them. Faulty perception leads to miscommunication.

Perceptual Filters & Frame of Reference Filters

Finally, we make sense of people's behaviors and events through a narrowed lens known as a perceptual filter. This external filter limits us from gaining an accurate perception of behaviors and events because perception is influenced by the self-concept which may be optimistic or pessimism in nature. As discussed in Chapter One, the frame of reference filters are internal filters that features everything a person knows about themselves. Everything a speaker says is filtered through their frame of reference, which is the combination of they're experiences, values, attitudes, and goals. The listener also has a frame of reference that messages filter through before being decoded. No two people have the same frame of reference, which explains why intentions are often misunderstood. Together, frame of reference filters and perceptual filters help us make sense of ourselves (internal) and people, as well as the world around us (external). Miscommunication between speakers and interpersonal conflict is too often related to perceptual differences and frame of reference differences.

SHARE YOUR EXPERIENCE

There is a person in your class that seems interesting because of comments he or she makes during discussions. You feel the two of you have a lot in common, and you'd like to get to know this person better. What constructs do you normally use when in this situation? In other words, how do you qualify a person as someone you'd like to know? Use this section on perception to respond.

_____

_____

_____

_____

_____

_____

Listening and Communication

"Wisdom is the reward you get for a lifetime of listening when you'd have preferred to talk."

—Doug Larson

What is listening?

Sound waves are all around us, it can be the ping of a text message or a person's voice. If we have healthy eardrums, we hear everything around us. Sound waves are a type of stimuli that stimulates hearing when they strike our eardrums. This is a basic explanation of how hearing occurs in the human ear. It is important to understand that hearing is not the same as listening. Even if you have healthy ear drums and can hear everything, it is impossible to pay attention to everything, because there is too much stimuli in our environments to attend to it all. Certain familiar or foreign stimuli (sounds) will attract our attention causing us to pay careful attention to it. The listening process calls for us to make sense of what we are hearing, understand it, decide what to do with it, and remember it for future references.

Example: *A kid is hanging out in on the couch playing her favorite video game when she suddenly hears the sound of keys rattling just outside the door. She selects that stimuli from the environment because it has captured her* **attention***; sensing that it's time for her mom to come home from work and she hasn't done your homework. Now that she has* **made sense** *of the sound and understands its meaning, her* **reaction** *is to quickly turn off the game, pick up the math book, and pretend to be deep in study mode. She will* **remember** *this stimulus because it can mean losing video game privileges if she gets caught in the future.*

Because the active process of listening requires us to select sounds from our environment to make sense of it in order to react to it, the listening process can be seen as "work." Therefore, listening does not simply happen! When we work to understand a message through the decoding process we are actively participating in the listening process. Another important aspect of listening is critical thinking as we set out to understand, we consider specific questions such as, "What does this message mean?" "Could it have a hidden meaning?" "How should I respond?" Most people are poor listeners due to a variety of challenges and faulty listening which we will discuss next.

Listening Challenges

Barriers to listening

1. *Encoding/Decoding Challenges:* Research has shown that humans can speak up to 600 words per minute but can only decode 75 to 100 words per minute. A problem occurs when encoding surpasses decoding. When a sender is encoding and sending messages rapidly, the receiver is challenged to decode each message at the same rate. This is not possible. People do not have adequate time to decode messages when they are sent rapidly. Perceptual filters are forced to work overtime because a message can have many meanings.

2. ***Information Overload Challenges***: In today's technology era, we are inundated with an overload of communication. On a daily basis, we take in information from advertising, smartphone technology alerts, conversations we overhear, lectures, social networking websites, etc.

   - Our short-term memory can only hold roughly 30 seconds of information at one time (such as a name or phone number); when the short-term memory fills up we find it hard to concentrate on listening. Our short term memory responds by purging information. This explains why we forget certain information as soon as we receive it. This can also explain why people often ask you to repeat simple facts only moments after you've communicated it. On the other hand, information that we hear often (such as names, multiplication facts, or processes) are stored in our long-term memory, which allows the information to be retrieved whenever we need it.

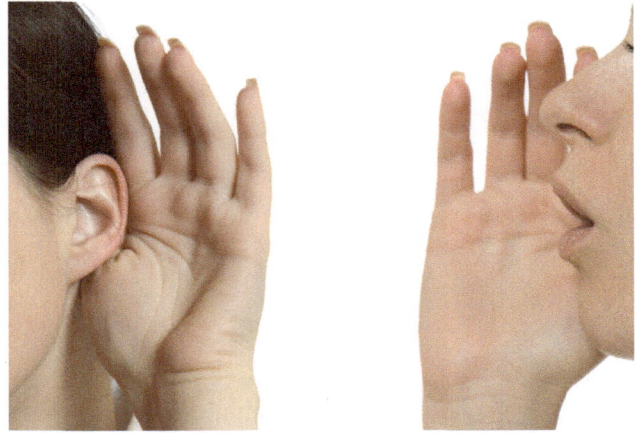

3. ***Listening anxiety***: Some people experience listening anxiety as a result of previous decoding failures.

   - Example: A student has listened to the teacher explain a mathematical process several times but is still not able to conceptualize how to calculate the problem. After the student experiences the same outcome few times, he or she begins to develop a fear of listening to mathematical instruction related to similar problems. Listening fears are common and often leads to poor listening behaviors.

4. ***Personal Concerns***: Chapter one presented two types of internal noise: psychological noise which is biological interferences such as hunger or fatigue, and psychological noise which are your personal thoughts. Psychological noise can contribute to poor listening because it blocks our ability to concentrate on the information that is being communicated to us.

   - Example: During a lecture your thoughts float to an unexpected situation that occurred earlier that day with your car. This distraction prevents you from listening to the lesson actively.

Faulty listening

5. ***Factual Listening***: Occurs when you listen for common facts and prematurely assuming you know what the speaker is going to say after hearing a few key words.

   - Can you remember a time when you thought you knew the point a person was attempting to make so you stopped listening? Instead, the person made a point that you didn't expect and you had to ask them to repeat it. This is an example of factual listening which is a primary cause of miscommunication. Because listening is work, people tend to listen for familiar words or phrases contained in a message to assign meaning.

6. ***Personal Biases toward the Speaker***: The old saying, *"Don't kill the messenger"* applies here. Too often, we stop listening, or practice factual listening, because we hold biases towards the speaker. The problem with this, is we do not know what type of information the speaker is preparing to share with us. In public speaking it is unethical to participate in biased listening, as every speaker has a first amendment right to be heard. Also, you never know what direction the message is headed in – it is possible that the speaker has had a change of heart!

7. ***Pseudo listening.*** Fake listening. This type of listening occurs when the receiver is distracted by more pressing thoughts or is bored with the topic. To avoid being rude, the listener will maintain eye contact with the speaker, nod at appropriate times and smile, but their thought are elsewhere. As students, you have probably participated in this type of faulty listening.

8. *Stage hogging.* Turn taking during a conversation can be challenging when the receiver of the message is thinking instead of listening to the speaker. Stage hogging occurs when the listener interrupts the speaker and attempts to insert their thoughts into a conversation. Studies show that individual who participate in stage hogging have low self-esteem. Such individuals have a need to be at the center of attention to feel important.

9. *Defensive listening.* Occurs when a listener takes a speaker's comments as a personal attack when it is not meant to be. Such insecurities provide glimpses of negative self-concept and self-esteem. Practicing useful critical thinking listening skills can assist in avoiding defensive listening behaviors.

10. *Ambushing* – At times a person will listen attentively to a speaker to collect information that will be used against them later, this is called ambush listening. Lawyers use this strategy when interrogating a witness. This type of listening can create defensiveness in the speaker.

11. *Insensitive Listening* – Taking a speaker's remarks for face value instead of looking under the words or subtle phrases to discover the true meaning of the message.

Listening Affects Communication

Effective communication skills work hand in hand with effective listening skills. Faulty listening skills leads to miscommunication. People listen to obtain information, for understanding, enjoyment, or to learn. How well you listen has a major impact on the quality of your relationships with others. When communicators practice active listening, they are better able to satisfy their basic and higher level needs especially relational development which we'll discuss later.

SUGGESTIONS TO BECOME AN EFFECTIVE LISTENER

- Pay attention.
- Look at the speaker directly.
- Eliminate distracting thoughts. Be conscious of your self-talk.
- Don't interrupt the speaker. Wait for the speaker to complete a thought before sharing your thoughts.
- Listen to the entire message to isolate key points.
- Relate the main idea to something you are familiar with to remember key points.
- Don't complete the speaker's sentences.
- Don't judge the speaker or message prematurely, listen to the full message.
- Talk less, decode more. Working to understand will help you stay focused on the speaker.
- Ask clarifying questions to actively participate in the speaker's conversation.
- Be conscious of your listening behaviors. It is easy to lose focus which activates pseudo listening.

Summary

The self-concept is a relatively stable set of perceptions that we hold of ourselves; it provides answers to the question, *"Who am I?"* Feedback that shapes the self-concept comes from individuals that we respect, look up to, or have authority over our lives. For example, *"I am a student,"* answers the question, *"Who am I?"* Self-esteem adds value to the type of student the person believes herself to be. *"I am an average student."* Ego-boosting and ego-busting messages from those we look up to shapes our self-esteem. Other influences are reflective appraisal, social comparison, self-expectations, and expectations from others, which are self-fulfilling prophecies. Ego boosting messages inspires a higher level of self-esteem than does ego busting messages. Such messages lowers self-esteem A person's frame of reference reflects their experiences, values, and traditions. It is a filter that shapes how they think and how they communicate. The frame of reference filter impacts every message that a speaker encodes and sends; both senders and receivers have frame of reference filters. When communicators frame of reference environments overlaps to some degree, communication is easier. When there is no overlap, communication is more complicated.

Perception refers to how a person understands others and the world around them. As a person interacts with people and situations around them, they develop perceptual constructs that are isolated boxes of understanding. Perceptual filters develop from these constructs which helps us understand behaviors of people and the world around us. Listening and communication are related because decoding messages accurately calls for effective listening skills. Hearing and listening are not the same: Hearing occurs naturally; but listening calls for critical thinking and perception checking to make sense of messages. The listening process calls for the selection of stimuli from an environment, attending to the stimuli by working to understand it, and assigning meaning to it. Once this is complete, the receiver of the message uses critical thinking skills to decide how to react to the message received. The final step is to remember the information. There are six reasons why communicators participate in poor listening which leads to communication breakdowns, and they include factual listening, encoding & decoding challenges, information overload, listening anxiety, personal concerns, and personal biases.

Key terms

Self-Concept

Self-Esteem

    Ego boosting messages

    Ego busting messages

    High self-esteem

    Low self-esteem

Reflective Appraisal

Social Comparison

Self-Fulfilling Prophesy

    Self-imposed expectations

    Expectations imposed by others

Perceptions

    Constructs

    Perceptual Filters

    Faulty Perception

Listening versus Hearing

Listening Process

    Select

    Attend

    Understand

    React

    Remember

Listening barriers

    Factual listening

    Encoding & decoding Challenges

    Information Overload

    Listening Anxiety

    Personal Concerns

Personal biases

    Faulty listening

    Factual listening

    Personal biases towards the speaker

    Pseudo listening

    Stage hogging

    Defensive listening

    Ambushing

    Insensitive listening

Looking Out: Communicating with Others

VOCABULARY BUILDERS: *Ruminate*, verb
To think carefully and deeply about something for an extended period of time.
"The question got us ruminating on the real value of wealth."

Ameliorate, verb
To make something (like a problem) better, less painful.
"When your back hurts, consider lying on a hardwood floor to ameliorate the back pain."

## CHAPTER 3

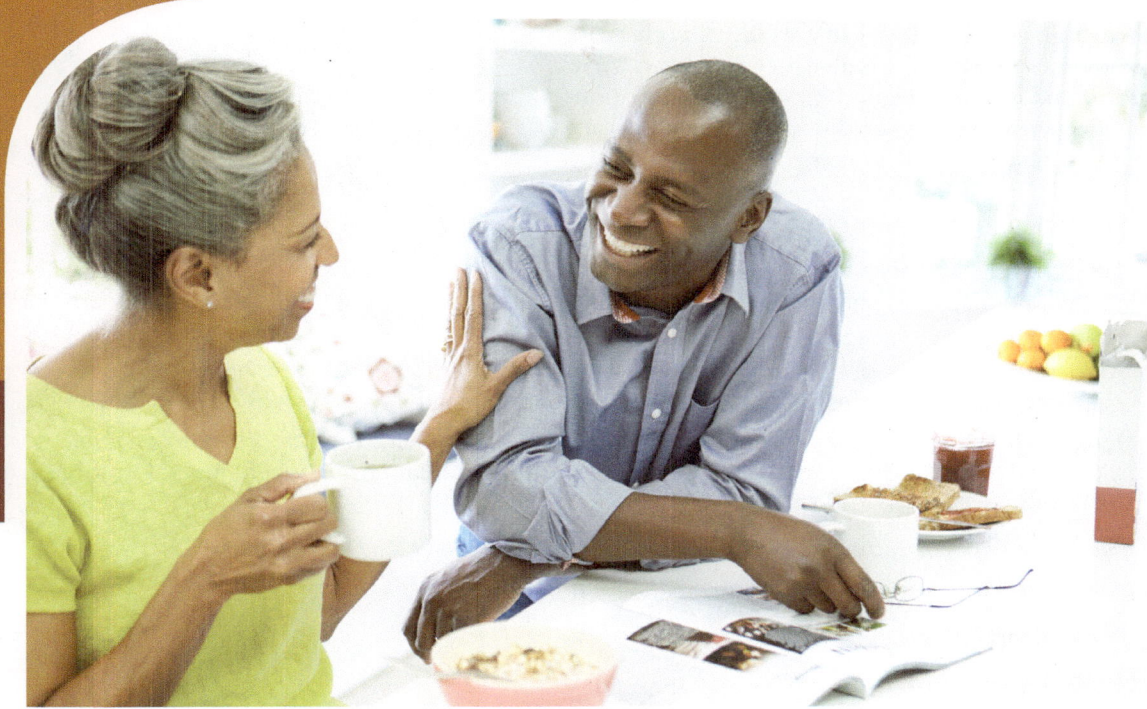

*"Sometimes it seems safer to hold it all in, where the only person
who can judge is yourself."*

—*Sarah Dessen*

Self-Disclosure Shapes Interpersonal Interactions & Relationships

We share parts of who we are with our family members such as our likes and dislikes. Other parts of who we are may be shared with close friends such as our fears and dreams. We'll share even less of ourselves with acquaintances. Never do we share all that we are with anyone; and as a result, the deeper aspects of our thoughts, feelings, beliefs, and experiences are kept private. The only time we may willingly share more private information about ourselves with others is to satisfy basic and higher level needs as discussed in Chapter One. The funny part of this withholding information is that not all is significant. Sometimes we simply do not wish to share all that we are with others. Self-disclosure is the process of intentionally sharing personal information about yourself to achieve a specific goal.

In this chapter, we will investigate self-disclosure to gain a clear understanding of how it is intentionally used to achieve specific goals; and, how it works to develop or destroy relationships. We'll also take a brief look at gender language patterns for a complete understanding of the complexity of human communication.

Understanding Self-Disclosure

Self-Disclosure is the process of **deliberately** revealing information about ourselves that would not otherwise be known. Self-disclosure is also the primary way that platonic and intimate relationships develop. Relationships deepen when parties disclose personal history, opinion, values, and experiences.

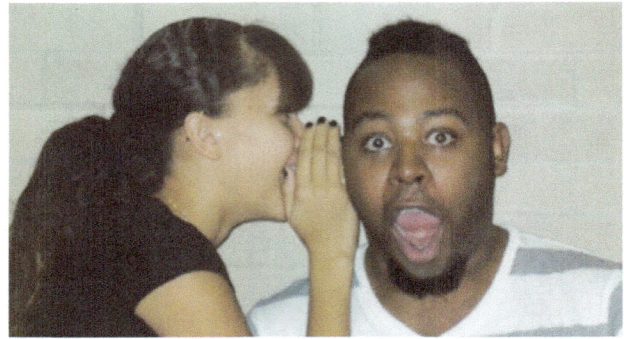

Self-disclosure occurs on three levels.

- **Lower level self-disclosure** is less risky and shared more actively shared during interpersonal interactions. Examples: *"I am a vegetarian!"* or *"I am a baseball fan."*
- **Moderate self-disclosure** occurs as interpersonal interactions become more meaningful and relationships develop. The parties begin to disclose at a more intimate levels such as goals or fears.
- **High level self-disclosure** involves more risky personal disclosure such as *"I had an abortion,"* or *"I have a criminal record."* This type of disclosure only occurs in a relationship where mutual trust has been achieved.

To qualify as self-disclosure, the information shared with others must meet the following criteria:

- Must be deliberate and not accidentally disclosed
- Must be significant, not trivial facts
- Must not be known by others

Self-disclosure serves many positive purposes in human communication:

- **Catharsis** – clearing the air by getting something off your chest that has been bothering you.
- **Clarification** – expressing a clearer picture to another person by disclosing more personal information.
- **Validation** – justifying ones actions by disclosing personal information that supports and explains their behaviors.

Characteristics of self-disclosure:

- Self-disclosure usually occurs in dyads (two parties talking).
- Self-disclosure is incremental (small snippets of information)
- Self-disclosure rarely involves sharing high level information.
- Self-disclosure usually occurs in positive relationships
- Too much self-disclosure can destroy relationships

SHARE YOUR EXPERIENCE!

Provide one example of how you have used self-disclosure to achieve: catharsis, or clarification, or validation.

_____

_____

_____

Social penetration theory

Social psychologists Irwin Altman and Dalmas Taylor defined two ways that communication can be more disclosing or less disclosing. Their model, the *social penetration theory* describes how interpersonal interactions move from topical to deeper meaningful ones through gradual and mutual self-disclosure. This sharing of mutual information often occurs in private dyads.

An onion model is symbolically used to explain Social Penetration Theory because like an onion our interactions has many layers. The outer layer of the onion can be seen as the *public self* where communicators share topical information that is socially appropriate. "It's really hot today," is an example of such sharings. The *private self* is represented by the inner layers of the onion. This is where personal information such as personal experiences, opinions, and personal feelings that reflects their self-concept are hidden and protected.

Altman and Dalmas further suggest that self-disclosure occurs in two dimensions: *breadth* and *depth* in five stages. Let's look at the first three stages of social penetration.

Social penetration theory phases

BREADTH outer layer of the onion **1. Orientation stage** *(low level less risky self-disclosure)*	We play safe with small talk and simple, harmless clichés like "It's going to be a scorcher today," following standards of socially desirability and appropriate behaviors. Neither party will disclose personal information at this stage.
DEPTH inner layers of the onion **2. Exploratory stage** *(moderate level self-disclosure)*	We begin to reveal ourselves by disclosing our opinions about moderate topics such as thoughts on college programs and career goals. Still, we do not share deeper feelings about the topics because trust has not yet developed. This is the testing stage where we feel the other person out by giving them general information about who you are. Many relationships never get past this stage; most will remain at this level or phase out altogether.
3. Affective stage *(high level risky self-disclosure)*	Self-disclosure takes a serious turn at this stage as the parties disclose real opinions about private and personal matters. This stage is touchy as the parties will openly share criticisms and arguments could result. On the other hand, if the parties share similar views of life a stronger trust relationship develops. If the parties get past this stage, the relationship will move to stabilization.

Johari's Window

A different way of understanding the importance of self-disclosure in interpersonal interactions is Johari's Window developed by Joseph Luft and Harry Ingram. The left column of this model contains everything you "know about yourself" (e.g. your likes, dislikes, interest, secrets, and aspirations). The right column of this model represents information that is "not known to self." The **open pane** contains information about us that is also known to everyone else. The **blind pane** on the left side of the model contains information about us that other people know, but we do not know. As people observe us, they see attributes in us that we are unaware of or have rejected because it does not support our self-concept. This information may be disclosed through feedback if a situation warrants such actions. The **hidden pane** contains information that we chose not to disclose unless a situation forces us to do so. The **unknown pane** contains what we are to become; self-actualization.

Known to self	Not known to self
1 **Open:** • General information known about you such as gender, intellect, creativity, talents, and other characteristics. • Know to you from feedback • Others also know this general information about you.	**2** **Blind** • Everything others know about you that you are not aware of. • You will only learn what others know about you through feedback. People withhold their view of you for different reasons.
3 **Hidden:** • Not known to others • Personal secrets • Will only disclose parts of this section when forced or to build trust relationships.	**4** **Unknown:** • Parts of you yet to be discovered • Growth potential • New experiences that create opportunities • Self-actualization

An important aspect of self-disclosure is that it is the only way relationships develop. The orientation, exploratory, and affective phases of social penetration is a useful way to understand how self-disclosure is used to build relationships. Mutual disclosure is critical as trust relationship develop. A negative aspect of self-disclosure is that it can also destroy relationships. We can look to social networking websites such as Facebook, Twitter, and Instagram to find examples of how risky self-disclosure harms relationships. Social networking users also create problems by copying unprotected private information from another person's page, and then disclosing that information for the world to see. This is unethical behavior. The lesson here is that self-disclosure on any level is risky, especially on the Internet where personal information can be distorted or used to create conflict. As such, great consideration must go into decisions to disclose in person, or via the Internet.

In public speaking, students must think critically when disclosing personal information they feel will help the audience understand points being made. An excellent rule of thumb to consider before disclosing personal information comes in the form of a simple question, *"What purpose will it serve to disclose this personal information? Is self-disclosure really required to make my point?"* At times, hypothetical examples are better choices as they allow you to avoid disclosing high risk information. Hypothetical examples are pretend scenarios that support or explain an idea.

Avoiding Self-Disclosure

So, far we've learned how interpersonal relationships develop through mutual self-disclosure. We also have examined how harmful effects of risky self-disclosure can lead to conflict and relational dissolution. What happens when a person feels uncomfortable disclosing information or when the risk of disclosing personal information outweighs the benefits? Most do not respond. To avoid self-disclosure, we often use behaviors that are similar to self-disclosure, but will only pretend to respond by disclosing personal information. Here are some options often used to avoid self-disclosure.

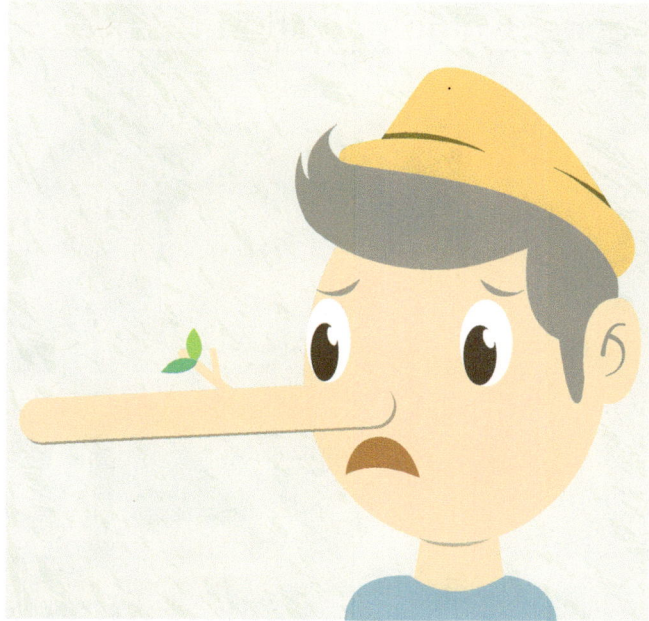

1. **Use Lies:** This strategy is used when trust is a concern. We may validate our moral decision as necessary to protect parts of our self-concept contained in the hidden pane of Johari's Window. For example, friends have gathered around to inspect the car you recently purchased. You have never felt comfortable discussing money, even with friends. And so when one of your friends inquires how much you put down on the car, you respond with a little white lie. *"I saved $2000 for a down payment."* You say this, knowing that you only put a $500 down payment on the car. This exaggeration helps you avoid embarrassment because your friend's have acquired more material comforts than you.

2. **Use nonverbal responses:** When we feel pressed to provide information that we are not comfortable sharing, we often use nonverbal cues in response. Hinting allows the person who is pressing for information to create his or her own answer. Such nonverbal responses include avoiding eye contact or nodding your head. This strategy is also used when a person is attempting to manipulate a situation by being vague.

3. **Withhold Information:** Masking our feelings or emotions allows us to withhold information without experiencing leakage. When others are pressing us for information that we simply don't want to share, we work to control our body language and facial expressions. A card player's term for this is "poker face." Past experiences normally warn us not to disclose information being sought by others. We might sense underlying repercussions or harms, or we may be protecting others from harm.

Guidelines for Self-Disclosure

- Think critically about a situation before deciding to disclose appropriate information.
- Disclosure of feelings is more revealing than disclosure of opinions; consider disclosing information as more opinion than personal facts.
- Consider your motivation for disclosing information (public or private) to avoid negative self-disclosure.
- Consider the risk of disclosing high level information. The goal is to decide whether the self-disclosure will solve a problem, make the problem worse, or create a new problem.

Gender Communication

Defining Gender Communication

Communication is a complex yet facinating social science; people may speak different languages but they manage to find the path to understanding during critical times. Author John Grey's novel "Men are from Mars, and Women are from Venus," purposes that the way men and women use language is "worlds apart" making communication between the genders complicated. Therefore, the focus of ongoing gender communication studies seeks to understand why miscommunication occurs between men and women by identifying how the genders use language differently to create meaning. The outcome of these studies reveled two distinct language patterns identified as female language patterns and male language patterns. Know also as communication style, personal language patterns is something that people see as natural. However, these patterns have many influences such as, environment, culture, genetics, and age.

Gender language patterns

A pattern is something that happens in a regular and repeated way. Therefore, gender language pattern studies sheds light on specific differences in how men and women create meaning and share information through distinct language patterns. What you might find interesting is men and women do not fall into gender specific categories. Some women display male language patterns, and some men display female language patterns in natural ways. People might feel that they communicate clearly, but this is not always true, especially the participants who express ideas through different language patterns. In general, men and women display a wide range of communication patterns. For example, male language patterns are more direct, authoritative, and self-centered; whereas female language patterns are more indirect, emotional, and selfless. Females use communication to develop rapport for family, friendship, and community building. And Males use communication for report endeavors; gathering information helps them compete or be seen as all knowing. Between the two extremes are variations in how men and women may blend gender communication patterns to create a unique styles of talking. This is not to suggest that one communication style is superior over the other – simply that they exist and provide valid reasons why men and women struggle towards mutual understanding. Therefore, it is important to investigate basic male and female language patterns in order to conceptualize how these patterns contribute to miscommunication. Take a few moments to take the brain gender quiz that follows to identify your gender language pattern. It should be noted that brain "gender" has nothing to do with sexual preference. Homosexual individuals typically score no differently in regards to brain gender language patterns than heterosexual individuals.

QUIZ - What Gender is Your Brain?

You can gain an idea of whether you tend to think in a predominately male or female style by answering and scoring this twenty-question quiz. While you may physically be a member of one sex; the way your brain is organized may result in you thinking like a member of the opposite sex.

<u>**Read the following personality traits and rate each using the following scale:**</u>

1 = you behave this way 0% of the time (rarely)
3 = you behave this way 50% of the time (half the time)
5 = you behave this way 100% of the time (almost always)

1. Talk about your emotions
2. Make decisions quickly
3. Put others before yourself
4. Take physical and emotional risks
5. Recognize the voices of people you have only spoken with a few times
6. Can point in a specific direction with ease
7. Are helpful to others even when not asked
8. Are competitive in most situations
9. Prefer intimate gatherings to large parties
10. Can easily back a car into a tight parking space
11. Can quickly locate where a sound is coming from
12. Find it easy to "tune out" external noise
13. Are sympathetic
14. Are ambitious and goal-oriented
15. Show affection for others
16. Prefer to be the leader
17. Remember names and faces of people you have just met
18. Are independent and self-sufficient
19. Spend time on your appearance
20. Are aggressive in actions and words

To determine your score, add up all your answers to the even-numbered questions, and then the odd number questions.

- The *even* number total is your *masculine score* and the *odd* number total is your *feminine* score.
- If your *even* score is significantly higher than your *odd* score (10 or more), it is possible that you behave according to male brain patterns. If your odd score is higher by 10 points your language pattern is more female.
- The greater the difference between your even and odd scores, the more likely you are to find communication with the opposite gender confusing and even frustrating.
- Some individuals may find that they have even male and female communication behaviors that are within 2 to 6 points. These individuals may find it easy to communicate with and understand both genders.

Please note that this quiz, while based on reputable research, is incapable of measuring deeper differences that would more accurately identify brain gender.

My odd number is ____. My even number is ____. My language pattern is _____

Common male and female language patterns

Male language patterns are seen as powerful.	Female language patterns are seen as powerless.
Direct language that is void of emotions and gets right to the point, this can cause hurt feelings but the message is clear.	Indirect language uses vague language filtered through emotion, this can be confusing and lead to miscommunication.
Sees disclosing feeling as a sign of weakness.	Sees disclosing feelings as a way to connect with others.
Uses language to exert authority and expertise.	Uses language to avoid conflict or hurting feelings.
Prefers problem-solving alone to think through options and challenges.	Prefers problem-solving with others to get different perspectives.
Reacts logically to incoming messages.	Reacts emotionally to incoming messages.
Share solutions that reflect his ability to problem-solve when others share personal issues.	Shares empathy or sympathy, showing the person that they are not alone.
Uses language to establish and retain status, maintain authority, or to compete (*to one-up another person*).	Uses language to nurture, socialize, establish relationships, and maintain harmony.
Spends more time communicating about sports, business, current events, and other men.	Spends more time communicating about personal or domestic issues, and other people.
Gossip focuses on sports figures, politicians, or television personalities.	Gossip focuses on family or close friends, and other individuals.
Moves into another's space, talks more with authority, interrupts, uses wit to command an audience.	Uses pauses to encourage others to take turns speaking.

The behaviors in common male and female language patterns as indicated in the chart are expressed through verbal and nonverbal means, leaving interpretation to the receiver. When direct communication methods are used, the message is often received as aggressive, unfeeling, rude, or selfish; yet, it is received with accuracy. When indirect communication methods are used, messages are more passive, vague, or confusing. The receiver's communication style will dictate how the message is decoded. When language styles match, communicators find it easier to understand each other. For example, April's communication style is direct and male-oriented, when she says to her brother, *"You're an idiot for telling your girlfriend that you would see her tonight. You know you have plans to go to the concert with your friends. Why didn't you tell her the truth?"* Her brother thinks about his sister's message and agrees that he used poor judgment. April's direct communication style did not offend her brother because his communication style a reflects male language pattern. On the other hand, if April displayed an indirect female language pattern, the message to her brother might not have been received clearly. For example, if April said, *"Your girlfriend really deserves better treatment"*, her brother may have dismissed her comment because he missed the underlying meaning of her message.

When two parties with opposite language patterns engage in conversation, many messages will be received the opposite way in which they were intended. This is called cross communication. Although male and female language patterns exist and can be observed through their interpersonal interactions, some male or female communicators will unconsciously display both male and female language patterns in a way that allows them to adapt to specific situations. You can understand this through the scope of managed identities as discussed in Chapter Two. For this reason, it is important to know your specific communication style in order to fully adapt your message when interacting with friends, family, co-workers, and romantic interest. When you are aware of your gender communication patterns, you are better prepared to encode and decode messages to be understood.

We naturally gather information about human behavior by observing other people. Therefore, if you pay attention to the language style of the person you are conversing with, you can interpret the person's message more effectively. Since we develop perceptual constructs that help assign meaning to experiences and events around us, it would also be beneficial to develop constructs that identify male and female language patterns. Public speakers should be aware of their communication language style to better engage and address various types of audiences.

In Part 1 of this textbook, you learned that humans use communication as a survival tool; also, how messages are sent, received, and distorted. You explored your personal communication behaviors and discovered their origins. In this chapter you investigated how carefully disclosing parts of your self-concept helps develop meaningful interactions and build relationships. Lastly, you learned your brain gender and discovered how men and women use language differently. As we turn our attention to Part 2 of this textbook "Communicating in Public Environments, it is important to have a clear understanding of your unique communication behaviors and style as a starting place towards effectively adapting your public speaking presentations to the diverse audiences.

Summary

Self-Disclosure is the process of intentionally sharing personal information that would not be known by others, but it serves positive purposes when used effectively. When people share personal information with others, they trust that the receiver of this information will equally disclose personal information to build relationships. Self-disclosure can be risky to the point of embarrassment or conflict when not used with care. The explosion of social networking websites has created a culture of unconscious self-disclosure that has opened the door for problems in interpersonal relationships and interactions. Social penetration theory, also known as the onion model, is another way to understand self-disclosure and relational development. The outer layer of the onion explains how communicators initiate interactions by disclose general information about a wide range of topics, but does not disclose personal opinions or experiences related to these topics. The inner layers of the onion model represent more in-depth sharing of information between two parties' as a relationship develops. At times, a person may not want to disclose personal information and will lie; use nonverbal hints; or completely withhold the information.

Understanding gender language patterns can help to avoid stressful communication. Encoding and decoding messages as they are intended tends to follow male and female language pattern styles. Male language patterns are seen as direct and void of emotion, while female language patterns are seen as indirect communication that embraces emotion. Gender language patterns do not always match the gender of the communicator. A male can display female communication patterns, just as a female can display male communication patterns. At times, a person may unconsciously display both gender language patterns. These language patterns are influenced by genetics, culture, age, and other people. In public speaking, the benefits of knowing your language pattern are enhanced awareness of how you approach different audiences, awareness of how the audience may receive and decode your messages, and influences how you structure each point for maximum impact.

Key terms

Self-Disclosure
    Catharsis
    Clarification
    Validation
    Low level disclosure
    Moderate level disclosure
    High level disclosure
Social Penetration Theory
    Onion Model
    Breadth and Depth

Initiating
Experimenting
Intensifying
Gender Communication
    Male Language Patterns
    Female Language Patterns
Report
Rapport

## PART 2

Communicating in Public Environments

Public Speaking: Ethics, Anxiety, and the Audience

VOCABULARY BUILDERS: *Disparaged*, verb
To describe (someone or something) as unimportant, weak, or bad.
"It is unethical to disparage another team's achievements."

Fastidious, verb
To be very careful about how you do something.
"She was fastidious in how she addressed the audience."

## CHAPTER 4

> *Live one day at a time emphasizing ethics rather than rules.*
>
> —*Wayne Dyer*

Ethics and Public Speaking

Ethics is a philosophical concept through which people consider what is right or wrong, moral or immoral. In communication, ethical speaking is critical to establishing credibility with your listeners. In general, ethical principles suggest that a speaker's main focus should not cause harm by misleading or deceiving the listeners. For example, presenting a speech that teaches the audience how to make a fake ID is teaching your audience how to break the law. Ethical questions will arise when appropriate decisions must be made. Often, such ethical decision focus on questions of honesty or dishonesty, moral or immoral behaviors, and fair or unfair treatment. History provides many examples of behaviors such as unethical speeches that resulted in horrible outcomes. Adolph Hitler for example promoted unethical anti-Sematic racism during his speeches that led to unspeakable horrors as described in history books. On the other hand, Martin Luther King's "I Have a Dream" speech triggered the start of racial unity in the United States. What we can learn from these speeches is that the power of the spoken word has the ability to destroy as well as inspire. As such, speakers must use ethical guidelines and practices presented in this chapter. Although the First Amendment of the United States Constitution protects free speech, there are a few exceptions such as speeches that slander, mislead, or defame.

Plagiarism

Another area of ethical responsibility is plagiarism. Claiming another person's original work as your own is wrong! But you already know this! Still, this unethical practice often occurs intentionally or as the result of carelessness.

Stealing someone else's ideas and presenting them as your own can have damaging effects on your grade!

In public speaking, three types of plagiarism must be avoided: global, patchwork, and incremental plagiarism.

When you take a speech that was written by someone else, rehearse it, and present it as your own.	**GLOBAL PLAGIARISM**
When speechwriters use sources from published documents to piece together a speech. A sentence from one book is copied and pasted into your speech document, followed by a sentence from another source. In the end, the entire speech is a collage of other people's originality without giving them credit.	**PATCHWORK PLAGIARISM**
Most students follow ethical guidelines to cite sources borrowed from others. But at times, a source may not be cited due to an oversight or carelessness. Although this is normally unintentional it is still unethical.	**INCREMENTAL PLAGIARISM**

Simply stated: plagiarism is wrong!

Ethical responsibility requires critical thinking because perception can shift situations as we'll see in the following scenario.

SHARE YOUR UNDERSTANDING: A true story

During a September 1998 video store robbery in Aurora, Colorado, a video store clerk was held face down at gunpoint by two young men as they robbed the store. 15-years later, the victim still suffers flashbacks from the robbery where he thought he would surely die.

In 2000, the young men were convicted on multiple counts of robbery, kidnapping and burglary charges. The judge also mandated that the felons serve each sentence back-to-back for a total of 98 years in prison. However, a problem occurred when a court clerk mistakenly wrote in one of the felon's files that his sentences should run at the same time – concurrently. Corrections officials at prisons use inmate's files to determine how much time each inmate should serve. Because of the clerical mistake in one of the young felon's file, he was released on parole in 2008 after serving just over 6 of his 98 years.

The freed inmate got a job, married his high school sweetheart, and had a son; he started his life over and vowed to never again live a life of crime. But by 2014, the authorities caught the clerical error and sent him back to prison. The concern in this case is that during his six years of freedom, he changed his life for the better. Now, 26-years-old, he attends church regularly and has become a productive citizen, husband, and father. He has also been raising his wife's older child from a previous relationship. Because of this, he and his wife believe that he has paid his debt to society, and that putting him back in jail will also sentence his family who had nothing to do with the crime. As a result, his family has posted an online petition to free him which has gathered over 500 signatures. This is an ethical dilemma. How would you respond?

NAME: _____   DATE: _____

Ethnocentrism

The belief that a person's culture or group is superior to all others is considered ethnocentric thinking. Ethnocentrism violates rules of ethics. Having pride in one's group or culture is natural. The problem arises, however, when a public speaker suggests that their group or culture's language, beliefs and traditions are superior to all others. Ethnocentric thinking occurs when judgments are made about group or cultural differences that are demeaning or patronizing. Example: When we talk about British drivers driving on the "wrong side of the road." Why not just say "opposite side of the road" or even "left hand side of the road?" To avoid ethnocentrism, a speaker must identify who the audience members are prior to the presentation and then adapt the message to that audience. Another example of ethnocentrism is a speaker who maintains that men are superior to women because they are stronger. The bottom line here, is offending others by implying that their way of thinking or acting is wrong will cause your listeners to stop paying attention.

Speaking Anxiety

Understanding Nervousness

Nervousness is normal. It means you care about the event or task that you are facing. Think about it:

- If you are nervous about an upcoming test, it means you care about passing the test.

- If you are nervous about what your friend thinks of you after an embarrassing event occurs, it means you care that they still see you as acceptable.

- If you are nervous about approaching a person with whom you are interested, it means you care about about being rejected and seen as undesirable.

- If you are nervous about speaking in front of people, it means you care about what they will think about comments; also because they are staring at you.

The technical term for public speaking or stage fright is glossophobia; glossa means tongue and phobos stands for panic or dread. Many people fear public speaking. A 2001, Gallup Poll asked Americans to list their greatest fears. A large percent of the participants identified speaking in public as their number one fear; this was exceeded only by fifty-one percent who said they were afraid of snakes. Since that time, other studies and surveys have produced the same outcome; the primary fear for most people is public speaking. In this section you will learn the causes of anxiety and how to control it.

Biological causes of nervousness

The primary culprit behind nervousness is **adrenaline** which is a hormone secreted by the adrenal glands, especially in conditions of stress. This influences increasing rates of blood circulation, breathing, and metabolism. Think of this adrenaline boost as a shot of extra energy that our body uses to address stressful situations that we should be concerned with. When the body has an overload of energy, the effects are nervousness which may or may not be visible to others. Each person's body responds differently to nervousness. Do you know how your body reacts to nervousness? Some common reactions include trembling hands or voice, sweating profusely, weakness of the knees, and a rapid heartbeat.

It is important to understand that speaking anxiety is not your enemy. Actually, that shot of adrenaline into your bloodstream can be used to vitalize you. When we become uncomfortable with what our bodies are experiencing, we allow this biological event to victimize us. What does this look like? It those peaky symbolic butterflies; they take flight and begin to break-dance in your stomach. There are methods that you can use to reverse this debilitating effect. It you practice the following anxiety controlling methods, you will soon find that your butterflies are flying in a smooth formation and you are feeling vitalized instead of victimized. Your negative nervousness will become positive nervousness that helps you focus on the task you hope to achieve. Positive self-talk is critical during these times of stress. Practice positive self-expectations during your self-talk.

Controlling Nervousness

"Best way to conquer stage fright is to know what you're talking about."

—*Michael H Mescon*

Here are five effective strategies useful in controlling anxiety:

When you practice:

- Rehearse your speech, presentations out loud with friends, family, work associates and anyone else willing to listen.
- Practice with all the equipment you're going to use.
- Work on your breathing, pauses, posture and voice.
- Practice with a timer so you can plan for the unexpected.
- Get familiar to your fear by visualizing everything that causes you anxiety.
- Avoid memorizing every word or reading word-for-word as that can cause additional stress and worsen anxiety.

Before you speak:

- Relax. Relaxation is vital before you present your speech.
- Exercise — go for a quick walk to calm your nerves.
- Get rid of any negative thoughts fueling your public speaking anxieties.
- Eat well, but don't force yourself to eat if you're not hungry.
- Avoid caffeine and sugar.
- Arrive early if possible and practice your presentation.
- Warm up your voice by talking and doing vocal exercises.
- Envision yourself presenting with a confident, loud voice, and envision your presentation being successful.

While you speak:

- Start strong. Use self-talk to control your butterflies.
- Think of your audience as your friends rather than strangers.
- Smile and be as natural as possible.
- Relax — take deep breaths and don't be afraid to pause.
- Move around a little to avoid shaking.
- Concentrate on what you're talking about, not on your anxieties.
- If you make mistakes, don't apologize, just keep going. Your audience probably won't even notice.

After you speak:

- Recognize positive points from your presentation even if you felt you had a bad experience.
- Don't reflect on negative things that happened as that can make you fear speaking publicly even more.
- If you made mistakes, relax and remember that everyone makes mistakes.
- Get more experience and practice as much as possible.

Audience analysis & surveys

In chapter one, we discussed four reasons why humans communicate: to satisfy physical needs, identity needs, social needs, and practical goals. In public speaking, the primary practical goal is to be heard; we want the audience to listen to what we have to say. In order to achieve this goal, a speechwriter must first investigate their audience to learn more about their beliefs, traditions, values, etc. It is important to learn what the audience knows about the topic, how they feel about the topic, what is the average age of the audience, and the gender of the audience? Once you, the speechwriter, has the answers to these questions, you can select appropriate examples and evidence that the audience will find interesting and understandable. This new information will also help you to select appropriate language; this will be discussed in an upcoming chapter. Next, we will discuss three types of audience analysis that are used to gather different types of information about the audience and speaking environment.

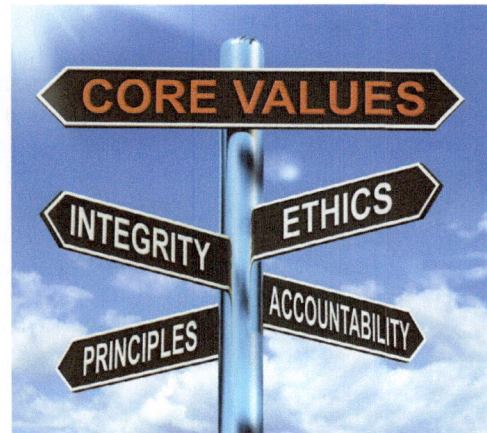

Demographic Audience Analysis

A demographic analysis provides the speechwriter with categories of information about the audience such as age, gender, sexual orientation, profession, ethnicity, special interest group affiliation, and socioeconomic level. When you think about the average age of your audience members you must consider distinct characteristics of each generation. Every generation has a different perception of human behavior and the world around them. This perception is strongly influenced by the mindset and historical events occurring during their developmental years: birth through roughly 25-years of age. If you remember, a person's self-concept develops during these years and locks in at roughly 25-years. Therefore, generational influenced constructs shape how people born in different generations assign meaning to messages and events. For example, women and men born prior to the baby boomer generation are known as traditionalists because they were taught to value hard work, loyalty, and clearly defined gender roles. These values are ingrained in their frame of reference and shape how they assign meaning to messages and behaviors. In other words, people from different generations will not always decode a message the same way nor will they agree on the meaning.

Adapting a speech to different audiences is challenging for speechwriters. At times your audience will be easy to relate to because everyone's frame of reference includes the same sizable over-lapping area. An example: the age of the speaker is similar to the audience's general age, all are college students, and most live near the college. Result, the speechwriter will find it easy to communicate the general idea (thesis) and supporting explanations to this audience. On the other hand, when the speaker's frame of reference has little to no over-lapping areas with their audience, the task of helping the audience understand will rest on the speechwriter's ability to creatively filter critical ideas through common shared experiences. We will discuss this later. In general, your audience will fall into a variety of different groups who understand and assign meaning to messages differently. It is the job of the speaker to find out what the audience knows and how they feel about the topic before writing a speech. Information contained in each demographic audience analysis is known as data. Once the speaker has analyzed the data from the demographics audience analysis, it may be necessary to dig deeper to identify the beliefs or values of the audience. Gaining information about your audience's beliefs can help the speechwriter to select more effective main points and supporting material, especially in persuasive speaking where the goal is to provide strategic counter-arguments that convince the listeners to understand and agree with their point of view. This type of audience analysis is called a *psychological audience analysis*.

Psychological Audience Analysis

At times a speechwriter needs to know more about the audience than their age, gender, sexual orientation, religion, ethnic group or social class. This general information is gathered by conducting a demographic audience analysis. When conducting a psychological audience analysis, the speechwriter's goal is to learn more personal information about the audience. Getting the job done requires you to become a seeker of knowledge by asking strategic questions that result in clear answers. This information will be used to better adapt the speech to the audience's interest or views. Every audience member holds personal beliefs that reflect their value system. A person's values are ingrained in their self-concept from birth. As discussed in Chapter two, these traditions, morals, and beliefs are taught by parents and other important people in the child's life. A psychological audience analysis is used most often in persuasive speeches where controversial topics are best approached and argued by first understanding why the audience holds opposing views on the issue. For example, if you are giving a speech in support of a woman's right to have an abortion, you must first identify audience members who disagree with you, and get a clear understanding of why they disagree before you can develop an effective counter-argument argument that speaks to and challenges their logical reasoning. We will discuss more about persuasion in Chapter 8.

Situational Audience Analysis

The final type of audience analysis is called a situational audience analysis which provides the speechwriter with critical information about the audience's feelings towards the speaker, topic, and event. Other information gathered during this investigation involves the time and location of the speech presentation. Knowing how an audience feels about the speaker, the topic, and the event, is instrumental to the effective outcome of a speech presentation. Information gathered using a situational audience analysis can help the speaker in the final stages of adapting a speech to the audience. The overall goal of public speaking is to capture the audience's attention and engage them throughout the presentation. If the audience has negative feelings about the speaker, the topic, or the event, they will be less likely to listen actively to the speech. There are methods that a speaker can use to address an audience that does not see them, the topic, or event in a favorable light. The speaker should first conduct a situational analysis to find out why the audience is unreceptive. This information can help the speaker address the issue in a diplomatic way to show the audience that his or her goals are ethical. It also helps to identify common experiences from which to filter important points that the audience can relate to. When the audience feels that they can relate to the speaker, the topic, or the event they are more apt to relax and receive the message.

Other information gathered in the situational audience analysis tells you about the size of the venue where the speech will take place. It is important to know what type of equipment is required to ensure that everyone can hear your voice, and have a clear view of you and your visual aids. Lighting will be important in rooms where there are no windows. Finally, the time of day that the speech takes place is important. Speeches that take place in the morning are often greeted by sleepy or hungry audience members, and speeches that take place in the evening may be greeted with fatigued audience members. Having this information in advance will help the speaker create an environment that is comfortable making it easier to engage them throughout the presentation.

Surveys

Now that you understand the three types of audience analysis used to gather data about the listeners, we will turn our attention to methods used to gather data when conductions any type of audience analysis. Three method-od used are: general observations, surveys, and interviews.

1. **General observations:** used to gather observable information about the audience. Such topical information will include age, gender, and ethnic group. This is the only type of viable information that can be gathered by observation. General observation of listeners can help with topic selection for informative or entertainment speeches. Persuasive speeches call for more in-depth information gathering.

2. **Surveys:** Three types of surveys are used to gather more in-depth knowledge about an audience. Advertisers use surveys quite often to learn more about consumer behaviors; you've probably been exposed to three primary types of surveys on many occasions as listed below.

Fixed-Alternative Survey	This type of survey limits the listener's responses to two or three choices. Example: *"Do you have an active Facebook account?"* *Circle one. [Yes - No]*
Scale Survey	A scale survey allows more opportunity for the listener to express their thoughts and feelings within a specific range. Example: *How often do you chat on social networking websites? 1 indicates "never," 3 indicated two to three times a week, and 5 indicating "every day."* Circle the number that best fits your answer. never [1 - 2 - 3 - 4 - 5] everyday
Open-Ended Survey	This type of survey is used when you do not want to influence how the person will answer. Instead, you pose a specific question and allow the respondent time to write an answer. Open-Ended surveys are useful to discover information you may not have considered, or may not have been disclosed by the audience member. The open-ended question method works best in cases where the speaker's views are strongly opposed. Focused questions offer a form of privacy were the audience member feels more comfortable discussing the issue in general. Information revealed may provide clues as to why the listeners oppose your thesis.

3. **Interviews:** A method used to gather information from individuals who have either experienced the topic that you are speaking about, or an expert who has spent quality time conduction research and case studies on the topic. Open-ended questions are normally used to gather information during interviews.

Gathering information to learn more about an audience requires the speaker to think critically about the questions posed on surveys or interviews. The goal of information gathering is to identify more revealing information, and this should be approached carefully. Remember, when people prefer not to disclose information, they will choose one of three options: lies, nonverbal hinting, or refusal to answer.

Critical thinking

Critical thinking is simply *"thinking about thinking!"*

Having the ability to think analytically is one of humanities greatest gifts when used properly. The act of thinking about your own thoughts should be approached strategically and logically in a way that seeks understanding for effective decision making. Thinking critically seeks to separate facts from opinions. When you think critically about the credibility of information that you read or hear, you are better equiped to make decisions based on proof and evidence that is valid and trustworthy. Everyone uses critical thinking to function in their day-to-day lives. When you get up in the morning, for example, you evaluate your clothing options based on certain criteria such as the weather, where you are going, or who you will interact with. This is critical thinking.

In public speaking, critical thinking is used to make every decision from the initial topic ideas to how the speech will conclude. As such, a speechwriter will not simply sit down and write a speech; the presentation will be developed in a step-by-step manor as the speechwriter thinks critically about the usefulness of each word, sentence, example, fact, and and other supporting detail used. Critical thinkers do not settle on the first piece of information they find because it relates to the topic, they will consider how it helps to explain a point made or provide an example of that point. Certain types of material may be appropriate to use for one group of listeners, but not for a different group of listeners.

Thinking about thinking is extremely important in speech writing!

When you conduct an audience analysis, it is important to use critical thinking to decide what types of questions to ask and what types of surveys to use. Afterwards, when you analyze the data that you've collected from your surveys, you will use critical thinking to create categories of meaning that help you understand what the audience is thinking. Using data that you gathered from surveys can be used in the speech but requires critical consideration. Statistics. for example, can be pulled from an audience survey to represent the listeners disposition. As you conduct your final revision to polish your speech you will think critically about the audience, remembering that the speech must be audience-centered; and therefore, every sentence should engage them in some way. Critical thinking is an important aspect of speechwritingg. Listeners must also listen critically as they seek to identify main points and connect reoccurring themes to help understand a speaker's point of view.

SHARE YOUR UNDERSTANDING: Building a Survey

The goal of this practice assignment is to provide you with an opportunity to practice building a survey. Remember, if you don't ask the right questions, you won't get the answers your looking for to help polish your speech. The question is the most important part of a survey. INSTRUCTIONS: Your instructor has asked you to write a short speech to teaching the class how to do something. The instructions are to select a hobby that you do at home or an activity that you have always wanted to do. Because you don't know how informed your classmates are on the topic you've selected, you must create and circulate a survey that will provide you with this information. You will use data taken from your audience analysis to assist in developing an audience-centered speech.

In the space provided below, use critical thinking to create a survey that will be used to gather data that shows how much your audience knows about the topic you've selected.

Select one type of survey: fixed-alternative, scale, open-ended

A final note about the audience. As we have learned, humans are not able to retain large amounts of information upon first hearing it. Short term memory cannot hold an entire speech. Because of this, professionals in the field of communication developed a strategy known as the 3Ts, "tell them what you are going to tell them in the introduction," "tell them everything you planned to tell them in the body," and "Tell them what you told them in the conclusion." The 3Ts method will help you structure the speech presentation in a way that helps the listeners hear the thesis and supporting themes in a variety of different ways throughout the speech. We will discuss how the 3Ts are inserted in different parts of the speech throughout the next chapter.

Summary

In this chapter, we discussed ethical speaking, understanding and controlling nervousness, and gathering data to help adapt your speech to the audience. Ethics is a philosophical concept where people decide what is right or wrong, or moral or immoral in human affairs. In communication, ethical speaking is critical to establishing credibility with your listeners. An ethical speaker would never write a speech to teach an audience how to create a fake ID, or one that seeks to harm others. Experiencing anxiety about public speaking is normal, as it indicates your concern for a positive outcome. Public speaking is rated as one of the primary types of anxiety for all people. Methods to control anxiety include accepting that it is normal and using anxiety to vitalize you instead of letting it victimize you. Also, you should allow for adequate time to practice and prepare your material. It is important to begin developing your speech as soon as you receive the assignment. Having adequate time to brainstorm, research, write, and revise means that you will interact with your speech several times before you deliver it. In doing so, you will become familiar with the material and feel more confident when it is time to share the information with your class. It is helpful to practice the speech three times a day, beginning three days prior to your presentation to help memorize it in sections. The more you rehearse, the more comfortable you will be during your presentation. Use your full speech outline on day one, and move to a delivery outline (discussed in Chapter 5), on the final day of rehearsal. You should be able to deliver your speech with limited use of the outline. Having a timer handy is always helpful during your practice periods. To develop a speech that is geared towards your audience, it is important to find out what your audience knows or does not know, as well as their opinions about the topic. This information can be analyzed to help you decide what type of information is required in your speech to successfully inform, persuade, or entertain the audience.

Key terms

Ethics
Plagiarism
Global
Patchwork
Incremental
Anxiety
Adrenaline
Visualization
Demographic Audience Analysis

Surveys
Fixed-Alternative
Scale
Open-Ended
Interviews
Psychological Audience Analysis
Situational Audience Analysis
Critical thinking

Four Steps to Writing a Speech

VOCABULARY BUILDERS: *Epiphany*, noun
To suddenly see or understand something in a new or clear way.
"I've struggled with this math problem for years; but today, I had an epiphany - I get it!

Succinct, adjective
Using few words to express a brief thought or idea
"His instructions for today's activities were quite succinct."

## CHAPTER 5

Speech Heading: Brainstorming

General Purpose:

The assignment and general purpose for giving the speech.

Narrowed Topic:

A narrowed topic must reflect the general purpose.

Specific Purpose:

A statement that indicates specifically what you want your audience to know at the end of the speech.

Central Idea:

A one-sentence summary of a speech which includes the thesis and a preview of the main points.

"A speaker should approach his preparation not by what he wants to say, but by what he wants to learn."

—Todd Stocker

Public speaking dates back 2,500 years to Ancient Greece and Rome where noble men made speeches to inform citizens about laws of conduct, economic issues, or to debate politics. Public speaking was important in everyday life to communicate important information to the citizens. Over 2,500 years ago, there was no Internet, television, telephones, newspapers, or mass-produced books. The only way to learn about anything newsworthy was through public speaking events. Aristotle, a Greek philosopher lived during this era and laid the framework for public speaking, also known as rhetoric, which is still applied today. We will discuss these principles throughout this section.

Writing a speech shares many of the same method as essay writing. Speechwriters brainstorm topics, conduct credible research to locate useful supporting material, develop a well-crafted thesis, and organize main points in the body that explains the thesis in a logical way. The difference between writing an essay and writing a speech is that the speaker must apply strategic verbal and nonverbal strategies in a speech whose goal is to engage the listeners and keep their attention from beginning to end. Whereas a written essay does not demand that you read it in its entirety at one time. This chapter presents the four important steps of speech development.

Step One: Speech Heading – Brainstorming

The speech heading is designed to guide speechwriters through a critical thinking process of brainstorming to develop four connected statements; each statement helps to build the next statement beginning with the general purpose of the speech. This speech heading strategy is designed to reduce topic selection frustrations and writers block. The four parts of speech heading are, general purpose, narrowed topic statement, specific purpose statement, and the central idea. Let's look at each of the four parts separately to understand the purpose of each part and how to develop effective statements.

General Purpose

The first step in writing a speech is to identify the type of speech you are assigned to develop and present. Because specific strategies and methods are used to build different types of speeches, it is important to be clear on the broad goal of the speech – the general purpose. In most cases, an instructor will give you the broad goal as an assignment, or organizers may provide you with a broad goal if you are speaking at a an event.

- If you are asked to give an informative speech, **the general purpose** is *"To Inform."*
- If you are asked to give a persuasive speech, **the general purpose** is *"To Persuade."*
- If you are asked to give an entertainment speech, **the general purpose** is *"To Entertain."*

Understanding the general purpose of a public speaking presentation will make it easier to select an appropriate topic.

Narrowed Topic Statement

Once the general purpose of an assignment is known, the next step is to identify a topic that fits the general purpose of the speech assignment. A topic is not the same as a title. A topic is a narrow statement that implies specifically what you will discuss in your speech. If written effectively, the narrowed topic statement will easily become the thesis. A title is a creative word or short phrase designed to attract attention, but a title does not tell an audience specifically what they will hear in a speech. Some instructors will provide students with a list of topics to choose from when assigning a speech while others allow students to select their own topics.

Guidelines for Topic Development

Should not be a fragmented thought	Must meet general purpose of assignment
Should represent one major theme	Must be audience-centered
Should not be vague	Must be able to meet time limits
Should not use figurative language	Must not be too trivial for audience

Many brainstorming strategies are used to help identify an appropriate topic; four methods are presented below.

Brainstorming strategies

1. Consider a topic that reflects your interests or experiences.	These types of topics should always be the first to consider because they are the simplest.
2. Consider a topic you always wanted to learn more about.	Most of us are curious about something that we have little or no knowledge of. This is an opportunity for you to research and learn more about the topic and then share what you've learned with your audience.
3. Consider a topic that you are passionate about (especially for persuasive speeches).	Topics that spark raw emotion make for great persuasive appeals, as you are vested in proving your point by supporting it with evidence, facts, and proof.
4. Consider interesting topics discussed in your other classes, current events, news, technology, etc.	The world provides us with a wealth of topic ideas. Every day there are news reports that focus on controversy, human interest stories, entertainment news, and world events that would make for interesting topics.

After you select a topic, you must narrow it in order to express exactly what you want to talk about. The reason for narrowing your topic is to shape it into a thesis statement which is the main or controlling idea of the speech. When you take time to think critically about your topic, most will use one or more of the strategies listed above. The outcome of your brainstorming session will likely result in a one or two word topic. The next step is to narrow that topic by asking yourself what you want the audience to know specifically about this topic. Your answer will become your narrowed topic. Sometimes the narrowed topic is not narrowed enough. You can access this by playing the "questions game." We will use "music" as a broad topic to help understand how this game works. Let's say you have always loved music and would like to present a speech about music. This means your initial broad topic is "music." The problem, is there are many aspects of music that you can focus on in a speech. Unfortunately, you cannot discuss every aspect of music in one speech because this violates the guidelines for topic development. This is where the questions game begins. Ask yourself this question, *"What aspect of music do I wish to share with my listeners?"* The answer will be a type of music that you grew up listening to; jazz. Now, that your broad topic has narrowed to "jazz music," let's ask the question again. *"What aspect of jazz music do I want to discuss with my listeners?"* This question will motivate you to think deeper in order to pinpoint the final answer. As you engage in a bit of self-talk about your love for jazz music, you realize that there are many types of jazz because that specific genre of music has changed quite a bit since your parent's era of jazz. BINGO! That's it! You are now prepared to answer the second question; "Jazz music has changed a lot over the last sixty years." This more complete topic statement is narrowed in a way that shapes the direction that you will travel in your speech.

Sometimes you may want to polish your topic a bit more by removing words that constitute clutter. This can be done by substituting the word "evolution" for "has changed a lot." Now you have developed a polished speech topic that will make it easy to proceed to the body of your speech where you will provide explanations of how jazz music has evolved over the past sixty years. Now, you should have a better understanding of how a narrowed topic easily becomes a thesis when developed fully. Look at the following example to get an idea of how a broad topic is narrowed to express the primary focus of the speech.

Original Topic: Music

Narrowed revision: Jazz music has changed a lot over the past fifty years.

Final polished topic: The evolution of jazz over the past fifty years.

Spending adequate time with topic development is the key to effective and satisfying speechwriting. The point here is to take topic development serious as it is the most important step in the overall speechwriting process.

One final comment about your topic supports the guidelines; you must think critically about methods to relate your topic to the audience to make them want to listen. With music, for example, you can show your audience how the different styles of jazz is integrated in many other genre's of music. Point to popular artist whose music reflects jazz influences. Now, it's time to practice what you've learned in this section.

SHARE YOUR UNDERSTANDING

For the two broad topics below, think about what you might like to talk about as it relates to each topic and narrow it to create a final polished topic. Use the example above.

TOPIC: <u>Fast Food</u>

NARROWED:_____

POLISHED (if desired): _____

_____

TOPIC: <u>Reality Television</u>

NARROWED:_____

POLISHED (if desired): _____

_____

Now that you understand the first two steps of speech heading development, you can focus specifically on what you want your audience to know about your topic.

Specific Purpose Statement

When working on your speech heading, you must answer the following question, *"What do I want my audience to know specifically about my topic at the end of my speech?"* This is called *the specific purpose statement*. Guidelines for generating a specific purpose statement are as follows:

- **The statement is one sentence that included an infinitive phrase: "To inform my audience ..."**
- **Must not be a question**
- **Avoids figurative and vague language**

The first four words of the specific purpose statement are called the infinitive phrase: *"To inform my audience."* The infinitive phrase is a statement that reminds the writer "who" he or she is giving the speech to – the audience. Note: The first two words of the specific purpose are the same as the two words in the general purpose: "to inform".

You will need to add a final word to complete the infinitive phrase before finalizing the specific purpose statement. Some common words that are used are "about", "how", or "to". You must decide which adverb or preposition fits best as you develop your specific purpose statement. And finally, bring down your topic to complete the specific purpose statement as shown below.

- General Purpose: **To inform**
- Narrowed Topic: **Spring break should be used to catch up on coursework or projects.**
    - Infinitive Phrase: **To inform my audience**
    - Choose an adverb: *about, how,* or preposition: *to*
            To inform my audience (that)
    - Add the topic: **Spring break should be used to catch up on coursework or projects.**

Specific Purpose: *To inform my audience (that) spring break should be used to catch up on coursework or projects.*

By combining the general purpose and the topic, you can easily create the specific purpose statement which will help you develop your speech. The goal is to refer back to this statement periodically as you piece your speech together to ensure that you do not lose focus of your specific purpose. It is easy to get off track, or forget "who" you are writing the speech for. Writer's block can be avoided when a speechwriter takes time to think critically about the specific purpose of the presentation.

Guidelines for developing the specific purpose statement

1. Must be a full sentence that begins with the infinitive phrase, (To inform my audience)
2. Must not include figurative language: "I told you *a million times* that I am not a basketball player!"
3. Must not use vague language such as something, things, stuff, etc.
4. Must not be written in a question format.
5. Must be limited to one specific idea.
6. Should not be too vague or too general

HOMEWORK

In the following partially completed speech heading scenarios, narrow the topic to fit your interest. Use the general purpose and narrowed topic to develop a suitable specific purpose statement. Be sure to add the infinitive phrase as you develop each specific purpose statement. You will compare your answers in small groups and with the class.

EXAMPLE:
General Purpose: To inform
Broad Topic: Reality TV
Revised Narrowed Topic: Reality TV is sending negative messages to teenagers about acceptable social behaviors.
Specific Purpose: <u>To inform my audience (how)</u> reality TV is sending negative messages to teenagers about acceptable social behaviors.

NAME: _____   DATE: _____

1. **General Purpose:** to inform

2. **Broad Topic:** Facebook

3. **Revised Narrowed Topic:** _____

4. **Specific Purpose:** _____
_____
_____
_____

1. **General Purpose:** to inform

2. **Broad Topic:** Careers

3. **Revised Narrowed Topic:** _____

4. **Specific Purpose:** _____
_____
_____
_____

1. General Purpose: to inform

2. Broad Topic: Math

3. Revised Narrowed Topic: _____

4. Specific Purpose: _____

_____

_____

_____

1. General Purpose: to inform

2. Broad Topic: Vacations

3. Revised Narrowed Topic: _____

4. Specific Purpose: _____

_____

_____

_____

1. General Purpose: to inform

2. Broad Topic: Fast Food

3. Revised Narrowed Topic: _____

4. Specific Purpose: _____

_____

_____

_____

1. General Purpose: to inform

2. Broad Topic: Cell Phones

3. Revised Narrowed Topic: _____

4. Specific Purpose: _____

_____

_____

_____

Central Idea

The fourth and final part of the speech heading is the central idea, which is a one-sentence summary of a speech that serves two purposes. The first purpose is to reveal the thesis and the second purpose is to preview the main points that will explain the thesis in the body of the speech. The central idea also represents the first "T;" tell's the audience what you're going to tell them."

Guidelines for writing a central idea		
Should not be written as a question	Should not be written as a fragment	Must be one topic expressed in one sentence.
Must not use figurative language	Must not use vague language	Must summarize speech

As mentioned earlier, the narrowed topic of the speech heading when written strategically will easily become the thesis of the speech. A thesis is the main focus of a speech, or *a* statement that the speechwriter wants to prove or disprove. The first part of your central idea is your narrowed topic or thesis, and the second part is a preview of how you plan to explain the topic. In order to create a central idea that is worded correctly and flows smoothly, you may rearrange, add, or subtract key words from your narrowed topic. You can use a semi-colon to connect your list of main points to the thesis to form one grammatically correct sentence. The main points can be implied in the central idea instead of listing them individually. It is important to consider your audience when selecting main points. Below are a few well worded central ideas that align with the guidelines.

- Thanksgiving is my favorite holiday because of family, food, and fun.
- We can help the fight against global warming if we recycle, avoid using aerosol sprays, and conserve water.
- Physical activity has proven to be a stress reducer; today, I will discuss three primary types of stress reduction activities.

SHARE YOUR UNDERSTANDING

Identify the error in each central idea?

I. The first thing to do when you get a new pet is to purchase food. You must also purchase a leash.

II. Pets are expensive and pets can be great companions.

III. The Blue Angels.

Explaining the Thesis

To select appropriate audience-centered main points, you must consider what type of information will best explain or prove your thesis while engaging the audience. Main points are used to explain your thesis and must be selected with the audience in mind. A speech normally includes three main points, but may have more or less depending on time limits. Because the practical goal for a speechwriter is to be heard, selecting main points must be approached creatively and logically. Two questions to consider when deciding what your main points should be are: "What might the audience already know about my topic?" And "What types of main points will engage my listeners as I explain my thesis?"

For beginning speeches such as self-introduction and informative speeches, you can make general observations of your audience to answer these questions. Persuasive speeches, however, will require you to dig deeper by analyzing the audience with surveys in order to answer these questions. Main points should be developed as a full sentence statement, not a fragmented thought and should be organized in a logical order.

To finalize your central idea, you must blend the thesis and main points into one grammatical correct sentence; often a compound complex sentence connected with a semi-colon. The final outcome will summarize your speech. At that point, your job is to explain each main point in the body of the speech by using lots of examples, facts, interviews, or statistics that will help the listeners understand your thesis. Inserting a few of your experiences will help personalize the speech making it more interesting to the audience. The central idea must also meet all of the guidelines listed previously. Here are some final thoughts to consider when structuring your central idea.

1. The main points can be listed or implied as shown below:
   Listed: *Jazz music has evolved greatly over three eras; 1960 to 1970, 1971 to 1985, and 1986 to 2010.*
   Implied: *Jazz music has changed greatly over the past fifty years.*

2. Main points must be explained in the same order that you've listed them in the central idea.

3. You may also rearrange the wording of your thesis to create a more conversational central idea statement. *"The jazz music tradition has undergone many changes; today, I will discuss three eras of change over the past fifty years."*

Most students find it easier to list the main points because it helps them focus on the pre-assigned main points. You know exactly what you will explain to your audience. When you allude to the main points that explain your thesis, you may have general thoughts about the main points you plan to use to explain your thesis. However, this has the potential to become an unexpected case of writer's block as you try to define each main point when developing the body of the speech.

Organizational Patterns

Before moving your main points from the central idea to the body of the speech where they will be explained, you must decide which main point to present first, second, and last. Main points must be organized using logical patterns that helps the audience follow with ease. Four common types of organizational patterns used in speech-writing are explained below.

Chronological order: Main points are organized in a timeline pattern. For example, historical events or narratives are best understood when presented in the order in which they occur.
Main Point I. In the summer, my family loves to participate in daring water sports like jet skiing and surfing.
Main Point II. In the fall, my family turns to hiking, fishing, and camping in wooded areas.
Main Point III. In the winter, my family loves to snowboard and ski.

Topical order: Allows the writer to decide the order in which main points are presented. Often, the most important main point is presented first while the least important main point last. This order may be reversed if the writer wants to save the most important point for last. Consider the audience when using topical order.
Main Point I. Going on a blind date is a frightening experience.
Main Point II. Some blind dates have turned out pretty good, while others have been unpleasant.
Main Point III. When someone sets me up on a blind date, I ask them to text me a photo of the person and their full name so I can Google them and look them up on Facebook.

Spatial order: Main points are organized in a directional pattern. For example, if you are giving a speech on the Hawaiian Islands, you might organize your main points as follows.
Main Point I. The oldest and _northernmost_ island in the Island chain is graced with natural beauty.
Main Point II. Molokai is located near the _center_ of the Hawaiian Islands and has preserved its connection to the past and its love for the outdoors.
Main Point III. Larger than all of the other islands combined, Hawaii Island, or Hawaii, or the Big Island, is the _southernmost_ island and vast enough to hold 11 of the world's 13 climactic zones.

Causal order (_cause and effect_): Has two or more main points. Causal order is arranged to help the writer prove that a relationship exists between two or more vairables. This can be an event that has already happened (what caused or triggered it to occur), or an effect that could occur in the future (what are we doing today that will cause this effect to become a reality in the future?) The second main point offers evidence that proves the first main point to be true – a cause contributed to a specific effect, or an effect was caused by a specific action. This organizational pattern is used with both informative and persuasive speeches.
Main Point I. (effect) Today, more school age children are obese than fifty years ago, which is due to easy access to fatty foods.
Main Point II. (cause) Childhood obesity can be attributed to lower priced fast foods and unhealthy school lunch offerings.

SHARE YOUR UNDERSTANDING

Practice what you've learned. Use the information provided to develop your own central idea. Be creative and use critical thinking.

EXAMPLE

General Purpose: To inform
Narrowed Topic: Specialty coffee shop advertising has inspired a new generation of coffee drinkers.
Specific Purpose: To inform my audience how specialty coffee shop advertising has inspired a new generation of coffee drinkers.
Central Idea: Specialty coffee shop advertising has inspired a new generation of coffee drinkers by using young adults in their commercials, creating dessert-like coffee drinks, and using European terms to describe their products.

General Purpose: To inform

Narrowed Topic: Visiting the dentist twice a year can save teeth

Specific Purpose: To inform my audience that visiting the dentist twice a year can save teeth.

Central Idea: _____

_____

General Purpose: To inform

Narrowed Topic: People are getting married for the wrong reasons

Specific Purpose: To inform my audience that people are getting married for the wrong reasons.

Central Idea: _____

_____

SHARE YOUR UNDERSTANDING

Use the central idea given to identify the general purpose, narrowed topic, specific purpose, and main points. The general purpose can be to informative or persuasive. Each statement must be written in full sentences, and you will need to add words to the main points to create a full statement.

General Purpose: _____

Topic: (Narrowed): _____

Specific Purpose: _____

_____

Central Idea: *The three major steps in responding to an emergency are surveying the scene, contacting an emergency medical service, and starting CPR if needed.*

Main Point: I. _____

_____

Main Point: II. _____

_____

Main Point: III. _____

_____

General Purpose: _____

Topic: (Narrowed): _____

Specific Purpose: _____

_____

Central Idea: *The effects of falling off of a bike without a protective helmet can result in a fractured skull, brain damage, and paralysis.*

Main Point: I. _____

_____

Main Point: II. _____

_____

Main Point: III. _____

_____

Step Two: Developing The Body - Annotation Symbols

The second step in writing a speech is to develop the body; now you'll "tell them your audience what you plan to tell them" - the second of the 3Ts. Each each main point selected to explain the thesis must also be explained fully using a variety attention keeping strategies. Remember, speech development is structured in an essay format; introduction, body, conclusion. There are several outline formats used to help the speechwriter develop a speech. Outline formats for speech development also include symbols that communicate the specific role each sentence serves in the speech. These are known as annotation symbols.

Annotation symbols are important in speech development as the writer must think critically about the usefulness and placement of each sentence.

As you develop your speech, it is important to assign appropriate annotation symbols that communicate the relationship between sentences in each section. The first step to outlining a speech is to learn the four tiers of annotation symbols indicated below. Understanding and applying each annotation identification symbol appropriately, when developing your speech will help connect the points you seek to make.

Roman numerals	I, II, III	Communicates the sentence is a main point
Capital letters	A, B, C	Communicates the sentence is a subpoint
Numbers	1, 2, 3	Communicates the sentence is a sub-subpoint
Lowercase letters	a, b, c	Communicates the sentence is a sub-sub-subpoint

Subpoints

Just as your thesis is explained by main points, each main point must also be explained by using subpoints. Capital letters are used to identify a subpoint. In looking at the pattern presented so far: main points explains the thesis, and subpoints explains main points; we can easily add a third level that explains "subpoints." This third level of annotation is called sub-subpoints as shown in the box above. Most speeches will have lots of sub-subpoints as they are the sentences that explain each subpoint. Think about a paragraph format where you have one opening sentence (the subpoint) followed by several supporting sentences (sub-subpoints) that explains the opening sentence. The sentences that follow (i.e. sub-subpoints) should further explain the subpoint. Annotation symbols are arranged using a hierarchy alignment that shows the relationship between the sentences in a paragraph. Subpoints, for example, are indented under each main point to show that they are related. Each new subpoint must be assigned a new capital letter.

When copying your main points from the central idea into the body of the speech outline, minor adjustments must be made. Each main point listed in the central idea will be a fragment and must be developed into a full sentence in the body of the outline. See the examples below.

Fragment: Incorrect	Full Sentence: Correct
I. People love pizza.	I. Pizza is of one of America's favorite fast foods.
II. Different pizza crust.	II. There are three types of pizza crust; thin, hand tossed, and deep dish.
III. Different toppings	III. There are many toppings to choose from when creating a pizza.

Annotation symbols are also assigned to each main point. In the example below you'll notice how each main point is identified by a roman numeral. Also represented in the example are subpoints that explain each main point.

Central Idea: *One of America's favorite fast food is pizza because you can personalize it.*

I. Studies show that pizza is one of America's favorite fast foods.
   A. I was not surprised to learn this fact during my research, since my friends and I eat pizza almost every day.
   B. Pizza.com fun facts reports 94 percent of Americans eat pizza regularly.
   C. According to the National Association of Pizza Operators (NAPO), approximately 3 billion pizzas are sold in the U.S. each year.

II. There are three primary types of pizzas: thin crust, hand tossed, and deep dish.
   A. The Chicago thin crust is crispier and crunchier than the New York style and is normally cut into squares rather than diagonal slices.
   B. Hand tossed pizza dough is one of the more common types of crust that you will see.
   C. According to Foodtravel.about.com, in the 1940s, Pizzeria Uno in Chicago developed the deep-dish pizza, which has a deep crust that lines a deep dish, similar to a large metal cake or pie pan.

III. There are many toppings to choose from when creating a pizza.
   A. Topping a pizza is a creative adventure for the pallet.
   B. Common pizza toppings are mozzarella cheese, Italian sausage, or pepperoni.
   C. Gourmet toppings range from vegetables, pineapple, or anchovies, to more elaborate steak and potato wedges toppings.

As you develop each sentence of your speech a few questions should be considered: *"Have I selected audience-centered subpoints help explain each main point?"* and, *"Have I used critical thinking when selecting words in my sentences for maximum impact?"* Lastly, in essay writing, every paragraph ends with a closing sentence that wraps up the point made. The same is true for speechwriting, every main points must also have a closing statement; this normally occurs in the last sentence or two. Next we'll look at the last two types of annotation symbols.

Sub-subpoints and Sub-sub-subpoints

Subpoint "A" from the speech excerpt above; *"I was not surprised to learn this fact during my research, since my friends and I eat pizza almost every day,"* requires further explanation. In fact, each subpoint in the excerpt above requires further explanation. To do so will requires the use of the third and fourth levels of annotation symbols: sub-subpoints represented by numbers and sub-sub-subpoints represented by lower case letters. Below is an example of how the four levels of annotation look in outline format.

• **Sub-subpoints** explain the subpoint directly above it.
 	
 • **Sub-sub-subpoints** explain the sub-subpoint that is directly above it.
	I. Main point
	   A. Subpoint
	   B. Subpoint
	     1. Sub-subpoint
	     2. Sub-subpoint
	       a. Sub-sub-subpoint
	       b. Sub-sub-subpoint
	 Notice how each level of annotation symbols are indented to express a hierarchy of related thought.

The excerpt from a speech below provides us with an example of how the four levels of annotations symbols are used in hierarchy order to show how each sentence is related to the one above it and below it.

Central Idea: My morning began on a positive note, but quickly turned into a nightmare.

I. I got up early and left my apartment at 7:00 am in order to get to work early.
   A. However, when I got to my car I was greeted with three aggravating problems that prevented me from leaving my parking spot.

1. First, I noticed that there was a big circular object locked to my front tire.
   a. I slapped my head remembering the warning letter I'd received last week warning if I didn't pay my parking ticket, my car would be booted.
   b. And now, there it was – a bright yellow boot locked to my rear tire.
2. The second reason I couldn't leave my parking spot was my car keys.
   a. The doors were locked, and I could see my keys laying in the compartment between the front seats where I'd tossed them last night as I gathered my bags.
3. And to make matters worse, I wouldn't be able to leave the parking spot even if I had my keys and my tire was free of the boot.
   a. Two cars were parked right on my bumpers, one in the front and one in the back.
B. At that point, I knew I was going to be late for work and my boss would not be happy.
   1. I was already on probation due to excessive late arrivals.
   2. So, I ran to the corner to catch the next bus only to discover that it was delayed due to construction traffic.
   3. It was two hours past my starting time when I finally arrived to work; needless to say, my boss immediately terminated me.

HOMEWORK

A challenging aspect of outlining a speech by using annotation symbols confidently: subpoint, sub-sub-point, and sub-sub-subpoint. The easiest way to become comfortable using annotation is to practice.

Instructions: The speech excerpt below includes three main points with supporting subpoint, sub-sub-points, sub-sub-subpoints. **Your challenge:** Use a separate sheet of paper to fully annotate this speech excerpt. Be sure to indent to show the hierarchy of thought. It's useful to identify the three main points first and, leave space between each main point for the subpoint, sub-subpoints, sub-sub-subpoints.

Central Idea: *Most of my college classes are okay; but my favorites are public speaking, art, and sociology.*

My favorite class this semester is the fundamentals of speech communication because I am learning how to organize my thoughts to avoid being misunderstood. Being misunderstood has always been a problem for me. I guess it's because I'm a musician who is kind of "out there," or so people say. Learning how to outline my thoughts has helped me to think strategically before I open my mouth. The most important thing that I think about before I open my mouth is "Who am I talking to" because answering this question helps me chose my words carefully to make sure that person understands me.

Another thing that I think about is speaking in full sentences to communicate everything I'm thinking about. Prior to taking this class I spoke in fragments all the time. No wonder why people didn't understand me! I keep most of my thoughts in my head. It was hard to organize my thoughts when I first started the class because I just like to talk. But public speaking has taught me how to slow down and think before letting words fall out of my mouth.

My second favorite class this semester is art. When I registered for art 101, I thought it was going to be a piece of cake. I was wrong. Professor Candle had us researching the history of different types of art to learn about their origins. I thought I'd be painting and drawing. But, once I stopped complaining and conducted my research I learned a lot about the different processes used to create 3-D abstracts and strategies used to mix paints. In the end, I was glad that Professor Candle made us read first because it helped me develop more skills to improve my drawing and painting abilities.

My third favorite class is sociology because it studies how people live and behave in different cultures and environments. I'm the kind of person who loves to people-watch to observe their behaviors. It might sound crazy, but it's not – people do amazing and strange things when they think no one is watching. Sociology also helps me understand myself, and that is a good thing.

Connectives

During a speech, the speaker will share significant amount of information with the audience in order to explain the thesis. As learned in Chapter Two, short-term memory prevents us from holding more than thirty second of information at a time. This makes it challenging for the audience to remember important points shared as the speaker moves through their presentation. Because of this, speechwriters must remind their audience of important themes shared as they move through their presentation.

Connectives are used for this purpose. As the name suggests, connective are used to connect the speaker's thoughts in a way that helps the listener understand and remember how one thought is related to the next. Connectives are also used to summarize information previously shared or to preview upcoming information. Speechwriters insert connective throughout their speech during the developmental process. The final use of connectives is to help the speaker keep track of where they are in the speech during the actual presentation. We will explore four types of connectives in this section.

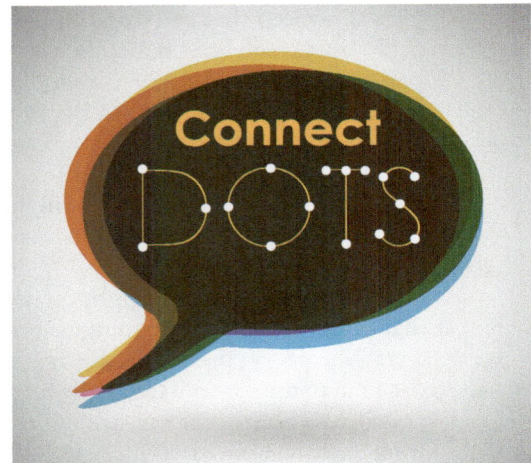

#1. Transitional words and phrases: tells the audience that one though has ended and new thought is beginning.

Adding more information:	also, again, as well as, besides, furthermore, in addition, likewise, moreover, similarly, in fact, indeed
Contrast and Comparison:	contrast, by the same token, instead, likewise, on one hand, on the contrary, rather, similarly, yet, but, however, still, nevertheless, in contrast
Summarizing:	all in all, all things considered, briefly, in any case, in any event, in brief, on the whole, in short, in summary, in the long run, to sum up, to summarize, finally
Generalizing:	as a rule, as usual, for the most part, generally, generally speaking, ordinarily, usually
An Example:	for example, for instance, in particular, particularly, specifically, to demonstrate, to illustrate
A Result or an Effect:	accordingly, finally, consequently, hence, so, therefore

#2. Signposts: similar to road signs that tells the audience where the speaker is in the speech.

The first …	A…	To begin …
The second …	B …	Next …
The third …	C …	To end …

#3. Internal Summaries:

Used when a lot of information has been shared. The speaker will summarize the main theme of that section before proceeding to the next point. Although most internal summaries occur at the end of a main point, in technical speeches internal summaries often occur in the middle of the main point.	Example: *"So far, I have shared the importance of Maya Angelo's thought provoking poetry and novels which earned many literary awards."*

#4. Internal Previews:

Used to tell the audience where the speech is headed next. An internal preview is normally used between main points or after a lengthy subpoint.	Example: *"Next, I will share one of Dr. Angelo's most notable poems read at President Clinton's inauguration."*

SHARE YOUR UNDERSTANDING

Time to practice using transitions and signpost. Read each excerpt below for clarity. Next, consider how you could add transitions or signpost to connect one sentence to the next. Use the blank spaces beneath each speech excerpt to re-write it with the addition of connectives.

I. Many people use social networking websites.

    A. Facebook is of one of the most popular social networking websites.

        1. More businesses advertise on Facebook today.

        2. Families who live in different states or countries can talk to each other on Facebook.

I.

1. Working a full time job and going to school is hard.

    A. There's no time for relaxation.

    B. I can't get all of my reading and homework done.

I.

As you can see, the body of a speech requires the speechwriter to focus on many different areas of development to create a speech that flows smoothly from one thought to the next. The body of a speech is the actual speech whose primary purpose is to explain the thesis. The introduction and conclusion of a speech presentation is not the speech, but serves an important role in the overall presentation. Next, we will look at the third and fourth steps of speech development: the introduction and the conclusion.

Step Three: The Introduction

The introduction of a speech is the most important part of the speech because its overall goal is to capture and keep the attention of the audience while strategically leading them to the central idea. Because of this, the speech introduction is often referred to as the "lead in." You should not write your introduction until you have completed the body of the speech. While conducting research on your topic, creative ideas will emerge for introduction material. Because the goal of an introduction is to gain the listener's attention and lead them to the central idea, this section should only cover roughly twenty percent of your speaking time.

Four goals of the introduction are:

- to grasp your audience's attention
- to show that you are credible (trust worthy) to speak on the topic
- to give your audience a reason to listen by relating the topic to them
- to introduce your central idea

Strategies to grasp your audience's attention

In general, speakers have three seconds to grab the attention of their audience before they stop listening. Speechwriters must learn and use a variety of strategies whose goal is to capture the listener's attention at the start of the speech. The "hook and bait" method of attention gaining is often used to achieve this goal. This strategy suggest that: just a fisherman baits his hook with interesting bits of food that attracts fish to bite onto the baited hook, so too does a public speaker. Bait used by a speaker comes in many forms as indicated in the chart below. Once you have hooked your audience with interesting bait that has captured their attention, you must slowly lead them towards your central idea. Attention gaining is the most important aspect of a speech presentation because the audience must feel motivated to listen; remember listening is work.

Use a topic-related quote.	Tell a topic-related joke.
Tell a shocking or fascinating story that is related to your topic	Reference current events related to your topic
Share some startling facts related to your topic	Describe a problem that the audience should be, or are aware of
Ask rhetorical questions that lead to your topic	Reference a previous speech

Credibility statement

To persuade listeners to accept information presented as valid and true, you must tell them why they should believe you. A credibility statement informs the audience that information presented in the speech comes from valid research and sometimes personal experience. Example: *"I've always been curious about ongoing global warming warnings. I wondered what it really meant and why people were so afraid of it. So, I researched the topic and discovered some interesting facts about global warming and our future that I will share in this speech."*

Give audience a reason to listen

Once you have engaged your audience by using a strategically creative attention getter and explain what qualifies your information as credible, the next step is keeping your audience engaged by connecting the topic to the listeners. This calls for more in-depth critical thinking as you consider some aspect of the topic that a general audience can relate to because they've experienced it. *"You"* language should be used to achieve this goal. Example, *"Have 'you' ever eaten something so cold and it gave you brain freeze, and the only thing you could do was wait until it passed? Well that's how my gums every time I eat cold food because I have sensitive gums."*

Present your central idea

The final goal of the introduction is to provide your audience with a summary of the speech – the central idea. This is the same summary statement that you generated in your speech heading. Your audience will be more apt to listen if they know where the speech is going. This is why it is critical to develop an effective one-sentence central idea that includes a clear thesis and a preview of the body. Copy and paste your central idea from the speech heading into the introduction section of your speech outline. When presenting the central idea, it is critical that you state it exactly as you worded it in the speech heading to avoid confusing your audience. Below is the introduction to the speech excerpt from page 84 and 85. Study this brief introduction example for understanding. Know that some introductions may be longer.

Example: Introduction

I. **Attention Getter:** I am not a morning person, so getting up early to report to work at 7:00 AM has been stressful!

   A. When my alarm goes off, I always hit the snooze button several times and then over-sleep; I know some of you probably do the same thing.

   B. Most of the time I'm up late completing an assignment for one of my college classes; so I only get a few hours of sleep.

II. **Credibility Statement:** My mom suggested that I take a time management class; she knew I was on a 30-day attendance probation at work because of of my late night study sessions.

   A. So, I Goggled "time management" classing in my area and did some research to find out what I would learn.

      a. I was surprised to find a free class right on my campus!

   B. To be honest, I wasn't really interested in going but I needed to keep my job; plus, I was on the verge of failing most of my classes.

      a. I didn't really have a choice.

III. **Give Audience a Reason to Listen:** Have any of you ever been in a situation like this?

   A. Maybe it was other responsibilities that you struggled to balance with your class load because there wasn't enough time!

   B. I know I'm not the only one who has struggled with time deadlines since we're all college students.

   C. After taking the class, I actually made a time management schedule and began following it.

      1. After two weeks of getting to work on time my boss complimented my efforts; and, I even got caught up on my school assignments.

         a. I was feeling pretty good.

   D. I stopped hitting the snooze button on my alarm clock because it became easier to get up early when I wasn't up late completing assignments.

   E. On the last day of my attendance probation at work and I had to meet with the human resources director and my boss to end my probation; I was excited.

IV. **Present Central Idea:** My morning began on a positive note, but quickly turned into a nightmare.

Step Four: The Conclusion

The conclusion of a speech serves three primary goals.

- To signal the end of the speech.
- To summarize the main theme of the speech that will lock in your residual message.
- To provide listeners with a satisfying end.

Signal the end of the speech

Some speakers signal the end of a speech with the phrase, "In conclusion". This is not the best way to wrap up a speech because members of the audience may stop listening when they hear this phrase. Therefore, it is important to signal the close of your speech in a way that motivates the audience to continue listening. A speech often ends by returning to the introduction to wrap up a story that began in the introduction, or to reinforce the thesis. Below are some useful phrases that will help achieve this goal.

- "So, as you can see …"
- "Now you can see how …"
- "Remember the story I told you in the beginning of this speech? (add the ending of the story)"
- "All-in-all"

Summarize the main themes of the speech

A summary of your speech is the residual message. The *residual message* is the primary theme you want your listeners to take away from your speech long after the speech is forgotten. Example: In Martin Luther King Jr.'s "I Have a Dream" speech, the residual message is that he had a dream that all people would be equal and the world would be a better place. The residual message summary is a short statement that also expresses the last of the 3 T's concept, "tell the audience what you told them." If you focus on punctuating the residual message throughout the speech, it will be remembered as you close with it.

Connect back to the introduction for a satisfying end

The closing statement is just as important as the opening statement in your introduction because when developed well, it leaves the audience with a satisfying ending. The *residual message* of the speech is more likely to be remembered when a speech includes a satisfying ending. Because listeners generally remember the first and last statements in a speech, the closing should always tie back to the introduction in a meaningful way.

Three useful strategies to connect the conclusion back to the introduction:

■ When sharing a brief story in the introduction, withhold how it ends until the conclusion.
■ Refer back to the introduction with a quote or by referencing the attention getter that you used.
■ Pose a rhetorical question in the introduction and answer it in the conclusion.
■ Close with a quote that supports the residual message.

Example: Conclusion

I. **Signal the end of the speech:** All-in-all, I tried to correct a bad habit before I suffered the consequences of my actions; I lost.

II. **Summarize the main theme and the residual message:** What I learned from this experience is the importance of using some type of time management schedule to organize my personal and public life; especially important due date and deadlines.

III. **Connect back to the introduction in a circular manner for a satisfying end:** I'm still not a morning person, but this experience has changed how I plan my day. My next job will not start before 9:00 AM, and I'll be sure to take evening and weekend classes.

Summary

Developing an effective speech requires the writer to pay specific attention to detail. The speech heading is designed to guide speechwriters through a brainstorming process that provides critical information to help formulate the central idea. Skipping these steps can lead to writer's block. Understanding the general purpose of a speech can greatly assist the writer in selecting and narrowing the topic. Once the topic is locked in, the writer must decide specifically "what" she or he wants the audience to know or do at the end of the speech. A central idea summarizes the entire speech in one sentence that includes a thesis and two or more main points that explain the thesis. When working on the body of the speech, it is important to assign annotation symbols to show the relationship from one sentence to the next. Annotation marks also communicate a sentence's relationship to the sentence above it. Connectives such as transitional words and phrases and organizational patterns help listeners follow the speaker's thoughts easier. The introduction and conclusion of a speech should not be written until last, because the body of the speech provides creative ideas to use to open and close a speech. The job of the introduction is to grab the listener's attention; present a credibility statement; give the audience a reason to listen; and introduce the central idea. The conclusion has three goals: to signal the end of the speech, to summarize the residual message, and to connect back to the introduction for a satisfying end.

Key terms

Speech Heading: Brainstorming
General Purpose
Narrowed Topic
Specific Purpose
Central Idea
Introduction
Body Conclusion
Main Points
Annotation Symbols
Connectives

Transitions
Internal Previews
Internal Summaries
Sign Post
Chronological Order
Topical Order
Spatial Order
Causal Order
Residual Message

Your First Major Speech: Informative

This chapter will address the following concepts:

Informative Speaking

Outlining your speech

Delivering your speech

VOCABULARY BUILDERS: *Disingenuous*, adjective
Not straightforward or candid; insincere or calculating
"Disingenuous individuals usually become successful by misleading others."

Loquacious, adjective
Very talkative, smooth conversations
"My loquacious brother keeps interrupting me while I work. This is the reason working from home is just not a good idea."

## CHAPTER 6

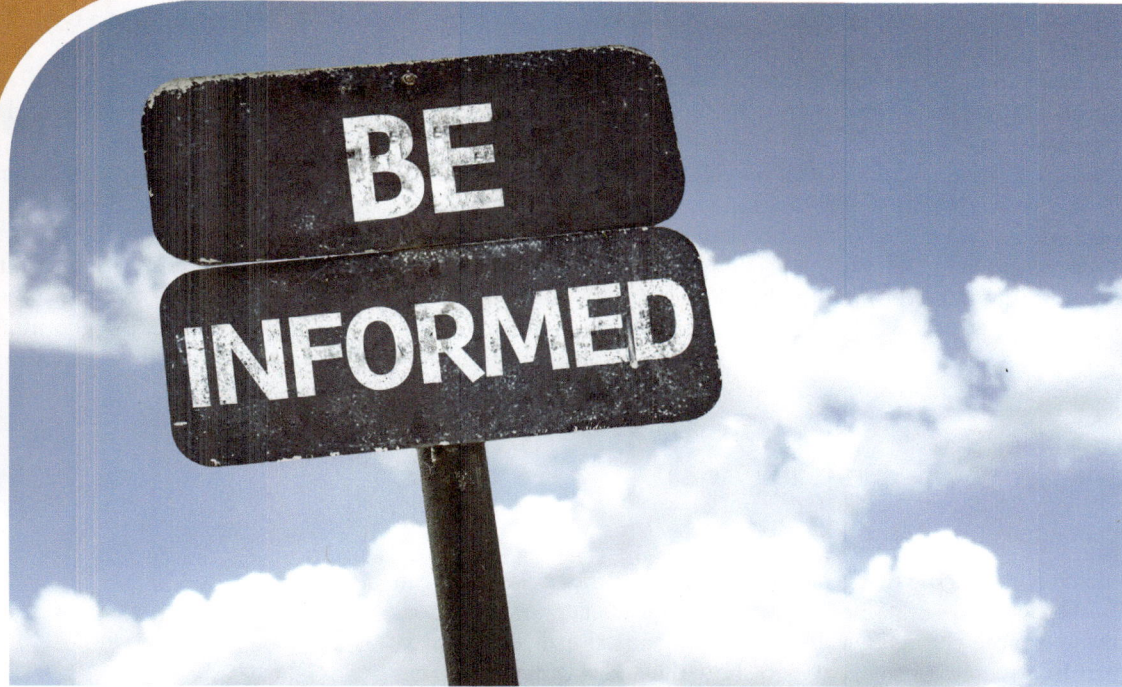

"Sharing knowledge is the first step to wisdom, sharing it is the first step to humanity."

—unknown

In public speaking courses, the first major presentation is normally a simple speech whose goal is to share information or knowledge with others, as a teacher does. This type of speech is called an informative speech. A self-introduction speech is also an informative speech because the speaker shares some aspect of who they are with their classmates. You may have already given this speech at the beginning of the semester. People use informative speaking in their everyday lives to share general or pressing information with others. Any time you begin a sentence with, "Did you know ..." you are participating in informative communication. This chapter will introduce you to different categories of informative speaking; the outline format used to develop and present an informative speech, non-verbal communication that plays a vital role in the speech delivery and important delivery methods.

Informative Speaking

When we share information that we consider interesting or important, we are participating in a type of communication known as informative speaking. Informative speaking is used to communicate information, knowledge, and understanding to others. Examples of people who participate in this type of communication daily are news reporters and teachers. Informative speaking does not involve telling others what to think or do, as this would be persuasive speaking.

When writing an informative speech the general goal is to fill in gaps of knowledge that your audience may not know or to share new information with them. When developing an informative speech, it is helpful to think of yourself as a teacher sharing knowledge with your listeners. You must also consider the audience as you craft your speech to help select appropriate words, engaging examples, and images. Too often, people communicate by sharing fragmented thoughts that does not fully communicate meaning. A public speaker must present their thoughts fully to achieve an end product of mutual understanding. As learned in Chapter one, communication does not occur until there is an end product of mutual understanding. Next, we will investigate the different categories of informative speaking as each has a different focus.

Informative Speech Categories

Speeches about objects

An object is something that is tangible in form, in other words, you can see and touch it. Main points in this type of speech are best organized by using topical, chronological, or spatial organizational patterns. Example: In a speech whose goal is to show the audience how different ingredients create the nutritional value of pre-packaged cookies, the speaker may use a topical organization pattern. In doing so, the speaker is able to decide which main point to present first, second, and last in a logical manner. Since the overall goal is to explain how a blend of ingredients create the and nutritional value, the first main point will set the stage showing that all pre-packaged cookies are not the same nutritionally. The second main point might discuss cookies with high caloric content, and the third with low caloric content.

Central Idea: The nutritional value of different types of cookies is not the same; I'll explain how ingredients such as natural grains, additive, fillers, artificial flavors, and preservatives create the nutritional value of a cookie.
   I.   Prepackaged cookies are a popular snack food .
   II. Cookies with a high caloric content have little to no nutritional value.
   III. Some cookies with a lower caloric content have a healthier nutritional value.

Speeches about processes

A process speech is also called a "how-to" or "demonstration" speech because it provides the audience with a step-by-step presentation of how to do or make something. Common process speeches can include how to prepare your grandmother's special vegetable soup, or how to change the oil in your car. The challenging part of developing and presenting a process speech is that the speaker must take time to show the audience every detail required to achieve the end goal. Process speeches usually require visual aids, the speaker must decide what type(s) of visual aids will get the job done. We will discuss the proper use of visual in chapter nine. It is important to note that the speaker should allow adequate time to practice delivering the speech with visual aids.

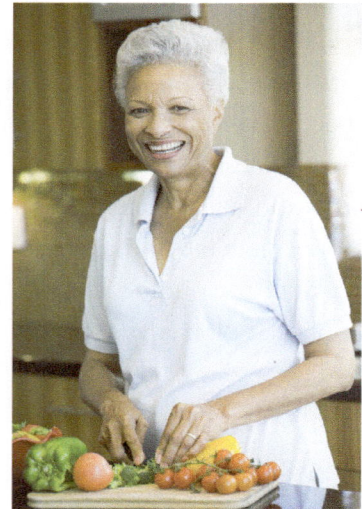

Process speeches are normally arranged in a topical order. Grouping similar material into three or four main points helps simplify the explanation as shown below.

This example includes subpoints to show how the material can be grouped.
Central Idea: Preparing my grandmother's special vegetable soup can be achieved in three easy steps
   I. The utensils required to prepare this soup are: a stock pan, long handled spoon and ladle, colander, wooden cutting board, potato peeler, and a sharp chopping knife.
     A. Stock pans, cooking spoons and ladles come in a wide variety.
     B. There are different types of colanders and cutting boards.
     C. The potato peeler and chopping knife can be traditional or high-tech.
  II. Grandma uses different types of root vegetables in her soups such as: potatoes, carrots, squash, sweet potatoes, and onions; non-root vegetables used are celery, cabbage, corn, green beans, and tomatoes.
     A. Root vegetables are used to create the rich base or broth.
     B. Non-root vegetables are used to fill the base or broth with sweet yumminess!
 III. The cutting and cooking process is simple but can take up to three hours.
     A. The cutting process calls for organization, time, and patience but is so satisfying.
     B. The root vegetables are cooked slowly until they become a blended broth.
     C. Once the broth is done, the other vegetables are added with herbs and spices.

Speeches about events

Any occurrence that happens is considered an event. During the warmer months there are many special outdoor events around the world. From celebration parades to fairs, people simply love to plan events during warmer months. Other events may be more serious in nature such as the September 11, 2001 when two airplanes flew into the World Trade Center towers in New York, or the tragic shooting at an elementary school in New Town, Connecticut. Whether the event is festive or tragic, it is important to present factual details and accounts of the event in the order in which they occur. The overall goal is to transfer your feelings about the event to the audience through the use of creative wording and imagery. Engaging your audience's senses is a skill that can be achieved with practice. Organizational patterns used for this type of speech are chronological, topical, or spatial.

Central Idea: Each year, December brings an exciting month filled with holiday celebrations such as Hanukkah, Christmas, and Kwanza.
   I. Hanukkah is a Jewish holiday celebrated for eight days and nights.
  II. Christmas is a Christian celebration of Jesus' humble birth to a virgin in a stable in Bethlehem.
 III. Kwanza is a secular festival observed by many African Americans as a celebration of their cultural heritage and traditional values.

Speeches about people

People's behaviors, achievements, and activities make for interesting speech topics because people are interesting and unique. Therefore, speeches about people describe their essence, achievements, contributions, or uniqueness. Informative speeches written about people could be a person who has inspired you, such as President Barak Obama, Mexico's President Enrique Peña Nieto, or a famous sports or music personality. Main points for this type of speech generally use a topical organization pattern that highlights two or three aspects of why you think this person makes for an interesting topic. A chronological organizational pattern can be used if your goal is to highlight key points in this person's life using a timeline.

Central Idea: President Barak Obama will forever be a prominent figure in American history.
    I. Barak Obama was born in Hawaii to a white American mother and black Kenyan father.
   II. He became the first African American president of the United States in 2008 with an estimated 66.7 million popular votes and 365 electoral votes.
  III. In 2010 President Obama signed a health care reform bill into law.
  IV. According to a July 2015 article written by Adam B. Lerner, "President Obama in many ways has helped start the same kind of political revolution that Reagan did."

Speeches about concepts

A concept speech is the most complicated of all informative speeches to develop. A concept is something that is intangible, meaning you cannot see or touch it. Examples of concepts are: beliefs, theories, notions, principles, or ideas that are often seen as abstract because they reflect a person's views. Examples of concepts can be religious principles, space travel notions, astrological beliefs, parenting theories, or political views.

The challenge for speakers when developing a concept speech is to find concrete ideas that make more abstract ones relatable and tangible to the audience. Concept speeches should break down complex ideas into manageable groups of information in a way that helps the listeners understand.

Causal speaking falls under the concept speech category. The speaker's general purpose is not to simply discuss a concept, but to also provide evidence that supports their belief that one specific event triggered another event to occur, or could trigger another event to occur in the future. Causal speaking is also used in persuasive speaking.

Whether used in an informative or persuasive speech, the primary approach that a speaker must use when developing a causal speech is to strategically prove that there is a clear relationship between a cause and its effect or effects through evidence. This type of speech requires quite a bit of supporting evidence to be successful. The following thesis statement below is causal and must be proven in the speech.

    Example: *Many students did not pass the exam because the questions were tricky.*

For this thesis to be accepted as true, the speaker must eliminate other variables that may prove to be the true cause. As you investigate facts during your research, you may uncover key information that supports the truth of your thesis. In the example, the truth might be that students do not pass exams for two equally important reasons: they do not study, or they do not know how to study.

The following example includes a full speech heading to provide you with a clear example of how a causal speech is developed.

General Purpose: To inform – causal
Specific Purpose: To prove to my audience that people suffer from depression during the late fall and winter because there is less daylight hours and more darkness.
Central Idea: During the late fall and winter many people suffer from depression because there is less daylight hours and more darkness.
    I. Studies suggest that half a million Americans experience feelings of depression, irritability, and fatigue during the late fall and winter when there is less daylight.
   II. The cause of these problems is actually a disorder known as Seasonal Affective Disorder.

Here are a few general guidelines for informative speaking:

1. Think of ways to relate your topic to your audience using common experiences.

2. Use everyday language and avoid using words that are too technical, vague, or abstract.

3. Because words are powerful and have the ability to capture an audience's attention, you must be creative in how you personalize your ideas.

4. As you learn more about your audience during the audience analysis, be careful not to bombard them with information they already know. Instead, try to provide the audience with new knowledge that you may have recently discovered.

Outlining your speech

"My father always said that too many words cheapened the value of a man's speech."

—Patricia Briggs, Raven's Shadow

The human mind is filled with an abundance of rapid thoughts called self-talk. Sometimes we are able to sort through our jumbled self-talk to communicate clearly. Other times we fail to encode these thoughts accurately which results in frustrating miscommunication. Learning how to organize your thoughts before communicating them to others is a skill that will extend to every aspect of your life. Outlining is a method used to help sort out your thoughts on paper. Students who have taken English classes should be familiar with the outlining process as essay writing uses an outline format. In an outline each sentence is evaluated for its usefulness in making or supporting specific points that explain the thesis. All sections of the outline format is designed to organize the speaker's thoughts and feelings in a linear fashion. In chapter five you were introduced to four parts of the speech outline, which are the speech heading, introduction, body, and conclusion. In the next section we will transfer those sections directly into a speech preparation outline.

Preparation outline

A preparation outline is used to develop informative or special occasion speeches. Speeches are usually developed one complete thought at a time in a full sentence format. This makes it easy to see how each sentence relates to the next sentence by creating a continuous flow of logical thought. When sentences are written in fragmented thought, it can be difficult for the speechwriter to assess the coherence between key points that they are attempting to make. Additionally, when you write full sentences, you become more familiar with the content of each section making it easier to memorize later on. The preparation outline template that follows provides a visual image of how each section of the outline is arranged. As you study the following preparation outline, notice how it begins with the four-part speech heading followed by the introduction, body, conclusion and annotation symbols. Notice how the annotation symbols are indented to form a hierarchy of continuous related thought. Once you insert your main points into the preparation outline template, from the central idea, it is important to select an appropriate organizational pattern before you begin to explain your main points. Double space your preparation outline to allow space for revisions as you polish your speech draft.

Speeches are not written in a manuscript format as you would an essay. Outlines are used for drafting, revising, polishing, and delivering a speech. The delivery outline will be presented later in this chapter.

PREPARATION OUTLINE TEMPLATE: for informative or entertainment speeches only.

General Purpose: _____
Narrowed Topic: _____
Specific Purpose: *To inform my audience* ( ) _____
Central Idea: (thesis & main points) _____

INTRODUCTION
I.   **Attention-Getter:** Use the hook & bait method to engage your listeners.
II.   **Personal Credibility:** Tell audience how you learned about your topic (*your research and experience*).
III.   **Give Audience Reason to Listen:** Use common experiences and "You" language to engage.
IV.   **Central Idea:** (Copy and paste one sentence central idea from the speech heading.)
Transitional statement letting audience know your speech is beginning

BODY
I.   First main point that explains the thesis; (taken from the central idea)
        A. First subpoint that will explain the first main point
            1. sub-subpoint; sentences that continue to explain the first subpoint (I-A)
            2. sub-subpoint; sentences that continue to explain the first subpoint (I-A)
            3. sub-subpoint; sentences that continue to explain the first subpoint (I-A)
            * *There is no set amount of sub-subpoints. Think of paragraph sentences. Some subpoints will not
              have sub-subpoints, but every main point will have subpoints.*
        B. Second subpoint that will explain the first main point
            1. sub-subpoint; sentences that continue to explain the second subpoint (I-B)
            2. sub-subpoint; sentences that continue to explain the second subpoint (I-B)
            3. sub-subpoint; sentences that continue to explain the second subpoint (I-B)
        C. Third subpoint that will explain the first main point
Transition into main point 2
II.   Second main point that explains the thesis; (taken from the central idea.)
        A. First subpoint that will explain the second main point.
            1. sub-subpoint; sentences that continue to explain the first subpoint (II-A)
            2. sub-subpoint; sentences that continue to explain the first subpoint (II-A)
            3. sub-subpoint; sentences that continue to explain the first subpoint (II-A)
        B. Second subpoint that will explain the second main point.
            1. sub-subpoint; sentences that continue to explain the second subpoint (II-B)
            2. sub-subpoint; sentences that continue to explain the second subpoint (II-B)
            3. sub-subpoint; sentences that continue to explain the second subpoint (II-B)
        C. Third subpoint that will explain the second main point.
            1. sub-subpoint; sentences that continue to explain the third subpoint (II-C)
Transition into main point 3
III.   Third main point that explains the thesis; (taken from the central idea.)
        A. First subpoint that will explain the third main point
            1. sub-subpoint; sentences that continue to explain the first subpoint (III-A)
            2. sub-subpoint; sentences that continue to explain the first subpoint (III-A)
        B. Second subpoint that will explain the third main point
Transitional statement letting audience know your speech is ending

CONCLUSION
I.   Cue audience that your speech is ending.
II.   Reinforce the residual message by summarizing the main theme of your speech.
III.   Provide a satisfying ending by referring back to the introduction or use a thesis-specific quote.

Study the speech that has been inserted into a preparation outline template. Notice how the speech heading appears first. The positioning of the speech heading helps the writer focus on the general purpose, specific purpose, and central idea throughout the speech development process. Connectives are highlighted in blue.

FULL INFORMATIVE SPEECH EXAMPLE: Category-Event!

Basic Preparation Outline Template

GENERAL PURPOSE: To inform
NARROWED TOPIC: Bullfighting is known around the the world as an exciting and entertaining sport.
SPECIFIC PURPOSE: To inform my audience (about) bullfighting which is known around the world as an exciting and entertaining sport.
CENTRAL IDEA: Bullfighting is known around the world as an exciting and entertaining sport; it includes lavish entertainment, torturing a bull to its death, and celebrating the matador for his bravery as the survivor of the battle.

INTRODUCTION

I.   **ATTENTION-GETTER:** We are all familiar with the yearly running of the bulls which takes place in Pamplona, Spain.
   A.   Televised news reports the event, and the end results in brave men who challenge the bulls.
   B.   We see sane men face off with wild bulls in a game of "catch me if you can."
      1.   Sometimes the men get caught because they trip and fall with disastrous results.
      2.   Bullfighting is totally different from the running of the bulls.
      3.   The bull fighter stands before the bull and taunts it by saying, "Gore me if you can."

II. **CREDIBILITY STATEMENT:** While vacationing in Mexico, a local man persuaded me and my sister to attend a bullfight.
   A.   He told us this was a once in a lifetime opportunity to witness a real Mexican bullfight – an experience that should not be missed.
      1.   "You will love it" he told us, "You will never forget it."

III. **GIVE THE AUDIENCE A REASON TO LISTEN:** He was right; I will never forget that bullfight because it was one of the most heart wrenching, cruel, and thrilling spectacles I have ever experienced.

IV. **CENTRAL IDEA:** Bullfighting is known around the world as an exciting and entertaining sport; it includes lavish entertainment, torturing a bull to its death, and celebrating the matador for his bravery as the survivor of the battle.

BODY

Transitional statement: *First, I'll talk about the pre-entertainment that hypes up the crowd.*

I.   **The most important objective of bullfighting is to entertain the crowd.**
   A.   **The event began** when couples came out in elaborate costumes and performed traditional Mexican dances accompanied by a Mariachi Band.
      1.   Everyone enjoyed the music and those who knew the songs sang along at the top of their lungs.
   B.   **Next,** the men came out on horses for a rodeo.
      1.   The cowboys demonstrated the skills of their horses while the riders demonstrated their expertise and self-discipline.
   C.   **Up to that point,** the entertainment had been really exciting just like the man had promised.

II. **The main objective of bullfighting is to kill the bull.**
   A.   **First,** the bull was released into the ring; he ran around snorting and acting like – a bull.
      1.   His entrance was met with shouts of excitement from the crowd, *"Toro! Toro! and Toro!"*
      2.   Then, out rode a man carrying a long steel lance.
      3.   His horse was covered with a heavy blanket draped over its sides.
      4.   The picador rode around the bull in the ring until he had a good angle to aim at the bull's throat, then he rammed the lance into the bull's jugular.
         a.   I almost passed out!
      5.   The bull immediately stumbled as blood gushed from his throat.

B. **After that** happened, the banderoles appeared.
   1. They are handsome young men who aspire to be matadors; and until that time, their job was to assist the matador.
   2. The banderoles were also dressed in elaborate costumes.
      a. Each one carried two swords festooned with ribbons that matched their costumes.
   3. As we watched, they ran to the stumbling, snorting, bleeding bull and attempted to plant their swords in the bull's shoulders.
      a. This act further weakens the bull.
      b. By stabbing their swords in the bull's shoulders, the banderoles showed their bravery and strength.
   4. The crowd suddenly began to count out loud.
      a. I realized that they were counting the number of swords in the bull's shoulders.
   5. They cheered shouting, "Toro! Toro! Toro!"
C. **Finally,** when the bull was raging mad and foaming at the mouth, out came the matador, the star of the show.
   1. He appeared resplendent in gold and silver.
      a. He wore a tie, a thick belt, and a Montero, which is a stylized hat.
      b. The matador carried an elaborate cape draped over his shoulders as the crowd shouted *"Toreros! Toreros! Toreros!"*
D. The applause a Matador receives is based on how close he gets to the bull's horns without getting gored.
E. **At that point,** the picador, and the banderols - prodded the bull into charging the matador who lourished his cape and maneuvered his body in a way that put him closer to the bull.
   1. After tiring the bull to the point where he was so enraged and weak, the matador ran the sword he'd hidden under his cape between the eyes of the bull killing him.

III. **When it was over, a rope was tied around the bull's legs, and the mighty Toro – the bull - was dragged from the stadium by his feet.**
A. It was a strange fight to the death between a bull and the matador.
   1. This time, the matador walked away.
   2. Although I was glad that the Matador walked away unscathed, I was also very angry and very sad.
   3. In fact, I had a royal meltdown with uncontrollable sobs.
   4. For a while I was inconsolable.
   5. It all seemed so cruel to me.
B. **Then** a beautiful woman came over and held my hand and explained that Toro would always win the fight because he was stronger and braver than any man.
   1. So to level the playing field and give matador a chance to prove his bravery, helpers were needed to weaken the bull so they may be matched equally in strength.
C. **After she concluded her explanation,** I looked at her and thought about the exciting entertainment I'd enjoyed before the bull appeared to be tortured, and just shook my head in confusion.

Transitional statement: As you can see, bullfighting is a thrilling, yet cruel entertainment-focused sport.

CONCLUSION
I. **Signal the end of the Speech:** I hope you have learned more about bull fighting events.
II. **Summarize the Body:** The bull fighter does not fight the bull alone; he has helpers that weaken the powerful bull to even the battle.
   A. The crowd is hyped up through different forms of entertainment before the bull fight begins.
III. **Leave audience with a satisfying end by reconnecting to the introduction:** I will never forget that experience; it was the most heart wrenching, cruel and thrilling spectacle I have ever experienced.

Delivering Your Speech

"There are always three speeches, for every on you actually gave. The one you practiced, the one you gave, and the one you wish you gave."

—*Dale Carnegie*

A good delivery can turn a mundane speech topic into an exciting adventure. The delivery of a speech is fifty percent of a presentation and is often more important than the verbal message. Delivery is a nonverbal form of communication. When a speaker has worked hard to develop, revise, and polish the speech, those efforts will be communicated in both the verbal and nonverbal aspects of the presentation. Delivering a speech requires the speaker to do more than present the facts that support the thesis. The audience must also be engaged. Strategies discussed in earlier chapters to engage an audience includes filtering main point through common shared experiences, and through the use of arousing examples. Let's look at the components of nonverbal communication as they relate to delivery.

Nonverbal Communication

The primary difference between verbal and non-verbal communication is:

- Nonverbal communication is simultaneous allowing us to send several messages at one time.
- Whereas we can only send one verbal message at time.

In a speech presentation, for example, the speaker sends multiple non-verbal messages along with each single verbal message. This occurs because the speaker's facial expressions, body movement, and vocal intonations are constantly communicating what the speaker is thinking or feeling at each moment of the speech. Nonverbal communication assist communicators because they server many functions.

Nonverbal communication serves many functions

- **Repeating:** When a person of high esteem appears to give a speech, the audience stands and applauds until the speaker says, *"Thank you, please have a seat."* A hand gesture accompanies the verbal request that indicates, "Sit."
- **Reinforce:** When giving a person directions, you might say, *"Go that way!"* and then point towards the direction.
- **Substitute:** Instead of saying *"Stop!"* you might hold out your hand.
- **Accenting:** Using vocal intonation to accent a word or phrase is a form of nonverbal communication.
- **Contradicting:** You can express two different messages at one time through verbal and nonverbal means. For example, when asked whether you ate your friend's last cupcake, you might respond, *"No,"* but your facial expression communicates guilt.

Because of the many functions that nonverbal communication serves, and the possibility of leakage, it is important for speakers to be aware of messages that their voices and bodies are sending.

During a speech presentation, the speaker's voice and body is used in a variety of ways to strength the presentation by punctuating key points.

Delivery: What the speaker's voice communicates	
Volume	When the volume of a speaker's voice is too soft, this might communicate shyness or anxiety. The opposite is true for a voice that is too loud, which could communicate too much confidence (arrogance).
Pauses	Brief moments of silence during a presentation may communicate several things: the speaker is gathering his or her thoughts, the speaker is addressing anxiety, the speaker is using the pause as a dramatized effect to punctuate a point made, or the speaker is using the pause as a transition to a new thought.
Rate	Those who speak at a higher rate of speech often communicate anxiety or excitement.
Pitch	The human ear responds differently to high or low pitches. Therefore when the speaker's voice is too high or too low, the audience may become distracted by the pitch and stop listening to the message.
Inflection	A change in vocal pitch is called inflection and communicates the speaker's interest in the topic. Vocal inflection also helps to engage the audience.
Vocal variety	Using a variation of pitch, volume, inflection, or rate of speech provides expressiveness that can engage the audience. Vocal variety can assist in communicating excitement, passion, or tension.

Vocalized pauses

When people are nervous or at a loss for words, they use fillers called *vocalized pauses*. These pauses include utterances such as *"um," "you know," "uh," "ah," "you know what I'm saying,"* or *"stuff like that."* Such fillers are extremely distracting to the audience and should be avoided. Silent pauses should be used in place of distracting vocal fillers, as pauses give speakers time to collect their thoughts by engaging in self-talk which also helps control anxiety.

Nonverbal Delivery: What the speaker's body communicates	
Personal appearance	Dressing appropriately for a speech communicates that you care. Appropriate attire also helps listeners see you as confident, trustworthy, and credible. Appropriate attire should be selected to help achieve your specific goals as a speaker.
Gesturing	Movement of the body (especially the hands) reflects one or more functions of non-verbal communication as previously discussed.
Eye contact	Conveys a level of comfort, confidence, and secures audience attention. Eye contact helps speakers build a general trust relationship with their audience. When a speaker avoids eye contact it can communicate discomfort or deceit.
Movement	Some speakers walk while talking because it helps them think or control anxiety. When a speaker takes a few steps away from the podium, stops, and continues to speak, the audience will not be distracted. This type of movement can be used to retain the listener's attention. However, pacing or exaggerated body movement creates great distractions for listeners.
Facial Expressions	Facial communication shows how the face can unconsciously communicate many emotions such as surprise, fear, anger, sadness, disgust, interest, contempt, and happiness. Speakers should always be aware of their facial expressions to avoid misleading the audience.

Delivery Types

Different events call for different methods of speech delivery. There are four types of speech delivery used: impromptu, manuscript, memory, and extemporaneous.

Impromptu speaking

Impromptu speaking is often called "off-the-cuff" speaking. This type of speech is not prepared in advance, but the speaker has knowledge of the subject and is asked to share that information with an audience. For example, at a Peewee Football banquet a coach may share details of an exciting play that led his team to a first-place victory. During his remarks, the coach remembers that John, his assistant coach was standing near the end zone when the unexpected touchdown occurred. He asks John to share his account of the play with the audience. John agrees although he has no time to prepare a speech. As he approaches the front of the banquet hall, he thinks of key points that he will use to explain the details of that final play. This is an example of how we use self-talk to help organize our thoughts. The assistant coach uses a conversational style of delivery as he describes the events that led to their victory. He will also maintain eye contact with the audience in a way that motivates them to remain engaged. If the speaker is passionate about the topic, that passion will be felt by the audience through his vocal variety and body language because emotions are contagious.

"It takes one hour of preparation for each minute of presentation time."

—*Wayne Burgraff*

Manuscript speaking

When an event requires a speaker to be exact, a manuscript speech is normally used. This drafted speech is carefully crafted and revised several times to ensure that the details are communicated accurately and logically. Once a speaker is satisfied with the draft, final polishing touches will be added. These additions include transitional words and phrases, figurative language, and a creative introduction and conclusion. During the presentation the speech will be read verbatim to avoid missing critical content or misrepresenting facts.

Memory speaking

Speeches presented from memory are normally short but requires the same developmental process as a manuscript speech. The difference between manuscript and memory speaking is the speaker presents this speech word-for-word from memory while maintain eye contact with the audience.

Extemporaneous speaking

An extemporaneous speech combines elements from each of the three speeches discussed. It is presented in a conversational way that engages the audience similar to an impromptu delivery. It is well-crafted, revised, and edited similar to a manuscript delivery. And, it is memorized in sections similar to a memory speech. The goal is to become familiar with the content of each section of the speech by rehearsing each section several times and then delivering the speech with the assistance of a key word outline or note cards. The goal of an extemporaneous delivery is to be familiar with the content to avoid reading – eye contact cannot be achieved if the speech is read. Mastering this skill can help with job interviews and other interactions that require listener engagement. Next, we'll explore the key word outline which supports an extemporaneous delivery.

Keyword Delivery Outline

Extemporaneous speakers use delivery notes that provide them with a skeleton outline to use when presenting a speech. The keyword delivery outline is never read verbatim during the speech presentation. Instead, the speaker pause from time to time to and consult their key word outline, or note cards, to be reminded of the next point. Quotes or oral citations are alway read verbatim and should be written fully in the keyword outline. The content of a keyword outline includes: key words and phrases, connectives, and expert citations that are logically structured to assist the speaker. A keyword delivery outline is a whittled down skeleton of the full speech. This skeleton outline serves as a roadmap that jogs the speaker's memory should he or she forget where they are in the speech. The only assistance that a speaker has at the podium to help during the presentation is a skeleton of the speech. Therefore, it is important to think critically about words or phrases used in a keyword outline. When too many important words are removed from the full speech outline while developing the keyword outline, the speaker may not have adequate support to jog their memory should they forget the point they were attempting to make.

The keyword skeleton outline also includes connectives that reminds the speaker where he or she is going in the speech. Another helpful addition to the keyword outline are delivery cues. Here are a few examples: "Look at audience," "speak up," "don't use fillers," "slow down," "mistakes are ok, just keep talking," etc. These delivery cues are normally written in colored pen or marker to capture the speaker's eye as he or she progresses through the presentation.

Example: ineffective and effective method to scale down a sentence

From the full preparation outline.	A. First, the bull was released into the ring; he ran around snorting and acting like – a bull.
Less effective	A. First, the bull was
More effective	A. First, bull released- snorting

The easiest way to create a keyword delivery outline is to copy and paste the fully typed preparation outline speech onto a blank page that will be used to scale down the content. Before deleting any word/s from the sentence, think critically about key words that will trigger your memory should you forget your next thought during your presentation. Some speechwriters will delete an entire sentence and replace it with a brief thought that sums up the essence of the sentence. Others might delete several sentences because they reflect general information that is easy to remember. Whatever the case, you must decide what scaled down method is best for you. The goal is to get the full outlined speech scaled down to a two page key word outline to use at the podium. A full speech preparation outline should never be used as a keyword outline during the delivery of your presentation If you wish to use note cards to deliver your speech, transfer the content from the key word outline that you developed to note cards. Whether you plan to use the two-page format or note cards, it is important to test your keyword outline several times during rehearsal. A question to consider each time you rehearse the speech is, "Did the keyword delivery outline help me remember points that I forgot?" If the answer is "No," then you must revise your delivery outline again by inserting key words into sentences or sections where your memory was most challenged.

The rule for using note cards is to limit them to the following: one for the introduction, one for each main point, and one for the conclusion. Having too many note cards at the podium can end in disaster. Speakers might drop one or two, mix them up, or misplace them. These unfortunate occurrences will leave the speaker with inadequate support during the speech. Compare the keyword delivery outline that follows to the full preparation speech outline on bullfighting presented earlier in this chapter.

Keyword Outline

INTRODUCTION
I. **ATTENTION-GETTER:** We are all familiar with - running of the bulls - Pamplona, Spain.
   A.   Televised news reports
   B.   We see sane men face
       1. Men get caught.
       2. Bullfighting is totally different.
       3. Bull fighter taunts bull.
II. **CREDIBILITY STATEMENT:** While vacationing in Mexico
   A.   Once in a lifetime opportunity.
       1. "You will love it" he told us, "You will never forget it."
III. **GIVE THE AUDIENCE A REASON TO LISTEN:** I will never forget.
IV. **CENTRAL IDEA:** Bullfighting is known around the world as an exciting and entertaining sport; it includes lavish entertainment, torturing a bull to its death, and celebrating the matador for his bravery as the survivor of the battle.

BODY
Transitional statement: *First I'll discuss the pre-entertainment that hypes up the crowd.*

I. **Primary goal - entertaining crowd.**
   A.   Event began, couples in elaborate costumes - Mexican dances - Mariachi Band.
       1. Enjoyed music - sang along loudly.
   B.   Next, rodeo.
       1. Demonstrated horse's skills - riders demonstrated expertise & self-discipline.
   C.   Entertainment really exciting.

II. **The main objective kill the bull.**
   A.   First, bull released into ring – a bull.
       1. *"Toro! Toro! Toro!"*
       2. Man has long steel lance.
       3. Horse - heavy blanket draped over its sides.
           a.   Called a Picador, - matador's helpers.
       4. The Picador - good angle of the bull's throat, - rammed lance bull's jugular.
           a.   Almost passed out!
       5. Bull stumbled - blood gushed.
   B.   Next, banderoles appeared.
       1. Young men aspire - matadors; until that time, - assist matador.
       2. Banderoles - dressed - elaborate costumes.
           a.   Carried two swords - ribbons - matched - costumes.
       3. Approached stumbling, snorting, bleeding bull - stuck swords shoulders.
           a.   Further weakens bull.
           b.   Banderoles showed their bravery and strength.
       4. The crowd counts.
           a.   Counting swords in bull's shoulders.
       5. "Toro! Toro! Toro!"
   C.   Bull was raging mad and foaming at the mouth, out came the matador, the star of the show.
       1. He appeared resplendent in gold and silver.
           a.   Wore tie, thick belt, Montero, - stylized hat.
           b.   Matador carried cape over shoulders - *"Toreros! Toreros! Toreros!"*

D. Applause matador receives - how close - bull's horns - getting gored.
E. Picador, banderols - prod bull - charge matador - flourished cape – got closer to bull.
   1. Bull enraged and weak, matador jammed sword between eyes of bull killing him.

III. **When it was over, rope tried bull's legs, - mighty Toro - dragged from stadium by his feet.**
   A. Strange fight to the death a bull - matador.
      1. This time matador won.
      2. Glad matador survived, - angry and sad.
      3. Meltdown.
      4. Inconsolable.
      5. So cruel.
   B. Then beautiful woman explained - Toro would always win - stronger - braver - man.
      1. To level playing field - matador prove bravery, helpers weaken bull - matched equally in strength.
   C. Thought about exciting entertainment enjoyed before bull tortured, felt confusion.

Transitional statement: *As you can see, bullfighting is a thrilling, yet, cruel entertainment-focused sport.*

CONCLUSION

I. **Signal the end of the Speech:** I hope you have learned more about bull fighting events.

II. **Summarize the Body:** The does not fight the bull alone; has helpers weakens powerful bull even the battle.
   A. Crowd hyped up - entertainment before fight begins.

Leave audience with a satisfying end by reconnecting to the introduction: I will never forget that experience. ... it was the most ...

Summary

Informative speaking is defined as sharing knowledge and understanding with others. This type of speech is normally the first major speech assigned in a public speaking course. Five categories of informative speaking were introduced in this chapter: speeches about objects, speeches about processes, speeches about events, speeches about concepts, and speeches about people. In informative speaking, speaker's job is to share new information with the audience or to add to their existing knowledge.

The general preparation outline's goal is to help speechwriters outline their thoughts in a way that makes it easy for the listeners to follow. This outline has four parts, speech heading, introduction, body, and conclusion. A method used within the outline to help the speechwriter analyze each sentence is called annotation. These symbols are used to rank the relationship between sentences using a hierarchical format. Roman numerals are used to communicate main points; capital letters are used to communicate subpoints which explain main points; numbers are used to communicate sub-subpoints that explain subpoints; and lower case letters are used to communicate sub-sub-subpoints that further explain sub-subpoints. Each type of annotation symbol is indented to form the hierarchical relationship in each section. Every main point must have subpoints that explain them.

When a speech has been outline effectively, the speechwriter considers delivery strategies. The delivery of a speech communicates fifty percent of the overall presentation. Delivery is the nonverbal part of the speech and includes facial expressions, body movement, and attire. Nonverbal communication serves several functions: repeating, reinforcing, substituting, accenting, and contradicting. At times, speakers will use vocal pauses to fill in empty space during the presentation. Utterances such as, "um" "er"" "uh" stuff like that," and "you know" can be distracting and should be avoided. Four types of delivery methods are used by public speakers: impromptu speaking, manuscript speaking, memory speaking, and extemporaneous speaking. Student of public speaking use extemporaneous delivery because it is a blend of all three and allows for audience engagement. Extemporaneous delivery style is conversational and engaging, carefully drafted and revised, and memorized. Speakers present extemporaneous speeches with the assistance of a key word delivery outline to help jog their memory should they forget where they are in the speech.

Key terms

Informative speaking
Categories
   Speeches about objects
   Speeches about events
   Speeches about concepts
   Speeches about people
Preparation Outline
   Speech heading
   Introduction
   Body
   Conclusion
Annotation symbols
Delivery
Nonverbal communication
Nonverbal communication functions
   Repeating
   Reinforcing
   Substituting
   Accenting
   Contradicting

Vocalized pauses
Delivery: the voice
   Volume
   Pauses
   Rate
   Pitch
   Inflection
   Vocal variety
Delivery: the body
   Personal appearance
   Gesturing
   Eye contact
   Movement
   Facial expressions
   Attire
Impromptu speaking
Manuscript speaking
Memory speaking
Extemporaneous speaking
Keyword outline

Explaining or Proving Your Thesis

This chapter will address the following concepts:

Searching for Knowledge
Selecting Sources to Support your Ideas
Internet Research
Library Research

Oral Citation

Written Citation: Bibliography
APA Format

VOCABULARY BUILDERS: *Vacillate*, verb
To swing indecisively from one side to the other; being indecisive.
"If you vacillate between two positions, there is no way you will win the debate."

Ubiquitous, adjective
Existing or being everywhere at the same time: constantly encountered
"The city council wants to make Wi-Fi ubiquitous in the city by the next two years."

## CHAPTER 7

"Research is formalized curiosity. It is poking and prying with a purpose."

—Zora Neale Hurston

Curiosity is a normal human behavior because humans want to understand what makes a person, object, or event behave in unique ways. Sometimes we'll ask others to explain our observations, while other time we turn to google or the library to search for answers. When people participate in this type of digging to uncover answers, they are conducting research. When we conduct credible research, a wealth of new information is acquired. In doing so we become wiser because our knowledge base expands - our brains grow. From our earliest years, feedback from other slowly filled our "knowledge baskets." When we enter school, this basket begins to expand at a faster rate as it receives valid educational information about people and the world. Unfortunately, too many people stop acquiring valid credible knowledge when they leave school; their views and opinions represent a limited understanding. The solution to this is to become a life learner by becoming "information literate." This means knowing when it is time to conduct brief yet credible research to find answers. In today's Internet era, getting this done is as simple as typing "Google.com" into a browser and selecting answers that come from credible organizations.

Searching for Knowledge

Have you ever wanted to learn more about a hobby that you've always been interested in like building dresser or making a cheese cake? Curious minds will find instructions by asking a person who is an expert in these processes or by looking for instructions on the Internet. Before the explosion of Internet search engines, people had to go to the library to find answers to their questions. Today, when a person wants to know how to make a cabinet, bake a cheese cake, or know more about a prominent figure, the first place they normally go is google.com. In the past this posed a lot of problems because of credibility concerns. However, with the expansion of online learning institutions, libraries, and special interest organizations, the Internet offers more credible information. Still, research via the Internet must be approached with caution because there are still a lot of websites that are not credible but may appear to be. For example, a website that says "Dell Computer Tech Support" does not always come from the official Dell corporation. If you look at the second line, you will see the name of this company that has posted under the Dell name "www.guruaid.com/Tech-support-for-Dell." This is not a credible website as it is posing as the official Dell computer's website. Other times the website will come from a valid person or organization who may not experts in that field but may have personal experience. Proceed with caution as people do not experience an event the same; the information may be biased.

In this chapter we will explore popular methods used to search for knowledge that is informative and credible. In public speaking, this type of information is used to explain or support important claims made in the speech. A claim occurs when a speaker makes a statement they propose to be true. Such statements must be accompanied by evidence in order to be received as valid.

Selecting Sources to Support Your Ideas

It is not enough to merely tell your audience what you know about topic. People are generally skeptical about the trustworthiness of new information. Therefore, it is important to back up your thoughts with evidence and proof. For example, if you tell your audience that a person with bad credit can purchase a home without a down payment, you would have to prove that claim by providing a lot of proof in the form of evidence from credible sources. In a persuasive speech, if a speaker attempts to convince the audience that the answer to gun violence is arming all citizens with guns, the speaker would have to provide credible evidence and proof.

Sources used in a speech must meet the following criteria:

- Must not be second hand information; should come directly from the source.
- Must not be outdated information as this misrepresents new emerging views on the issue.
- Must come from a credible source that is an expert in the field, or has experience on the matter.

There are different types of supporting material to use in a speech. More common types are, facts, examples, statistics, and interviews. Study each type of supporting material below to better understand how each are used.

1. **Facts:** a piece of factual information used as evidence or proof used to support a claim.

2. **Examples:** There are three types of examples used to explain a point.
   - Brief examples are used in passing as you move from point to point.
   - Extended examples are often required to help the audience better understand a situation or a concept. These examples are normally full narratives.

- Hypothetical examples are pretend illustrations the provide the listener with a realistic example of the story the speaker wishes to share.

3. **Statistics:** used to quantify expressions. If the speaker is attempting to inform the audience that a lot of people still smoke cigarettes, it would be better to quantify the phrase "a lot" numerically. The phrase "a lot" is vague because it would could mean 500 or 500,000. To find credible statistics to express this thought, a speechwriter could look for statistics on website hosted by the National Lung Association because medical professionals and researchers who represent this organization conduct ongoing surveys to assess the number of people who still smoke. The oral citation below express the speaker's though by using quantifiable expressions and informing the audience that the statistics come from a credible organization. *"According to a 2013 survey conducted by the National Cancer society, 30 percent of Americans still smoke at least one pack of cigarettes a day, and another 10 percent have stated that they smoke at least three cigarettes a week."*

Statistics should always be rounded to help the listener decode and remember them. It is easier to remember four million than it is to remember 3,399,587million. Rounding makes decoding and remembering much easier and should always be used with numerical expressions. Be careful not to overuse statistics as your audience may become overwhelmed and the extemporaneous presentation will sound more like a detailed report than a conversational sharing of information.

4. **Interviews:** Two types of interviews can be used to gather information in support of your speech.

   - Expert interviews: Many professionals in their fields have knowledge about certain conditions that fall within their area of expertise. Supporting material gathered from a credible professional whose focus is related to your topic is valuable. For example, if you are informing your audience of the effects of lightning on the human body, you would probably want to interview a person who has conducted extensive research on the topic.

   - Non-expert interview: this type of interview is conducted with a person who has personal experience on the subject of your speech. For example, to get a different understanding of the effects of lightning on the human body, you might want to interview a person who was actually struck by lightning to get a first-hand perspective.

Using supporting material in a speech

Once you have gathered a sufficient amount of information from your research that has provided you with more insight, it is time to analyze each piece separately to assess its usefulness. Not all information discovered during research will be used in your speech. Remember that supporting material must be audience-centered in a way that helps your listeners relate to each point that you make. Some information discovered during research is used to teach the speechwriter more about the topic. Research begins by considering what you know and do not know about your topic. Audience interest and knowledge must also be considered. Finally, it's time to dig through the Internet and library systems to uncover specific credible facts about your topic. Before inserting information you've discovered into your speech, you must answer the following questions: "will this information will help explain a point, present facts or statistics to prove a point, or provide a different angle to to help my audience consider my view on the issue. Also, as you assess each claim made in the speech, look for statements that are not fully explained or proven by evidence. These little slip ups can have negative effects on the listeners. Always search through your speech draft to identify statements that require addition explanation to fully support your thesis. The nature of humans involves various levels of skepticism; therefore a speaker's views must never stand alone. Information that you gather must be current and not outdated. During research, students will often select the first article or book they come across. Use the critical questions listed above to help select useful supporting material.

Guidelines for qualifying supporting material

1. Information is provided by a respected expert in their field or peer who has experience on the issue.
2. Information is up to date and provides current trends or changes
3. Information must come directly from the source; cannot be second hand information.
4. Information must be audience-centered to help listeners relate
5. Information must be appropriate to the occasion, topic, and audience
6. Use a variety of supporting material to engage the audience and avoid biases.
7. Look for supporting information that explains or proves claims made in each main point.

Begin your research early to learn more about your topic and to identify supporting material in a timely manner. Begin by conducting a general Internet search as soon as your instructor previews an upcoming speech assignment, or distributes the assignment. You can use your smart phone, tablet, laptop, or desktop computer to conduct topical research. The possibilities are endless in the technology era in which we live; there is no valid reason to skip the research process.

Internet Research

Currently, research often begins for most people by logging onto the Internet to find useful information using search engines such as Google, Bing, Ask, or Yahoo. Search engines pull together information from the Internet that matches the words you type into the browser. "Work smarter, not harder," is an over used cliche" that still holds merit. Take a few extra moments to look at the second line of websites you find to qualify them as credible. The website address tells you to exactly where the information is coming from. Credible websites useful for research include; online educational sites, government sites, and professional institutional websites such as the Mayo Clinic website. All of these organizations upload current studies and facts that supports their area of expertise and focus. It is your job to qualify websites as credible before using information provided by them.

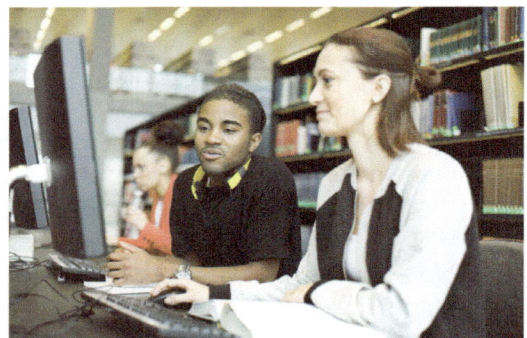

Qualifying a website as credible:

Check the URL: *.edu, .gov, .org*	Websites from educational or government sources can be validated as credible. Special interest organizations also host websites to share their information. Some of these sites are credible and some are not. Read on to learn more about these sites.
Qualify the author or sponsor of the article or website	Websites that are sponsored by a person or organization that specializes in a specific area such as, the National Lung Association can be seen as credible because they are medical experts.
Qualify the author or website is unbiased on the topic.	Some authors or websites are more concerned with supporting their beliefs or products. These types of sources are biased as they only share views that benefit their goals. This type of source cannot be used as proof or evidence.

Library Research

Library research has changed quite a bit since your grandparents era. The Internet has made it possible for libraries to upload their entire collection for use online. Such virtual libraries make it easier to research from the comfort of your home. Library databases can be found online but the user must be affiliated with the institution to access them. Databases house a collection of discipline specific articles published by professionals in their respective fields. Hard copies of these articles can be found in journals or periodicals in the library. Online databases are highly useful because they have more up to date information than books.

The library may not be used in the tradition ways of the past, but still offers lots of useful resources to support of your speech. Other sources that can be used for research are newspapers, magazines, books, and reference works. Reference works include encyclopedias, area specific dictionaries, your textbooks, and other types of reference books. An under-utilized feature of a library is the reference librarian; this is a person whose primary job is to help you fine tune your search to discover specific material that will strengthen your speech. I encourage you to visit your campus library soon!

Bibliography & Works Cited Listings

To avoid plagiarism, speakers must create a list of all facts, examples, statistics, interviews, and visual aids used in a speech that is not their original work or idea. Facts, examples, statistics, interviews, and visual aids all known as "supporting material" because each is used to explain or prove points made by the speaker. An APA (American Psychological Association) style bibliography or works cited page is used to list the supporting material in alphabetical order.

A *bibliography* page is an alphabetical list of supporting material used in a speech, and supporting material that you consulted to learn about your topic. Whereas a *works cited* page includes only supporting material that you actually cited orally in your speech. The APA style of listing your supporting material has some similarities and some difference when compared to MLA (Modern Language Association) style of listing sources. Many English courses use MLA style; but public speaking courses use APA style.

Let's build an APA formatted bibliography for a book using this textbook.

1. First indicate the last name of the author followed by the initial of their first name. Punctuation is very important, notice how the coma and period is placed. **Nabors, V.**

2. Next, add the year the book was published enclosed in parenthesis; a period follows the closing parenthesis sign as indicated. **Nabors, V. (2014).**

3. Now, we add the title and edition of the textbook. The title is italicized followed by a period. The edition of the text is in parenthesis followed by a period. **Nabors, V. (2014).** *Know what I'm saying.* **(1st ed.).**

4. Finally, we'll add the geographical location and name of the publisher; notice the punctuation marks. **Nabors, V. (2014).** *Know what I'm saying.* **(1st ed.). Dubuque, IA: Kendall-Hunt.**

Supporting material will come from a variety of documents; books, articles, magazines, Internet websites, etc. Each must be listed according to APA style as shown in the examples below. When an entry is longer than one line, each line after the first must be indented. Pay close attention to how punctuation is used to separate the information for different types of entries.

APA Format

Book with one author
Calimee, J. N. (2010). *Raising Da Family* (1st ed.). Boston, MA: McGraw-Hill.
Book with two or more authors
Portrum, H., & Gant, H. (2000). *Lost Moments.* Chicago, IL: X Press
Magazine article
Nabors, G. (2011, June). *Steve Harvey's Empire.* Essence, 45(3), 107-112.
Online journal article
Sullivan, K. (2002). *Doing It My Way.* Women's Health, 74, 89-111. Retrieved from http://www.ebscohost.com/
Personal interview
Williams. A. (2013, April 7). *Building a Culinary Business. Personal Interview*
Newspaper
Williams, C. (2005, March 15). *College Education Should Be Free!* Atlanta Times, pg. 5.
Online article one author
Adams. D. A. (2013 December 16). *Finding the Perfect Job!* Retrieved March 22, 2005, from http://www.workforce.com/articles/search-for-the-perfect-job-strategy
Online articles group or corporate author
Gant Clan. (2011). *Letting Go.* Retrieved July 22, 2011, from http://www.keen.com/documents/works/articles/spiritual/renewing-your-life-.asp
Television program
Dixon R. D. (Host). (2009). *Rocking Personal Growth* [Documentary]. The History Channel cable television.
Blog
Shawn C. N. (2014, October 1.)) *Let me help you help yourself* [Web log comment] Retrieved from http://pshchotherapy.net

HOMEWORK

If money were not an option and you could go anywhere in the world to vacation, where would you go?

The goal of this assignment is to practice using research methods and to create an APA formatted bibliography page. The vacation location you choose cannot be a place that you've visited in the past. You must use eight different sources to create your APA formatted bibliography. Appropriate punctuation marks and indentation is required.

Hypothetical Situation: Although money is not an issue, you have always been frugal with your spending. For this reason, you are to approach your vacation by conducting an Internet research to identify a destination that you would like to visit.

IMPORTANT: Wikipedia may not be used.

Once you have selected a vacation destination, you'll need transportation and lodging accommodations. Flights to your destination and lodging are best researched through travel websites. You are to submit a one paragraph typed description of your finalized vacation get-a-way, and develop an APA formatted bibliography that lists all websites that you researched to gather your information in support of this vacation. Include the following information: name and address of the hotel/rental where you will be lodging, name of the air carrier, flight number, and the arrival and departure date & time.

Oral Citation

Students who have gone through required English courses should be accustomed to creating a bibliography or reference page. This information tells the reader where the cited information used in an essay came from. It gives credit to the originator of the information. In public speaking however, the audience will not read the actual written speech and therefore will not have access to bibliography information. For this reason, public speakers must provide oral citations to achieve this goal.

Oral citation can be communicated in a variety of ways. What is important is the information that is being communicated. Just as with written citations, the author's name and organization that the author is affiliated with are important to communicate. Also, the name of the article or book, along with the month and year of publication must be shared orally. As demonstrated below, citations can be expressed in a scholarly manner or a relaxed conversational manner. Each speech excerpt below includes an oral citation indicated by italics.

Children are not alike, some mature faster than others. *According to Dr. John Thomas, author of the book Every Child Can Learn, "Children are not dumb; it's just that some take longer to open their books."*
Men who served in violent wars often come home with undiagnosed posttraumatic shock disorder, also known as PTSD. *Sgt. Maj. Gen. Helen Fraser, a doctor with the United States Marine Corps wrote an article August 25, 2012 titled Undiagnosed War Wounds, shared her similar observations of Marines who were leaving service with clear signs of undiagnosed PTSD because they refuse to acknowledge that had been traumatized by the horrors of war.*
Yesterday, I was reading the Cityville Express newspaper when I ran across an *article written by Sarah Lynne called When the World Gives You Lemons Make Lemonade. In this June 6, 2014 article* Sarah shares her struggles to come out of financial ruin after filing bankruptcy.
Roughly 25percent of all community college students will have to take developmental math, English, or reading courses to help develop college level skills. *These statistics were taken from the US Department of Education's website, on August 15, 2013*

Summary

Research is the heart of developing an effective speech presentation. Without research, speakers would share opinions that are biased and not supported by factual supporting material. Most people are skeptical of opinion-based information. For most college students, the Internet is their one-stop shopping place to research supporting material for speeches and essays. Supporting material includes facts, examples, statistics, or testimony. The Internet has changed over the years as more online universities and professional resources move to an online platform. Although this is true, sources must still be qualified as credible as some may be biased or distorted. Library systems are still offers the most credible resource available for research. Citing sources requires knowledge of APA format, which is used for public speaking courses. Also, speakers are required to cite their sources orally because listeners do not have access to the written speech and supporting bibliography. Information cited should include the person's name, affiliated institution, name and date of the article, or website address.

Key terms

Internet Research	Facts	APA format
Search engines	Examples	Oral Citation
Library Research	Statistics	Bibliography
Supporting Material	Interviews	

The Art of Persuasion

VOCABULARY BUILDERS: *Acquiesce*, verb
To accept, agree, or allow something to happen by remaining silent –
not arguing,
"Her employer demanded that she work the weekend shift, and she
acquiesced."

Pretentious, adjective
Having or showing the unpleasant quality of people who want to be
regarded as more impressive, successful, or important than they really are.
"Celebrities often suffer from inflated egos, and live pretentious lives."

## CHAPTER 8

> *"He who wants to persuade should put his trust not in the right argument, but in the right word. The power of sound has always been greater than the power of sense."*
>
> —*Joseph Conrad*

Public speaking in used to achieve a wide range of goals. It is the primary method used to satisfy practical goals introduced in chapter one. Although history has provided us with an abundance of great speeches presented by notable orators, we can look to current speeches to understand the power of the spoken word today. For example, the 44th President of the United States, Barak Obama, was a newly elected representative from Illinois in 2008 when he delivered a speech so powerful that it changed a nation. His success was attributed to one primary fact: He researched his audience to get a better understanding of their concerns. One of only a handful of presidents who writes there own speeches, President Obama thought critically about how to speak to his audience's logic and emotions to achieve the outcome he desired. A memorable statement made by Mr. Obama during this speech was, *"We are not a collection of red states and blue states we are the United States! If one party goes down, we all go down."*, and the crowd went wild.

What caused such a powerful reaction from the live and televised audience? It can be attributed to creative wording used in a timely manner, filtering key points through common experiences to help the listeners relate, and understanding the core of the problem as a result of in-depth research. In this chapter we will learn these strategies and methods for persuasive speech writing.

Introduction to Persuasive Speaking

When we attempt to *reinforce or change* other people's *values, beliefs, attitudes, or actions,* we are engaging in persuasive communication. We use persuasive strategies nearly every day. For instance, in the morning you might persuade a bus driver to wait for you by yelling "Wait!" as you run towards the bus that is pulling away from the curb. Your nonverbal message strengthens your request as you look pleadingly at the driver while standing in the median of the street, waiting for traffic to let you cross. You watch for the bus driver's response with bated breath, and a moment later, you exhale a sigh of relief when you notice that the doors have opened indicating that he will wait for you. Another way that you most likely use persuasion is to get family or friends to say "Yes" to requests that they would normally say "No" to.

To better understand the effects of persuasive appeals, we can look to our own experiences. How do you get others to say "Yes!" when they often say "No"? To answer this question, think about how you are persuaded by others, especially advertisers. What is your weakness? How does sales campaigns convince your to purchase a product or service that you're not in the market for? Are you persuaded more through your emotions or your logic? Take a few moments to respond to the questions below before we move on.

SHARE YOUR EXPERIENCE

Provide an example of the last time you were persuaded to do or purchase something. What was the selling point? (Your response will be shared in small groups or with the class as a whole)

How Does Persuasion Work?

Persuasion is not a simple matter of getting listeners to agree or disagree. Several degrees of persuasion exist as people think about situations they are observing, considering, or hearing. Listeners often formulate opinions that may or may not support the information they are receiving. By the end of your speech, some audience members may strongly disagree or strongly agree with your thesis. Between these two extremes are audience members who may feel neutral on the subject, and those who are moderately against or moderately supportive of the ideas you've presented. Audience members who are neutral about a topic have not experienced it, or have decided to make it a non-issue.

Successful persuasive speaker are able to shift their listeners views on their topic one degree to the right ... towards the speakers views. Rarely will a speaker be able to shift a listener's views from strongly or moderately disagree to strongly agree. Persuasion occurs in increments. The model below shows a scale of five degrees of persuasion where listeners may stand at the start of a speech.

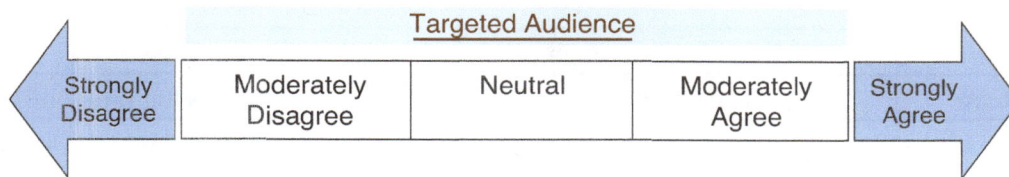

Targeted Audience				
Strongly Disagree	Moderately Disagree	Neutral	Moderately Agree	Strongly Agree

The audience's opinion of your thesis can range from strongly disagree to strongly agree. A persuasive speaker must also identify their targeted audience – the part of the audience they most want to persuade. Topic-specific surveys are used to gather information from the audience to provide the speaker with data on their values, beliefs, and attitudes surrounding the thesis. After analyzing the surveys, the speaker will have a more accurate idea of listeners who are strongly against their thesis, and those who are strongly in favor. These two groups should be eliminated from the targeted audience. The remaining eighty percent of your listeners will become the targeted audience for your speech; those who moderately disagree, are neutral, or moderately agree.

Listeners who strongly disagree with a speaker's thesis normally do so because of their values which are rooted in the self-concept. As learned in Chapter One, values are ingrained from birth. You will never persuade a listener whose values are rooted in religious doctrine to agree that capital punishment and abortion are just. Questions on your surveys must be specific to understand *why* the listeners feel the way they do to help you develop a strategic persuasive argument that *refutes* (counter-argue) their views.

A persuasive speech is considered effective when it shifts the *target audience's* thinking or actions incrementally to the right. Let's say that a few audience members are neutral on a topic because it doesn't affect their lives. The speaker is challenged to provide proven information that is filtered through common experiences to motivate this group of listeners care. A strategic speaker will help audience members who are neutral on their subject relate to it by showing them how the issue can or does affect them or a loved one. If the speaker's strategies are successful, they will be able to shift those listeners from neutral to moderately or strongly agree.

Mental dialoging with the audience

As an audience listens to a persuasive speaker, they respond internally to statements made by agreeing or disagreeing with the speaker. Sometimes they may even argue in their thoughts against a point the speaker has made. This type of internal response occurs naturally as parties are engaged in everyday conversation. There is a difference between everyday conversation and public speaking when it comes to disagreements. In everyday conversation, the speaker and listener can express opposing viewpoints as they argue in support of their position. In public speaking, however, listeners are bound by an ethical obligation not to interrupt the speech. Still, listeners are not sitting quietly accepting the speaker's views as factual, some are arguing against the speaker internally. Because of this, a speechwriter must consider what the audience might think after hearing controversial views and respond to them in the speech. This concept is known as mental dialoguing with the audience. The power of a persuasive appeal rest in knowing how your listener will respond to claims that you make. Study the example of mental dialoguing below.

Mental Dialoguing with Audience Example:

Speaker states:	"Pit bull terriers are a dangerous breed and should be outlawed."
Listener thinks:	"That's not true; it's the owners who abuse the dog—that's the problem."
Speaker responds:	"I know some of you believe the owners are at fault, not the breed. Let me share some factual information about the pit bull breed with you."
Listener thinks:	"Here we go! I've heard it all before."
Speaker responds:	"According to the American Society for Cruelty to Animals, the pit bull is a descendant of the original English bull-baiting dogs—a dog that was bred to bite and hold bulls, bears and other large animals around the face and head. When baiting large animals was outlawed in the 1800s, people turned instead to fighting their dogs against each other. These larger, slower bull-baiting dogs were crossed with smaller, quicker terriers to produce a more agile and athletic dog for fighting other dogs."
Listener thinks:	"Wow, I didn't know that."

As you can see from this example, the speaker was able to retain the listener's attention by considering what the listener might think after critical statements. In the end, the listener was open to hearing more. As you research your subject and evaluate audience surveys, it is important to look for reasons why your audience disagrees with your views. When you understand your opposition, it is easier to develop counter-arguments that will speak directly to the listener's thoughts as they occur during your persuasive presentation.

Ethics and the Psychology of an Audience

Ethical responsibility is important in all public speaking presentations; however, it is critical in persuasive presentations. In chapter four, ethics was introduced and defined as a philosophical concept where people decide what is right or wrong, moral or immoral in human affairs. "Speak no harms to others" is an easy way to think of ethics in public speaking. Here are a few persuasive topics that might violate this rule:

1. Persuading listeners to think they have a right to take violent action against the closing of grammar schools with low enrollment.
2. Using faulty or biased information that leads an audience to believe that one group of people is of higher value than others. Example: *nerds vs. popular high school students*
3. Persuading an audience to believe that it is logical and even ethical to vote for a person who has a reputation of getting free food from their college cafeteria.

Challenges in Persuasive Speaking

During a speech, audience members will ponder the following thoughts, *"Why should I listen, what's in this for me?"* Listeners are egocentric because listening requires them to work; people feel that they should get something in exchange for their attention. As a result, a speech writer must be creative in how they engage the audience throughout the presentation. Surveying your audience and evaluating the information from the analysis will provide you with vital information to assist in developing creative engagement approaches. A key method used by speakers to capture their audience's interest is filtering important points through common experiences.

Study the following examples:

1. Have you ever been so cold that your body trembled uncontrollably? Well, that's how my body responded when I walked up on a huge bear while hiking in the mountains.

2. Imagine your stomach rumbling because you're hungry. You go to the kitchen to look for food but there's nothing there; just an empty refrigerator and cabinets. You look in your wallet but there's no money to purchase food either. How will you quench the hunger pains that are growing louder in your stomach? People who are paid minimum wage experience this daily. They may have a home or apartment to live in, but after paying their mortgage or rent, little is left for groceries.

Persuasive Speech Heading

General Purpose: To persuade

Narrowed Topic: There must be opposition to qualify as a persuasive topic.

Position: Statement that expresses how you feel emotionally about your topic

Proposition: *(two parts – State the problem as you see it & the solution you think will resolve the problem.)* This comes from your narrow topic.

The persuasive speech heading brainstorming section is constructed using the same building methods as the informative speech heading.

It begins with the general purpose, followed by the narrowed topic. The difference between the informative and persuasive speech headings is the specific purpose and the central idea. Because of the persuasiveness of the topic, the specific purpose is phrased more directly; it reflects the speaker's emotional reaction to the topic. For instance, a speechwriter may hate pit bull terriers because they have attack humans without provocation leaving many crippled or disfigured; and, a few die. The speaker's position on this issue would be, *"Pit bulls are dangerous"*. This direct statement expresses how the speaker feels about pit bulls. In addition, the position helps the speechwriter think critically about a logical and acceptable way to solve the problem. When the speaker locks in a solution that could work, the next step is to formulate a full proposition statement. The proposition is stated in two parts: the problem and its solution.

In the speech, the speaker may propose that breeding pit bull terriers should be outlawed for five years until scientific research can identify reasons why the breed's temperament can at times turns deadly. This will become the speaker's proposal that the audience is persuaded to support.

SHARE YOUR UNDERSTANDING

Read each scenario below to identify the true problem. The goal is to think critical about the reason the problem is occurring, and then develop a scenario-centered solution that corrects the problem. When you are satisfied with your decision, write a proposition statement on the line beneath each scenario. Also indicate your approach, will it be a proposition of: fact, value, or policy?

Scenario Number 1: The teenagers in your neighborhood are out of school for the summer. Some have found jobs for most have not. As a result, they're hanging out on the neighborhood streets annoying neighbors with noise, mischief, and litter. Even though a few of them have had run-ins with police for minor events, they are decent kids. Identify the true problem in this scenario and consider solution options before developing your proposition.

_____

_____

_____

Scenario Number 2: The local grocery store in your neighborhood has gone out of business leaving behind a huge vacant building with a large parking lot. Word around the neighborhood is that the property has been purchased by a company that is known for hosting huge parties and concert events. Although the property has a parking lot that provides plenty of space for party and concert rentals, the residents of your neighborhood are concerned about late night noise from the parking lot and the venue. After conducting a bit of research you discover that the neighborhood has no zoning laws against businesses of this nature. Identify the true problem in this scenario and consider solution options before developing your proposition.

_____

_____

_____

Three ways to approach a proposition:

When developing a speech, speechwriters generally have little to no knowledge about their audience's beliefs or attitudes towards the topic. Because of this, speechwriters must dig for answers before deciding how to approach their audience persuasively. At times, the audience may hold opposing views on the issue because they have partial facts about it. Other times the listener's views against your proposition may be deeply ingrained in their values. The only way to find out why they oppose your views is to ask them. The most useful tool available to help learn about your listeners beliefs and attitudes, before writing the speech, is the audience analysis survey. When specific questions are posed on these surveys, the data will reveal patterns of attitudes and beliefs that helps the speechwriter select an effective persuasive approach. There are three different approaches that persuasive speakers use, propositions of fact, value, or policy. Each are described next for your understanding.

- **Proposition of fact** is used when the speechwriter concludes that the audience's opposition to the proposition is due to missing chunks for factual information. Through informative speaking, the speaker fills in missing facts and works to connect points to ensure that no gaps remain. Before the audience will accept this new knowledge as true, the speaker must present them with credible evidence from respected sources. A proposition of fact is probably the easiest type of persuasive approach because the speaker persuades by teaching. Select proposition of fact when your audience analysis results show that your listeners disagree with you because they do not have all the facts on the subject. Persuasion occurs by filling in gaps of missing information to paint a complete picture that the audience can see.

- **Proposition of value** asks the audience to judge the worth of a person, event, or situation. A few topics that are approach persuasively by using a proposition of value are: capital punishment, abortion, and physician assisted suicide. Filtering persuasive appeals though a proposition of value is most difficult because you are asking the audience to shift their self-concept. As discussed in Chapter Two, the self-concept locks in at roughly 25-years of age and is resistant to change. Does this mean you can't win with this type of approach? No! Instead of attempting to change a person's values or beliefs, the speaker must focus on changing their actions by using logic and emotional appeal. During the 2004 National Democratic Convention, Representative Barak Obama was the keynote speaker. His goal was to unite a country that had been divided by democrats and republicans; the red and blue parties. After conducting research and analysis audience surveys to better understand the problem, he developed a speech that shifted the consciousness of a nation.

    In 2004, the country was in a huge recession; democrats and republican politicians were accusing each other of causing this recession. Instead of taking a side and challenging deeply ingrained values of party affiliation, he focused his speech on showing his audience that the problem was not with the red (republican) or blue (democrat) states. Instead, he worked to show the listeners that the entire country would suffer if the parties did not work together to correct the problem.

    In this speech, Obama shifted the actions of his listeners; but, their values and beliefs did not change. Propositions of value are best approached in increments.

- **Proposition of policy** is an approach that asks the audience to advocate for creating or changing policies or laws. The speaker strives to convince the audience that a problem exists that requires change through the development of new or stronger laws, or guidelines. Once the speaker persuades the listeners to accept that a problem exists, the next step is to propose a plan of action. This plan that you propose must be practical and must not create additional problems. The pit bull speech topic used earlier in this text, for example, would qualify as a proposition of policy as the speaker is proposing that a new law be put in place to prohibit the breeding of the dog for five years.

    A speaker's goal when proposing a proposition of policy is to convince the audience to take one of two forms of action passive agreement or immediate action:

    * Passive agreement speeches asks the listeners to agree with the speaker's views, but take no action.

    * Immediate action speeches asks the listeners to take action such as; signing a petition or taking to the streets in protest..

Facts are used in all speeches as they are considered supporting material. Do not confuse factual information use in speeches as evidence with a proposition of fact; they are not the same. In order to select an effective proposition approach, you must understand why your audience disagrees with you. This information is gathered through the data collected from surveys that shows what the audience thinks about your proposition, and why. This data will help you select the correct proposition approach.

SHARE YOUR UNDERSTANDING

Read the following scenario and decide which proposition approach you would use to persuade your audience to accept your views. All the information required to make a decision is contained in each scenario.

Scenario: A close friend has just shared disturbing news about a mutual friend's mother. It seems that she has some type of blood illness which requires a blood transfusion to save her life. You are quite familiar with this woman and have enjoyed her home cooking when you played with her son as a child. She is a nice woman who is dedicated to her religion. What concerns you most about her illness is that her religion does not allow for blood transfusions. The outcome looks bleak and you are fearful for her life because she will not go against her religious traditions—you just don't get it. If you were to write a persuasive speech to convince the members of her church to allow for this lifesaving blood transfusion, what type of persuasive approach would you take? Name the proposition approach that you would use (*fact, value, or policy*), and explain why.

_____

_____

_____

_____

_____

_____

_____

_____

_____

Persuasive Methods

Convincing others to accept your views on matters is an skill that has historical connections. Over three thousand years ago, a Greek philosopher by the name of Aristotle became frustrated with the lies and deceit that were commonly used during public speaking events. To address this problem, Aristotle proposed that every public speech be conducted in an ethical manor. To be considered ethical, the speech must include three criteria: ethos, logos, and pathos.

Ethos: Credibility

In chapter four, we touched on establishing credibility. This doesn't end with the credibility statement communicated in the introduction; credibility must be reestablished throughout the entire speech. For a speaker to be perceived as credible, the audience must feel that the speaker as trustworthy, competent, and confident. A speaker's credibility is judged before the speech begins, during, and after the speech ends. The point, is that the speaker is always being scrutinized by skeptical audience members. Therefore, a speaker must display professionalism and integrity at all times to maintain a high level of credibility. Credibility is also established throughout the speech by the types of evidence used to proves or disproves a claim. Faulty evidence will be rejected quickly causing the speaker will lose credibility.

Logos: Logic and Reason

According to Aristotle, logic should be used in a manner that helps the speaker reach the sought after conclusion. Logical arguments are supported by evidence that provides support to claims made. Four types of evidence commonly used are: facts, examples, testimony, and statistics.

- **Facts** are something that truly exists, or it has occurred and can be proven.
- **Examples** can be brief, extended stories, or hypothetical. Each type is used to provide listeners with a visual or mental image of a point made by the speaker.
- **Testimony** may come from experts who have conducted extensive studies on the subject or individuals who have first-hand experience.
- **Statistics** help to quantify information in a way that helps the audience understand numerical inferences. Example: "A lot of people still smoke cigarettes today." Versus, "Over five million people still smoke cigarettes today.' Statistics should be rounded to the nearest whole number and should not be overused.

The evidence used in a speech must come from primary credible sources, not secondary sources. Facts pulled from secondary sources may be tampered with. They may include biases, misrepresented or incorrect facts. It is also important to combine different types of evidence form different sources to avoid biased supporting material. One factual piece of evidence does not adequately provide enough information to persuade an audience. A combination of sources from credible and respected individuals or institutions is the best way to completely support each point that you make.

Burden of proof is defined as, *"A duty placed upon a speaker to prove or disprove a disputed fact."* This means a persuasive speaker is responsible for providing evidence that proves his or her claim just as a lawyer does in the courtroom. A claim is a statement of fact that the speaker wants the audience to accept as true. For instance, a speaker may state, *"A college education will result in higher wages throughout a person's life."* Before the audience accepts this unsupported claim as true, the speaker must provide evidence that removes all skepticism. The burden of proof will always rest with the speaker.

Fallacies: Faulty Evidence

At times, evidence used by a speaker will be faulty because of illogical thinking or an embellishment of facts. This type of faulty evidence is called fallacies. A fallacy is illogical reasoning used by a speaker to prove a point. They are the intentional use of little lies, exaggerations, or omissions of important facts to prove a point. Fallacies are unethical and will cause the speaker to lose credibility with the audience. Therefore, speakers must avoid using fallacies at all times. Some common fallacies are listed below.

Slippery Slope: a speaker suggests that taking a particular step will led to subsequent consequences that can't be avoided.
Bandwagon: occurs when a speaker suggests that because the majority agrees with an issue, it must be correct.
Hasty generalizations: occurs when the speaker jumps to a general conclusion based on partial evidence.
Red herring: occurs when a speaker introduces an irrelevant issue to divert the audience's attention from the main issue.
Either-Or: the speaker attempts to give the listeners two options when there are actually more options available.
Appeal to tradition: speaker proposes that traditional ways of thinking or acting is more effective.
Appeal to novelty: speaker proposes that new age thinking and acting is more effective.

SHARE YOUR UNDERSTANDING

Write a statement that reflects each fallacy below. If you cannot think of one, go to the Internet to find an example.

Slippery slope: _____

_____

Bandwagon: _____

_____

Hasty generalization: _____

_____

Red herring: _____

_____

Either-or: _____

_____

Appeal to tradition: _____

_____

Appeal to novelty: _____

_____

Reasoning: Argumentation Style

In the courtroom, lawyers use a specific reasoning strategy to present their argument. Reasoning is a specific style of argumentation. Public speakers must make sure their reasoning is sound; logical and supported by evidence. They must also persuade their audience to agree with their reasoning. The most commonly used reasoning methods for persuasion are inductive, deductive, causal, and analogical.

- **Inductive Reasoning**, also known as specific instance. The type of argument can be understood as a triangle where the speaker begins the argument by providing one specific example of the problem. From there, the speaker will build a case by adding more and more instances of the same problem occurring. The goal is to convince the audience to agree that there is a problem by showing the magnitude of its reach. When the symbolic "triangle" has been filled with similar occurrences, supported by factual evidence, a concluding proposition statement will be presented. The speaker must be strategic when presenting the proposal to solve the problem, it must reflect logic and critical thought. Propositions of fact, value, and policy can be argued using this method.

- **Deductive Reasoning** arguments are divided into three elements called a syllogism: a major premise, a minor premise, and a conclusion. Primarily used for controversial speeches where the proposition is withheld until the third main point. A useful symbol used to help describe this argument type is the upside down triangle. Deductive reasoning arguments are divided into three parts. First, the speaker begins with the major premise which is a general statement about the problem; evidence is provide to prove the major premise true. Next, the speaker's moves to the minor premise which narrows the general statement to a specific thesis also providing evidence that proves it true. If the major premise is proven true, and the minor premise is proven true, then the conclusion has to be true.

Example: Major premise - *My friends love the food at Burger World. Minor premise - My parents say the food at Burger World is the best. Conclusion - Burger World has great food.* The specific conclusion of this argument reflects your proposition. This is another persuasive strategy used by lawyers in the court room. A famous example of deductive reasoning comes from the famous O. J. Simpson trial when his lawyer stated, "If the glove doesn't fit, you must acquit!"

- **Causal Reasoning** is often called cause-and-effect reasoning. In causal reasoning, the goal is not to simply prove that there is a cause and effect, but to prove that one cause triggered a specific effect to occur. Causal reasoning focuses on proving that a relationship exists between something that has already happened, or something that could possibly occur in the future. It is up to the speaker to provide a burden of proof that helps the audience see the relationship. A causal argument uses two or more main points. The first main point will introduce a problem, such as the effect of something that has already happened – like gas prices rising, or the cause of something that could happen in the future – like global warming. In the second main point, the speaker must use critical thinking to uncover the hidden relationship between the effect or cause as presented in the first main point.

- **Analogical Reasoning** is a type of argument that looks at similar situations and proposes that if an idea that solved one problem was successful, then the same idea should be used to solve a similar issue. Analogical reasoning uses two to three main points which presents a comparison of similar problems supported by factual evidence that shows how the problem was solved in different situations using the same method.

Pathos: Emotional Appeal

Aristotle's pathos can be described as the emotional impact of a speech; persuasive speeches always requires emotional appeal. Nonverbal messages that accompany verbal messages convey lots of emotional appeal. When logic is combined with emotional appeal the speakers is able to make a more compelling argument. Emotional appeal used most often is: creating a sense of urgency, fear, excitement, loyalty, pride, time constraints, need, values, etc. Advertisers use emotional appeal to persuade their targeted audience to purchase products that they do not need or were not planning to purchase. Because humans are emotional beings, the use of pathos in persuasion is a powerful strategy.

Next, is a full persuasive speech for study purposes. Notice how the reasoning style, proposition approach and outline template use are listed at the top of the speech. When you write your speech it is important to be clear about the specific strategies, approach, and methods you plan to use.

FULL PERSUASIVE SPEECH EXAMPLE

STRATEGIES & MEHTODS USED: Inductive, proposition of fact, and problem/cause/solution outline template.

GENERAL PURPOSE: To persuade
TOPIC: College athletes should not be paid because it could have a negative impact on their studies.
POSITION: College athletes should not be paid because it could have a negative impact on their studies.
PROPOSITION: College athletes should not be paid salaries because it could have a negative impact on their academic focus; instead, I propose that a percentage of the profits from revenue-generating sports be deposited into locked savings accounts, in the name of each athlete, to be turned over to each athlete at the end of the school year.

INTRODUCTION
I. **Attention-Getter:** When you think about attending college, you think of an experience that prepares students for careers – not a money-making sports organization.

II. **Personal Credibility:** As a student worker, I am assigned to the athletic department where I meet lots of basketball players who have amazing skills. Many have scholarships that pay their full tuition. I see the scholarship as an even exchange; the athletes share their skills for a free education, including room and board. Recently, some college basketball players started a petition to be paid for their services. To learn more about their complaint, I researched this topic and was amazed at my findings; the athletes are not totally wrong in this matter.

III. **Give Audience a Reason to Listen:** When you work hard to develop unique skills that make you stand out from the crowd, those achievements should be rewards when used by others like college sports teams. The truth is that college athletes are rewarded for their above average skills; they receive free tuition, books and supplies, and room and board. This is proof that college athlete are paid for their skills ... Right? Non-athletes have to pay for all of this. Still, big universities today are making huge profits from ticket sales, donations, and endorsements.

IV. **Proposition:** College athletes should not be paid salaries because it could have a negative impact on their academic focus; instead, I propose that a percentage of the profits from revenue-generating sports be deposited into locked savings accounts in the name of each athlete to be turned over to each athlete at the end of each school year.

Transition: *Let's begin by understanding the problem.*

BODY

I. Most high school athletes dream of playing for a division I university who reward full academic scholarships.
 A. Division I universities are the top athletic schools known for grooming players to move into professional sports teams.
 1. If for some reason the high school athlete is not selected to play at the division I level, he or she will look to division II or division III universities for acceptance.
 2. Division II and III university offers full or partial scholarships to top athletes as well.
 3. If these options are not available, the athlete may consider playing for a two-year community college that offers smaller academic scholarships.
 B. Still, the overall goal for student athletes is to show division I universities that they are good enough to be recruited for their team, but only a few are successful.
 1. There is nothing wrong with having a dream of making it to a division I university with hope of being drafted to a professional team.
 2. Students athletes are not preparing for life after sports by obtaining a degree; this a problem.

II. **The cause of this problem** is the huge profits that major sports universities have been making over the last thirty years or so from revenue making sports like basketball and football.
 A. Every time they win games for their university or college, lots of donations and endorsements come in from alumni and other organizations.
 1. The truth is that colleges and universities are getting rich from money-making.
 2. According to James Door's 2011 online article, *"Athletic Scholarships"*, $2.1 billion athletic scholarships are awarded every year.
 a. That is a lot of money!
 3. The report goes on to explain how the money is divided to cover the athlete's expenses.
 B. Still, the financial reports from top athletic universities provide evidence that supports the players' accusations that colleges and universities are getting rich off of their sweat.
 1. In the article, *Time to pay college football players -- changing times, money say so*, published in the *National Columnists* online magazine, Greg Doyel, a proponent in support of paying college athletes wages discusses how times have changed, and how college sports have become multimillion dollar moneymakers for universities. Doyel writes, *"The business of college football has changed dramatically -- especially in the last few decades -- and it*

has changed for damn near everyone accept the players. Salaries for coaching staff, stadium seating, and ticket prices have skyrocketed. The compensation for the athletes we're watching? Stagnated!"

C. Greg Doyel's argument is that nothing has changed for college athletes; and it is sad, yet true – everyone else is getting rich off of their hard work.
   1. Still, I do not think that paying college athletes a regular salary is the answer.
   2. When college students start earning money, their attitude about graduating changes.
   3. A few of the basketball players that I interviewed admitted that "if they got paid to play, they would not complete their degree; and instead, they'd try to get drafted by professional teams when their scholarships ran out."
   4. This immature thinking is a problem for several reasons.
   5. College athletes must think about life after basketball or football – they must acquire skills that will allow them to find employment.
   6. As I mentioned earlier, not many will make it to division I institutions; and therefore, these athletes are dreamers who do not have a backup plan.

D. Currently, most college athletes continue to dedicate time and effort to their studies to retain their scholarships.
   1. Would this dedication change if they were given a regular paycheck to share in the profits?
   2. I think it would change enough to cause concern.

Transition: Now that you have a better understanding of the problem and its cause, I'd like to propose a solution.

III. **STATEMENT OF SOLUTION:** I propose that student athletes be allowed to participate in a profit sharing program with revenue making universities.
   A. **Description of solution:** Greg Doyel's research proves that everyone except the athletes are benefiting financially from upgrades to college sports.
      1. College sports have converted from a hobby to a multi-million dollar business.
      2. Treating the student athletes with respect means sharing some of the profits with them.
      3. However, it would be wise to withhold their profit sharing checks to ensure they graduate.
         a. **How the solution fits the problem:** This solution fits the problem because it addresses the athlete's demands to be compensated fairly and communicates a level of respect to the top notch athletes.
         b. **Example:** At the end of each school year, each athlete would receive a lump sum payment of their share of the profits for the school year.
         c. School-related deductions will not be deducted from these checks.
   B. **How the solution can be implemented:** This plan will take several months to a year to organize and implement.
      Plan of Action:
      1. The steps required to make my proposal a reality is as follows:
      2. The institutions must meet with their board of trustees, chancellor, and chief financial officer (CFO) to work out the details to develop an athlete profit sharing program that would share profits that are generated each year for their specific sports program.
      3. Only revenue-generating sports may participate in the salary program.
      4. The CFO will be responsible for setting up savings accounts with three names on each: the athlete, the CFO, and the chancellor.
      5. The athlete will be given legal documentation that the account exists, and will receive monthly balance statements.
      6. Athletes will not have access privileges to these accounts; the CFO and the chancellor are the only parties with this privilege.

7. With this new program in place, the university chancellor or CFO should meet with the athletic director to create a two-level payment incentive.
8. Level one athletes who have earned starting positions in their team sports will receive an 10 percent more than their teammates who do not have starting positions. This will create additional motivation for tier two athletes to work harder.
9. In order to receive profit sharing payments, student athletes must complete the school year with a "C" average or above. If this is condition is not met, the athlete will only receive 10% of the full amount owed to him or her.
10. The program should begin during start of the next academic year to allow adequate time for development and preparation.

C. **Picture results:** At the end of each school year, student athletes who complete their studies with a "C" average or better will feel respected because of the profit sharing payment. This end of year payment will serve as motivation to the student to stay focused on their studies.

CONCLUSION

I. All-in-all, student athletes deserve respect , but not all attend colleges and universities that are revenue generating schools.
II. Still, this solution will address the problem for student athletes at top revenue generation universities.
III. Being accepted into a four year college or university is an honor that not all athletes achieve; it's unfortunate that the skill of those who do make it becomes their blinders.

Step-by-Step Persuasive Speech Development

---

1. Develop persuasive speech heading:
- General Purpose
- Narrowed topic
- Position
- Proposition

---

2. How will you approach your proposition?
- **Proposition of Fact:** Your goal is to persuade listeners to accept a particular view of the disputed facts by presenting a lot of factual evidence.
- **Proposition of Value:** Your goal is to persuade the audience to agree with your views of an issue through the use of emotional appeal.
- **Proposition of Policy:** Your goal is to persuade your audience to accept a specific course of legal action to solve a problem.

---

3. ETHOS: How will you establish credibility throughout your argument?
- Trustworthiness
- Competence
- Confidence

---

4. LOGOS = Logic and Reason (proven evidence & argument style)
- **Inductive reasoning:** begins with specific instances of a problem and proves that the problem is bigger than the one event prior to reaching a conclusion.
- **Deductive reasoning:** Involves three parts – major premise, minor premise, and conclusion. It provides enough evidence to suggest that the major premise and minor-related premise is true. And, it concludes that if the major and minor premise is true, then it is probable that the conclusion is also true.
- **Causal Reasoning:** uses evidence to prove that a relationship exists between something that has already happened and something that may occur in the future. Proves that a specific cause lead to a specific effect.
- **Analogical Reasoning:** is a comparison of similar problems. It uses evidence to argue that if a particular solution solves one problem, it is logical to use that solution to solve a similar issue.

---

5. PATHOS: emotional appeal strategies to influence compliance
- Types of Emotional Appeal: fear, compassion, pride, anger, guilt, or reverence

---

6. Selecting an Organizational Pattern: Outline (presented on next page)

Persuasive Speech Outlines

Outlines that support reasoning types are strategically designed to guide the speech writer through the developmental process. Five persuasive speech outlines are explained followed by templates.

Problem/Solution Outline	Supports inductive or deductive argumentation where the speaker aims to prove that a problem exists, and then proposes the best solution to solve the problem. The problem/solution outline has two main points: • The first main point addresses the problem. • The second main point addresses a solution.
Problem/Cause/Solution Outline	Supports inductive or deductive argumentation where the speaker plans to prove that a problem exists, but must also explain the cause of the problem to effectively persuade an audience. The problem/cause/solution outline has three main points: • The first main point addresses the problem as the speaker sees it. • The second main point addresses the cause of the problem. • The third main point addresses the solution that will satisfy the problem.
Causal Outline	Used primarily for informative speeches, but the same "relationship proving" strategy is used in the second main point of a persuasive problem/cause/solution outline. In an informative speech, the first main point introduces the an effect to set the stage. The second main point proves what caused the problem to show a relationship. A third main point may be added if there are several causes or effects. In a persuasive speech, subpoints are used in the second main point to prove a relationship.
Monroe's Motivated Sequence	Supports a persuasive speech that seeks immediate action from the audience. This speech is organized in five steps instead of main points. 1. Attention 2. Need 3. Satisfaction 4. Visualization 5. Action
Comparative Advantage Outline	This pattern is similar to motivated sequence and is often used for business presentations. The big difference occurs in the *satisfy* and *visualization* steps. In those steps you have to compare and contrast two or more plans, solutions or alternatives.
Refutation Outline	Supports controversial persuasive topics such as social issues. You anticipate your opposition's objections when developing the speech, acknowledge each in separate main points, and then refute each by using subpoints. Your refutation must prove why your view is "better," "more effective," etc.

PROBLEM / SOLUTION OUTLINE TEMPLATE

GENERAL PURPOSE:
NARROWED TOPIC:
POSITION (How do you honestly feel about your topic):
PROPOSITION (problem & solution):

Introduction
   I.   **Attention material** (use hook and bait method):
   II. **Credibility material** (tell audience how you learned about your topic):
   III. **Connect to the audience** (use common experiences and "You" language):
   IV. **Proposition** (copy and paste the proposition from your speech heading:
Transition to body of speech

Body
   I.   Main point #1 (Statement of problem)
        A.   (Description of problem)
             1.   (Signs, symptoms, effects of problem)
             2.   (Example, narrative, or testimony)
        B.   (Importance of problem)
             1.   (Extent of problem)
             2.   (Facts/statistics)
             3.   (Expert testimony)
        C.   (Who is affected)
             1.   (Facts/statistics)
             2.   (Example/narrative)
        D.   (Consequences of problem)
             1.   (Expert testimony)
             2.   (Example/narrative)
Transition to main point 2
   II. Main point #2 (Statement of solution)
        A.   (Description of solution)
             1.   (How solution fits problem)
             2.   (Example)
        B.   (How solution can be implemented)
             1.   (Plan of action)
                  (1) (Step 1 of plan)
                  (2) (Step 2 of plan)
                  (3) (Step 3 of plan)
                  (4) (Step 4 of plan)
             2.   (Costs and efforts)
        C.   (Picture results)
             1.   (Describe expected results)
             2.   (When results expected)
             3.   (Additional benefits)
Transition to conclusion

Conclusion
   I.   Signal end of speech
   II. Summary residual message
   III. Memorable End

Bibliography in APA format goes on the next page.

Develop your persuasive speech heading here.

GENERAL PURPOSE:_____

NARROWED TOPIC: _____

_____

_____

POSITION (How do you really feel about your topic): _____

_____

_____

_____

_____

PROPOSITION (problem & solution): _____

_____

_____

_____

_____

_____

_____

_____

_____

_____

_____

_____

_____

PROBLEM/CAUSE/SOLUTION OUTLINE TEMPLATE

GENERAL PURPOSE:
NARROWED TOPIC:
POSITION (How do you really feel about your topic):
PROPOSITION (problem & solution):

Introduction
   I.   **Attention material** (use hook and bait method):
   II. **Credibility material** (tell audience how you learned about your topic):
   III. **Connect to the audience** (use common experiences and "You" language):
   IV. **Proposition** (copy and paste the proposition from your speech heading:
Transition to body of speech

Body
   I.   Main point (Statement of problem)
       A. (Description of problem)
           1. (Signs, symptoms, effects of problem)
           2. (Example, narrative, or testimony)
       B. (Importance of problem)
       C. (Extent of problem)
           1. (Facts/statistics)
           2. (Expert testimony)
       D. (Who is affected)
           1. (Facts/statistics)
           2. (Example/narrative)
       E. (Consequences of problem)
           1. (Expert testimony)
           2. (Example/narrative)
Transition to main point 2
   II.   Main point (Argument of Cause)
       A. Statement of the cause of the problem
           1. (Evidence for the link, statistics, expert testimony or facts)
           2. (Continued evidence)
       B. Development of how this cause can be overcome -- leading to the solution
           1. How the cause is being handled currently
           2. How this current condition is inadequate
           3. How it might be handled differently
Transition to main point 2
   III. Main point (Statement of solution)
       A. (Description of solution)
           1. (How solution fits problem)
           2. (Example)
       B. (How solution can be implemented)
           1. (Plan of action)
               (1) (Step 1 of plan)
               (2) (Step 2 of plan)
               (3) (Step 3 of plan)
               (4) (Step 4 of plan)
           2. (Costs and efforts)
       C. (Picture results)

1.   (Describe expected results)
2.   (When results expected)
3.   (Additional benefits)

Transition into conclusion
Conclusion
I.   Signal end of speech
II.   Summary residual message
III.   Memorable End

Bibliography in APA format goes on the next page.

Develop your persuasive speech heading here.

GENERAL PURPOSE:_____

NARROWED TOPIC: _____

_____

POSITION (How do you really feel about your topic): _____

_____

_____

_____

PROPOSITION (problem & solution): _____

_____

_____

_____

_____

_____

_____

_____

CAUSAL OUTLINE TEMPLATE

GENERAL PURPOSE:
NARROWED TOPIC:
SPECIFIC PURPOSE:
CENTRAL IDEA:

Introduction
I.   **Attention Getter:** connect to the topic, a statement of significance (why the topic is important)
II.   Credibility statement
III.   Connect to the audience
IV.   Central Idea

Transition from the introduction to your first main point goes here.
Body
I.   **Main Point - Cause:** a brief description of the problem that sets the stage.
    A.   The first subpoint or supporting material
        1. Narrative or further explanation that helps audience understand
        2. Facts, statistics, etc.
        3. Testimony or authority citations
    B.   The second subpoint or supporting material.
        1. Narrative or further explanation that helps audience understand
        2. Facts, statistics, etc.
        3. Testimony or authority citations
    C.   The third subpoint or supporting material, or delete this number if not needed
    D.   The fourth subpoint or supporting material, or delete this number if not needed.

Transition from your first main point to your second main point
II.   **Main Point - Effect:** a brief description of the effect/s of the caused by problem.
    A.   The first subpoint or supporting material
        1. Narrative or further explanation that helps audience understand
        2. Facts, statistics, etc.
        3. Evidence, proof
        4. Testimony or authority citations
    B.   The second subpoint or supporting material.
        1. Narrative or further explanation that helps audience understand
        2. Facts, statistics, etc.
        3. Evidence, proof
        4. Testimony or authority citations
    C.   The third subpoint or supporting material, or delete this number if not needed
        1. Narrative or further explanation that helps audience understand
        2. Facts, statistics, etc.
        3. Evidence, proof
        4. Testimony or authority citations
    D.   The fourth subpoint or supporting material, or delete this number if not needed.

The transition to the conclusion
There may be several effects that resulted from the cause, add additional main points.
Conclusion
I.   **Signal the close of the speech**
II.   **Summarize residual message:** The review of your main points goes here.
III. **Closing:** Your closing statement goes here.

Bibliography in APA format goes on the next page.

Develop your persuasive speech heading here.

GENERAL PURPOSE: _____

NARROWED TOPIC: _____

_____

_____

POSITION (How do you really feel about your topic): _____

_____

_____

_____

_____

PROPOSITION (problem & solution): _____

_____

_____

_____

_____

_____

_____

_____

_____

_____

_____

_____

_____

_____

_____

_____

MONROE'S MOTIVATED SEQUENCE OUTLINE TEMPLATE

GENERAL PURPOSE:
NARROWED TOPIC:
POSITION (How do you really feel about your topic):
PROPOSITION (problem & solution):

Introduction
   I.   ***Focus attention of problem***
   II. Tie to audience
   III. Credibility statement
   IV. Proposition

Transition: I will begin by …
Body
   I.   **Main Point**: Statement of ***need for action***.
      A. Description of problem
         1. signs, symptoms, effects of problem
         2. example, narrative, or testimony
      B. Importance of addressing the problem
         1. facts/statistics/
         2. quotes from experts
         3. example/narratives
      C. Who is affected most by issue
      D. Concession rebuttal

   Transition to second main point:
   II. **Main Point:** Present ***a solution*** that satisfies the need.
      A. Description of the solution
      B. How will solution satisfy the need?
      C. How will the solution be implemented

   Transition to third main point:
   III. **Main Point**: help listeners **visualize the results**
      A. Describe the expected result if action is taken
      B. Describe the consequences if no action is taken

   Transition to conclusion
Conclusion
   I.   Restate your main points and central idea.
   II. Reemphasize your call to ***action***: What should the audience do next?
   III. Don't fizzle out! Close with a bang!

Bibliography in APA format goes on the next page.

Develop your persuasive speech heading here.

GENERAL PURPOSE: _____

NARROWED TOPIC: _____

_____

_____

POSITION (How do you really feel about your topic): _____

_____

_____

_____

_____

PROPOSITION (problem & solution): _____

_____

_____

_____

_____

_____

_____

_____

_____

_____

_____

_____

_____

_____

COMPARATIVE ADVANTAGE OUTLINE TEMPLATE

GENERAL PURPOSE:
TOPIC: (Should compare and contrast two or more plans, solutions or alternatives to solve a problem)
SPECIFIC PURPOSE: To show my audience (which choice is best to solve the problem)
PROPOSITION: problem and preview of body (two or three possible solutions will be presented)

I. **Attention material** **(Communication need for action)**
II. **Credibility material** (tell audience how you learned about your topic)
III. **Connect to the audience** (use common experiences and "You" language)
IV. **Proposition** (copy and paste the proposition statement from your speech heading)

Transition to the body of the speech

(The first part of the Body lists and examines and then dismisses the competing options.)
I. **Main Point: First comparison - explain and eliminate by showing weaknesses**
  A. It has been tried. **(Describe the Plan)**
    1. Supporting evidence
    2. Supporting evidence
  B. It didn't work. **(Practicality)**
    1. Supporting evidence
    2. Supporting evidence

Transitional statement to 2nd main point

II. **Main Point: Second comparison - explain and eliminate by showing weaknesses**
  A. It is being tried. **(Plan)**
    1. Supporting evidence
    2. Supporting evidence
  B. It is not working to solve the problem **(Practicality)**
    1. Supporting evidence
    2. Supporting evidence

Transitional statement to 3rd main point

III. **Main Point: Introduce and defend your proposed plan – your proposition.**
  A. It is being used. [Plan]
    1. Supporting evidence
    2. Supporting evidence
  B. It works and will solve our energy crisis. [Practicality]
    1. Supporting evidence
    2. Supporting evidence

Transition to conclusion

Conclusion:
  I.   Restate your main points and central idea.
  II.   Reemphasize your call to *action*: What should the audience do next?
  III. Don't fizzle out! Close with a bang

Bibliography in APA format goes on the next page.

Develop your persuasive speech heading here.

GENERAL PURPOSE: _____

NARROWED TOPIC: _____

_____

_____

SPECIFIC PURPOSE: _____

_____

_____

_____

PROPOSITION (problem & solution): _____

_____

_____

_____

_____

_____

_____

_____

_____

_____

_____

_____

_____

_____

_____

REFUTATION OUTLINE TEMPLATE (Used to support controversial topics)

GENERAL PURPOSE:
NARROWED TOPIC:
POSITION:
PROPOSITION:

Introduction (don't tell all yet! Most listeners are against your proposition! Be strategic and creative.)
   I.   **Attention material:**
   II. **Credibility material:**
   III. **Connect to audience:**
   IV. **Proposition** (make a vague statement related to the topic and transition to the body)
Transition to body of speech
Body
   I.   First Main point states the problem which is in dispute
       A. Address the most important reason that your opposition disagrees with you.
           1. Use sources to explain what this opposing side believes and why.
           2. Provide an example or two from research
           3. Keep the opposition's attention by telling them why you are glad they are concerned about this issue (because you are too).
       B. Now prove why your view is correct!!!
           1. Give plenty of support from credible and respected experts! Examples of supporting proof and evidence are listed below.
               a. (Explain how evidence provides a counter-argument for this point)
               b. (Explain significance of refutation)
               c. (Facts/figures/expert testimony)
               d. (Example/narrative)
Transition to main point 2
   II. Second Main point should address another reason the opposition disagrees with you.
       A. Address the most important reason that your opposition disagrees with you.
           1. Use sources to explain what this opposing side believes and why.
           2. Provide an example/s from research
           3. Keep the opposition's attention by telling them why you are glad they are concerned about this issue (because you are too).
       B. Now prove why your side is most correct!!!
           1. Give plenty of support from credible and respected experts! Examples of supporting proof and evidence are listed below.
               a. (Explain how evidence provides a counter-argument for this point)
               b. (Explain significance of refutation)
               c. (Facts/figures/expert testimony)
               d. (Example/narrative)
Transition to main point 3
   III. Third Main point should address another reason the opposition disagrees with you.
       A. Address the most important reason that this side disagrees with you.
           1. Use sources to explain what this opposing side believes and why.
           2. Provide an example or two from sources
           3. Keep the opposition's attention by telling them why you are glad they are concerned about this issue (because you are too).
       B. Now prove why your side is most correct!!!
           1. Give plenty of support from credible and respected experts! Examples of supporting proof and evidence are listed below.
               a. (Explain how evidence provides a counter-argument for this point)
               b. (Explain significance of refutation)
               c. (Facts/figures/expert testimony)
               d. (Example/narrative)
Transition to conclusion
Conclusion
       A. Signal end of speech
       B. Summary (residual message)
       C. Tie back to the introduction to end

Develop your persuasive speech heading here.

GENERAL PURPOSE:_____

NARROWED TOPIC: _____

_____

_____

POSITION (How do you really feel about your topic): _____

_____

_____

_____

_____

PROPOSITION (problem & solution): _____

_____

_____

_____

_____

_____

_____

_____

_____

_____

_____

_____

_____

_____

_____

Summary

Persuasion is the process of creating, reinforcing, or changing the beliefs or actions of other people. There are many strategies and methods that people use to get others to comply. Before a speaker can persuade others, the speaker must conduct an audience analysis to learn why their audience disagrees with them, and how to strategically approach the audience with a proposition that will solve the problem. Propositions are formulated into questions of fact, value, or policy to address audience concerns. Public speaking presentations must convey ethos, logos, and pathos to ensure be seen as ethical and audience centered. Ethos is credibility which must be present throughout a speech. Logos is logic and reasoning. A speaker must present evidence to prove claims and select a strategic reasoning approach from which to argue a point.

Four types of argumentation are used by speakers: inductive and deductive reasoning are polar opposites; causal reasoning seeks to prove that one event caused another event to occur; and analogical reasoning is a comparison of two issues that suggests, if a proposed solution worked to solve the first problem, it should be used to solve the second problem. Six types of outline patterns are used to organize a persuasive speech: problem/solution, problem/cause/solution, causal, refutation, and comparative advantage.

Key terms

Propositions of fact
Propositions of value
Propositions of policy
Targeted audience
Psychology of the audience
Ethos
Logos
Pathos

Evidence
Fallacies
Emotional appeal
Inductive reasoning
Deductive reasoning
Causal reasoning
Analogical reasoning

Engaging the Audience: Visual Aids & Figurative Language

VOCABULARY BUILDERS: *Arcane*, noun
Understood by only a few.
"For arcane legal reasons, the actual ceremony must take place offline."

Proclivity, adjective
A natural inclination for something that is often considered bad; a predisposition.
"Your proclivity to only remember your side of the story is amazing!"

## CHAPTER 9

"Make sure you have finished speaking before your audience has finished listening."
—Dorothy Sarnoff

Anyone who has been an audience member can relate to the importance of feeling fully engaged. When a speaker is passionate about their topic and uses arousing mental imagery and visual aids to bring their point to life, the audience will respond positively. There are many strategies used to achieve this goal. In this chapter you will learn how to use visual aids and creative language to capture your audience's attention from beginning of the speech to the end.

Using Visual Aids to Engage

Visual aids can be a powerful tool when used in a timely manner to emphasize points made in the body of a speech. For example, a speaker may have a goal of persuading the audience to raise the legal driving age from sixteen to eighteen because the brain of a teenager is undergoing change through their early twenties. To further explain the importance of this proposal, the speaker will share a few factual examples of horrible vehicle accidents caused by teen drivers. Although the audience seems interested, they do not fully respond until the speaker shows a few images of the aftermath of these accidents. The shocking images will provide the audience with a more realistic understanding of the problem.

Statistical trends and patterns are best communicated through charts and graphs. Use a bar graph, pie chart, or line graph when using words that would be better understood in a numerical format. When you use terms like; a lot or many, the audience might wonder, "How much is a lot or many?" Graphs and charts provides the audience with visual images of key points the speaker makes. Visual aids also serve as attention getters. A general rule is to use a visual aid when a point is best understood visually.

Types of visual aids

Many types of visual aids are used in speech presentations. We will look at types that are more commonly used.

Pie Charts: used to show percentage or proportional data. The percentage represented by each category is provided next to the corresponding slice of pie. No more than six categories are generally used because more will overload the pie chart with too much data to be understood visually. In a speech, the speaker might use a pie chart to represent percentages of wages earned with different level of academic achievement: high school diploma, associate's degree, bachelor degree, etc.

Bar Graphs: used to display and compare the number, frequency or other measures for categories of data. Bar charts are one of the most commonly used types of graph because they are simple to create and easy to understand. Used in a speech, a bar graph can provide listeners with a visual aid that shows a decrease in heterosexual marriages over a twenty year period.

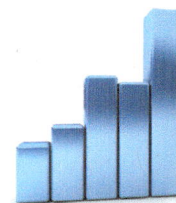

Line Graphs: used to show how one or more variables change over a continuous period of time. Examples of data presented in a line graph can be student graduation rates or snowfall levels over a certain period of time. Line graphs are also useful in identifying patterns in data such turning points in human behavior. Used as a visual aid in a speech, a line graph can show an incremental decline in cigarette smokers over a fixed period time.

PowerPoint Presentations

Currently, presenters are using presentation software such as Prezi and PowerPoint rather than the outdated poster board. Presentation software technology lets the speaker embed videos, pictures, and text, through computer generated software. When using PowerPoint or Prezi, do not insert your entire speech into the slides. Instead, use a minimal number of slides to help audience members understand key points that you are making. Use bullet points to limit text. When there is too much text on a PowerPoint slide the audience will be distracted by reading the information instead of listing to the speaker. Also, speakers should not face the PowerPoint presentation while interacting with it. It is important to practice with the presentation slides at home to become familiar with the lineup of each slide. Your keyword delivery outline should include the number of a corresponding slide, in each section, to make moving through your visual aid easier as you speak.

If a video is embedded into the PowerPoint slide it should be no longer than a few seconds and should not speak for the speaker. A video should only be used to provide an example of a point made by the speaker, not as a substitute for making the speech.

Objects and Models

An object is something that you can see in its three-dimensional form. An object can be a chair, a desk, or a cell phone. If the object that you want to use in your speech is too big or too small for a classroom, you can use a model. Models are scaled up or scaled-down versions of the real thing that can be used as a visual aid in a speech. If the speaker is giving an informative speech about her favorite baseball mitt, she might have the mitt with her to show the audience while explaining its importance.

The body

The human body can also be used as a visual aid. For example, if you've been studying the art of tai chi and want to show your audience different body movement, you could use a volunteer or your own body to demonstrate the moves as you explain them. Using your body as example is also a creative way to engage your audience.

Guidelines for using visual aids

- Practice your speech with the visual aid for accurate timing and comfort purposes.

- Have a backup plan in case your visual aid fails to work correctly.

- Do not pass around any objects or handouts during your speech because they distract your audience.

- Do not talk to your visual aid during the speech, keep your eyes on the audience while glancing briefly at your visual aid.

- Text or other visuals on PowerPoint slides or poster boards must be large enough to be seen by all audience members. Using technology to replace poster board is easier to learn and use. YouTube.com has lots of teaching video clips, or you can go to your student support center to get assistance.

- Text should be limited to a few words as possible on PowerPoint slides and poster boards. Use bullet points to highlight important thoughts; never full sentences.

- Arrive early to set up and test your visual aid to ensure that it works.

- The visual aid should take less than three minutes to setup and dismantle; and should be tested prior to the start of class.

Using Language to Engage

"Darkness cannot drive out hate; only light can do that. Hate cannot drive out hate; only love can do that."

—Rev. Dr. Martin Luther King, Jr

Word artists such as poets or lyricists understand the power of creative word usage. Word, when used figuratively can capture the soul, inspire, and move a person to action. Words have dual meanings; denotative and connotative.

- **Denotative meaning** is the literal dictionary definition of the word. For example, a dictionary might define the word "apple" as, "the round fruit from a tree of the rose family, which typically has thin red or green skin and crisp flesh."
- **Connotative meaning** is the emotional meaning of a word. For example, upon hearing the word "apple" you might think "pie" or "iPhone." When receiving a message, we also react first to the connotative meaning because of perceptual constructs. When we think about the full message, meaning will be reassigned as the speaker's denotative meaning is made clear.

Words used inaccurately can destroy a speech. There is no greater embarrassment than to mispronounce or misuse a word during a speech. The feedback from your audience can be frightening enough to activate the butterflies that you once had under control. Using words accurately is not difficult, however foreign or infrequently used words require research to help you become familiar with meaning and pronunciation. A dictionary or thesaurus is a good place to start; online dictionaries offer helpful audible pronunciation features. Language can be complex and challenge even the most fluent speakers; lets look at other important ways to consider language choices during speech development.

Familiar Words Are Cool!

It is helpful to use words that are familiar to you to avoid unexpected stumbles with pronunciation during the presentation. Speakers lose credibility when they stumble over a word in their speech because they come across as posturing. Many people believe that using scholarly or "big" words will make them appear smart; this is not true in all cases. Small common words used strategic will have the same outcome. Using scholarly or "big" words can also challenge the audience to comprehend meaning which can be distracting. When you come across an unfamiliar word during research, look up its meaning and substitute a more familiar word that will help you move through your speech without stumbling. When intentionally using foreign words, you must practice pronouncing the word by using online audio pronunciation assistance.

Concrete Words are Not Confusing

Abstract words work great in poetry and song lyrics but can be confusing in a speech. Speakers often use abstract words such as "things, stuff like that," or "something" as short cuts. Replacing abstract words with concrete words helps ensure clear understanding. Keep in mind that listening is work, and your goal is to motivate the audience to want to listen, by making this task easier through the use of concrete words. For example, instead of saying *"They all left for the concert."* Use more concrete words, *"The girl and her two friends left for the concert."*

Appropriate Words Encourage Listening

Word can be abusive or used in a way that excludes people. Using words that stereotypes groups of people according to gender, ethnic groups, sexual orientation, religious affiliation, or physical ability is unethical. Another way that word usage may offend is terms that involve gender. Using the word "men" or "man" to identify both men and women is sexists and must be avoided. Titles such as cableman or mailman, for example, are inappropriate to use when the service person is actually a woman. You can avoid using language that is sexist by substituting gender neutral words such as; *"mailman"* for *"mail person"* and *"cableman"* for *"cable technician."* The easiest way to turn your listeners off during a speech presentation is to minimize their gender or stereotype.

Other Types of Words to Avoid

Communicating in different environment requires us to select specific words that are understood in different environments. There are many ways to express our thoughts, but not all will be understood in every environment. Other times, our listeners will understand our word choices but will not take our communication serious because it does not reflect standard English. Examples of this can be seen in job interviews where your goal is to convince the employer that you are the best person for the job. Standard English is the language of business. Code-switching is a linguistic term used to describe the act of alternating between two or more ways of speaking. Code-switching can be observed in conversations where bilingual speakers move back and forth from their native language to their secondary language. Other examples can be observed when speakers of different English dialects switch from their native dialect to a more standard form of the English language. For example, a person from the southern part of the U.S. might code-switch from her southern dialect to a more understandable standard form of the English when conversing with a person from the northern part of the U.S. Instead of saying, "Y'all are welcomed here" code switch by saying, "Everyone is welcomed here." There are some people who prefer not to code switch as they feel their cultural norms should be understood by others. Still, you must consider who you are talking to and how important the outcome of your communication is to satisfying your personal needs.

- **Jargon** is language used exclusively by people in specialized environments. For example, technical terms used in a chemistry class will not be understood by people outside of that class. Code-switching is required.
- **Street Language** helps people bond with friends but can be distracting and offsetting in different environments. Knowing when to code switch when communicating in changing environments will assist in accurate message receipt. Instead of saying,"It's cool!" say what you really mean. "I missed my deadline, but it won't really hurt me in the long run."

Word Imagery Engages the Senses

A "wordsmith" skillfully uses words that create vivid imagery in the minds of the listener. Whenever you describe something by comparing it to something else, you are using figurative language. Figurative language such as metaphors and similes are important tools for skilled speechwriters. Add figurative language to your speech to help it "pop," because this form of speaking is a natural attention getter. You probably use some form of figurative language a few times a week. A few examples of figurative language is presented on the next page

Metaphor	A figure of speech in which a word or phrase is applied to an object or action that is not literally applicable. Example: *it was raining cats and dogs*
Simile	A figure of speech involving the comparison of one element with another of a different kind to make a description more emphatic or vivid. Example: *I was as hungry as a bear.*
Personification	Is the attribution of human qualities to something that isn't human. Example: *My computer throws a fit every time I try to use it.*
Repetition	Repeating the same words or phrases a few times to make an idea clearer. Example: *"Let freedom ring!"* From the "I Have a Dream" speech by Dr. Martin Luther King Jr.
Parallelism	The use of successive verbal constructions in poetry or prose that correspond in grammatical structure. Example: *"It was the best of times, it was the worst of times."*
Antithesis	Putting two opposing ideas together to achieve a contrasting effect. Example: *Money is the root of all evils; poverty is the fruit of all goodness*
Alliteration	The occurrence of the same letter or sound at the beginning of adjacent or closely connected words. Example: *Penny Peterson pitted plenty of prunes for a pie.*

Figurative language gives a public speech life; it paints mental pictures, engages thought, and promotes active listening.

SHARE YOUR UNDERSTANDING

Practice writing figurative statements below; if you cannot think of one, search the Internet.

Metaphor _____

Simile _____

Personification _____

Repetition _____

Parallelism _____

Antithesis _____

Alliteration _____

Summary

Speech presentations often require visual aid assistance to help the audience understand information being shared. Another benefit of using visual aids is helps to grasp the audience's attention allowing for deeper engagement. Some of the most commonly used visual aids are bar graphs, pie charts, diagrams, and PowerPoint slides. The body can also be used as a visual aid to demonstrate methods or skills. Models and objects help the speaker present scaled-up or scaled-down examples of objects. Words have dual meanings; connotative and denoted. Denotative meaning is the literal dictionary meaning of a word. When listeners receives message, they do not always assign the denotative meaning of the word when assigning meaning. At times, they may assign a connotative meaning to a word; this is emotional meaning that is triggered by past experiences. Speechwriters must think critically about word selection when developing a speech to avoid miscommunication. Words also have abstract and concrete meaning. Abstract meaning does not always provide listeners with enough information to understand the message. Therefore, it is important that speakers use concrete words to communicate clearly. Big words don't make the speaker look smart, simple everyday language will get the job done and should be used. Code-switching methods should be used in the place of jargon and street language.

Language used in a speech should be selected for its ability to engage. Using figurative language adds mental imagery to a speech. Imagery allows listeners to sense the picture that the speaker is attempting to paint through the creative use of words. Figurative language includes metaphors, similes, personification, repetition, parallelism, antithesis, and alliteration.

Key terms

Visual Aids
Charts and Graphs
Objects and Models
PowerPoint Presentations
the Body
Connotative Meaning
Denotative Meaning
Vague and Concrete Words
Code-switching
Jargon

Street Language
Figurative Language
Metaphor
Simile
Rhythm
Parallelism
Repetition
Alliteration
Antithesis

Appendix A

#1 Speaking for Special Occasions

In a stressful world, having opportunities to laugh and enjoy feelings of goodwill and camaraderie is critical to good health. Special occasion speeches are designed to bring people together to celebrate a person, institution, or event. The job of a special occasion speaker is to transfer her or his feelings towards a person, institution, or event to the audience by using rousing sentiments and creative wording. If the occasion is to celebrate a person's 100th birthday, the sentiments should evoke feeling of joy, amazement, and celebration. Lots of descriptive adjectives are used to achieve this goal. Some of the more common types of special occasion speech presentations are listed below with briefly described.

Introduction Speeches	This type of speech is normally brief as it is designed to prepare the audience for the upcoming speaker. Guidelines: Keep your remarks brief and remember the audience is there to hear the speaker, not you. Provide the speaker's name, and mention the occasion and the topic. You must connect with the audience in a meaningful way to gain their attention before the speaker is introduced.
Acceptance Speeches	A speech given by a person who has been publically recognized for a specific achievement. Guidelines: Thank the awarding organization and the person that presents the award to you. Be brief and to the point as you comment on your work and its importance to your life.
Tributes or Eulogies	Both speeches focus on highlighting the essence of a person, event, or group. Guidelines: The goal is to identify and share inspiring characteristics that made or makes the person, event, or group unique. It is important to provide examples through the use of sensory imagery that transfers your feelings to the audience. This is not a life story speech; it is an extended summary that paints a picture of the honoree in the mind of the audience.
After–dinner Speeches	This type of speech is usually connected to an event where a keynote speaker addresses an audience before, during, or after they have eaten a meal. Guidelines: The goal is to select a topic that is enjoyable and focuses on a theme normally given to the speaker by the sponsoring organization.
Toast	A brief speech designed to celebrate a person's achievements. Guidelines: The person presenting the toast must stand, and the person receiving the toast should sit; as you may have seen in a best man speech at a wedding reception. State the person's name, how you know the person/s of honor. Raise your glass after your commentary has concluded. Always end with an encouraging statement.

#2 Speaking in Small Groups

A small group generally involves three to eight members. Lets look to small group communication in the workplace. Most companies and organizations have people working in small teams to achieve an important goal. This has been found to be more effective and productive than having a single individual work long hours to complete a project. When you have a small group of people working on a project, you have the advantage: of having access to more ideas and solutions, of having more checking safeguards against hidden flaws in the plan, and of being able to establish more network connections. A small group is also more likely to take on and complete large-scale, complex projects. Another use for small group formation is debates, panel discussion, forums, and symposiums; all call for a more in-depth level of critical and analytical thinking. A group leader or moderator is assigned to keep the group on track, prevent state hogging, and insure that all members have an opportunity to speak. This person is assigned by the group or will volunteer.

When the task of a small group is to research a problem or event, the findings will be shared through a one of three small group presentation formats: symposium, forum, panel discussion.

- **Symposium presentation:** After the group has researched, discussed, and organized the findings of a problem or assignment each person will be assigned a small part of the finding to develop into a speech. For example, if a small group of five is assigned is to research and present a speech on the life of President John F. Kennedy, their findings will be divided into five sub-topics. Each member of the small group will take one sub-topic for speech development. On the day of the small group presentation, the speeches will address the following topics:
    o Young Jack Kennedy
    o John F. Kennedy's early political years
    o President John F. Kennedy's challenges as president
    o President John F. Kennedy's dark side during his presidency
    o President John F. Kennedy's assassination and legacy

  By the end of the small group speech presentations the audience will have gained more information about the 35th president of the U.S.
- **Forum presentation:** In a forum, all members of the small group have experience with the topic, or have conducted in-depth research on the topic and are prepared to respond to questions from the audience. A forum begins with opening statements on an issue by each member. Such statements reflects their opinions on the matter. The forum participants normally are seated at a table facing the audience.
- **Panel discussion or debate:** Members of the small group do not present speeches but have researched a specific topic/issue and has facts, statistics, or examples to learn more about the topic and identify credible evidence that supports their views. In a debate, small group members take sides on an issue and organize their evidence and proof in a way that provides effective counter-arguments. A panel discussion/debate calls for persuasive strategies and methods learned in chapter eight.

As the small group discussions begins, it is important to avoid groupthink. Groupthink occurs when the group reaches a consensus about something and everyone agrees without question – even if that idea is not actually the best one for the group. Sometimes group members are so eager to achieve consensus that they fail to explore other possibilities. Groups can reduce or avoid groupthink by devoting some time to brainstorming, research, and by thoroughly discussing the pros and cons of proposed ideas. As a group member, don't be afraid to disagree, as sometimes consensus can actually hurt the group.

Difficult Group Members Offer Real Life Learning Experiences

Group members who are lazy, over-scheduled, chatty, or bossy are difficult to work with. However, keep in mind that learning how to deal with these situations will be important in the working world. While these difficult group members aren't exactly doing you a "favor," they are providing you with a learning experience. Do your best to handle the situation, and when this problem reappears at work in the future, you'll be better equipped to act.

"So basically you are looking for books on changing everyone except yourself."

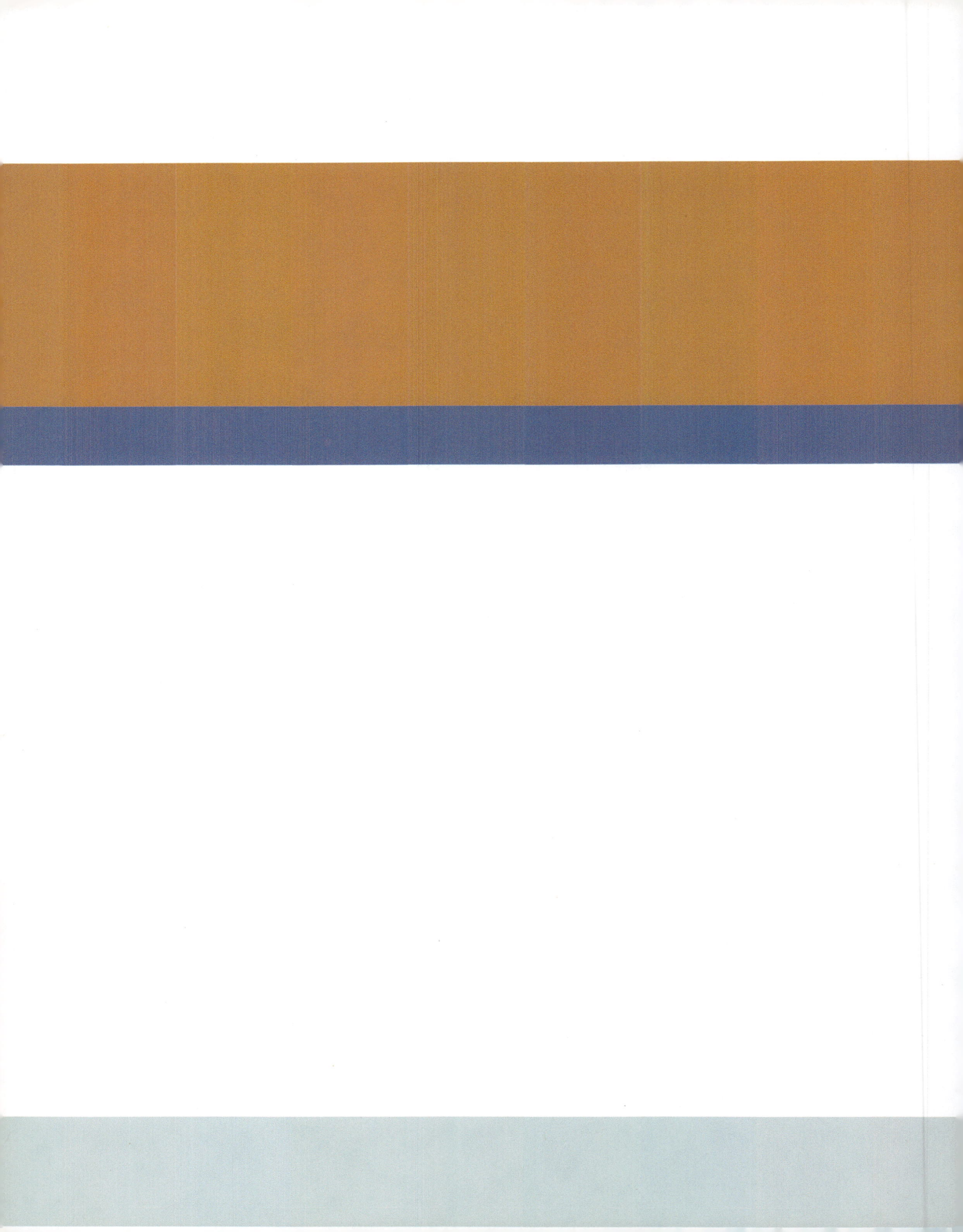

## PART 3

Speech Assignments, Rubrics, and Active Learning Activities

Appendix B: Speech Assignments, Rubrics, and Peer Critique Forms

#1 - Self-Introduction Speech

Name: _____

Presentations Begin	See syllabus
Typed Speech Draft Due	May handwrite speech, see syllabus for due date
Grading Scale	See syllabus
Evaluation	Simply follow the assignment to earn full points
Time Limits	1 to 3 minutes

The purpose of this speech is to help the class get to know you on a topical level, and to have some fun getting to know one another. During this 1 to 3 min. speech, you will introduce yourself; and then, briefly answer the questions below to help us get to know you. You may use the back of this assignment to draft your speech, or you can type it. Practice your self-introduction speech at home using a timer to make your speech fits within the allotted time window of 1 to 3 minutes. Speeches that exceed 3 minutes will be cut off.

Introduction

1. Begin by sharing the following information **using full sentences**:
   A. State your full name.
   B. What is your major or program?
   C. Have you taken a speech class in the past?
   D. Have you attended other colleges/university?
   E. What are your plans after graduation?

Body

1. First, rate your level of speaking anxiety:
   - (1) I'm normally not very nervous at all,
   - (2) I'm nervous in various situations,
   - (3) I'm extremely nervous about speaking in public.
2. Second, search the Internet to find a newspaper article from the day you were born, or a magazine article, such as Time or Newsweek, from the week or month you were born. Once you find newsworthy information from your birth year, select an article, advertisement, photograph, editorial, etc. that relates to your life in some meaningful way (in other words, something of interest to you). You will share this information with the class and explain why you selected it.

Conclusion

1. Conclude by answering the following question, "If I were an animal, tree, body of water, insect, or season, which would I be and why."

Always signal the end of your speech by saying, "*Thank you.*"

#2 – Informative Speech

Presentations Begin	See syllabus
Typed Speech Draft Due	See syllabus
Grading Scale	100 points (90/100 = A, 80/89 = B, 70/79 = C, 60/69 = D)
Evaluation	See Grading Rubric
Time Limits	4 to 6 minutes

Instructions:

For your first major speech, the goal is to share knowledge about a specific topic in a way that helps them conceptualize and understand. You must select a topic that meets the general purpose of the assignment. The topic that you select should not be too trivial (known by all); you might risk boring the audience. Be careful not to suggest that your listeners act or think a certain way as that is persuasive speaking and not the general purpose of this assignment. With the easy access that the Internet offers for research, I suggest you Google informative speech topics to get started. You can also learn more about your topic online. "Work smarter, not harder!"

Speech Requirements:

1.   Extemporaneous Delivery (Chapter 6)
     ➢   Use vocal variety to help engage your listeners.
     ➢   Speakers must maintain eye contact with the audience.
     ➢   Avoid fillers or distracting mannerisms.
     ➢   The non-verbal message must match the verbal message.
2.   Supporting Material Citation Requirements
     ➢   In the body of the speech, each main point must be supported with at least one citation.
     ➢   This citation must be typed into the full preparation outlined speech and keyword delivery outline where it will be spoken.
     ➢   You may not cite yourself as an expert.
     ➢   Wikipedia, encyclopedias, non-expert dictionaries, or non-expert print or web sources may be used to fulfill your citation requirements.

Managing Presentation Day Anxiety:

1.   Preparation: The most important strategy is to start early and leave time to rehearse, rehearse, rehearse.
2.   Strategies discussed in Chapter 4 on controlling anxiety control should be reviewed and applied.
3.   Some speakers do not feel the effects of anxiety until they stand at the podium and look at their audience. Do not underestimate the power of anxiety. Be prepared to counter-act it with self-imposed prophesies of success. Do not give way to the fallacy of perfection; you will make mistakes – it is okay.
4.   Attire: studies show that a person's attire has a strong impact on emotions. Take care with your attire on presentation day. The audience will make first impression judgments about your credibility, competence, and trustworthiness that can be seen and felt as you present your speech; can trigger anxiety.
5.   Lastly, know that your peers in the audience are rooting for your success.

On Your Presentation Day

You must submit the following documents:
1.   Full typed preparation outlined speech with attached APA formatted bibliography
2.   Keyword delivery outline or speaker's notes
3.   Informative speech grading rubric
4.   Two informative speech peer review forms
Speakers who do not submit a fully typed speech in a preparation outline format will not be allowed to present their speech.
Draft your speech heading on the next page

DRAFT YOUR INFORMATIVE SPEECH HEADING HERE

General Purpose: _____

Narrowed Topic: _____

_____

Specific Purpose: _____

_____

_____

Central Idea: _____

_____

_____

NOTES TO HELP BUILD THE BODY OF YOUR SPEECH

_____

_____

_____

_____

_____

_____

_____

_____

_____

_____

_____

_____

_____

_____

#2 – GRADING RUBRIC: Informative Speech

Name: _____ Topic: _____

	F	D	C	B	A
Introduction (20 pts.)					
Used hook & bait method to grab audience's attention	1	2	3	4	5
Provided a credibility statement	1	2	3	4	5
Central idea summarized speech	1	2	3	4	5
Transitioned to the body	1	2	3	4	5
Body (45 pts.)					
Subject Knowledge: depth of content reflects knowledge of topic	2	4	6	8	10
Provided adequate supporting material to explain each main point	2	4	6	8	10
Provided full credible "oral" citations to support all facts	2	4	6	8	10
# of full oral citations heard: _____					
# of partial oral citations heard: _____					
# of facts or statistics used without citations: _____					
Speech was audience-centered: attempted to keep listeners engaged	2	4	6	8	10
Used a variety of connectives throughout the presentation	1	2	3	4	5
Conclusion (15 pts.)					
Signaled the end of the speech	1	2	3	4	5
Summarized residual message	1	2	3	4	5
Closing statement reinforced proposition	1	2	3	4	5
Extemporaneous Delivery (20pts.)					
Used appropriate eye contact, brief reference to notes	2	4	6	8	10
Body: gestures and movement enhanced key points made	1	2	3	4	5
Voice: volume, rate, pitch, vocal variety, fillers	1	2	3	4	5

TIME (*4 to 6 minutes*): _____   **Points earned out of 100** _____

Strengths:	Areas to work on for next speech:

Penalties:
- Over/Under Time Limit: (-3 points per 60 seconds)   _____
- Read 50% of speech: (-20% of points earned)   _____
- Partial speech outline submitted/essay format: (-10 points)   _____
- Missing APA formatted bibliography: (-10 points)   _____

Total Penalties subtracted: _____ *- point's earned* _____ = _____   Grade: _____

#2A – Peer Critique Form: Informative Speech

Your Name: _____ Your Topic: _____

INSTRUCTIONS: Familiarize yourself with this critique form before speeches begin. As the speech progresses, you should check off each item covered effectively by the speaker. You must provide written comments that communicate the speaker's strengths and weaknesses. This will help them identify area to work on for the next presentation.

Introduction:
_____ Speech began with a strong attention-getter that established the topic.
_____ Strong personal credibility was established.
_____ Central idea was clearly stated.
_____ Transitioned effectively to the body.

Body:
_____ Organizational pattern made it easy to follow speaker's progression of ideas.
_____ Information given was all relevant to explain the thesis.
_____ Speaker attempted to filter key points through common experiences to engage listeners.
_____ At least one expert source was cited to support each main point.
(___) Full oral citations heard during presentation. (Use tally marks: _____)
_____ Oral citations included required information to qualify as credible.
_____ Connectives were used to help listeners make logical connections to points made.
_____ Topic narrowed to cover an appropriate amount of information for the time limits.
_____ Avoided skimming over points rapidly or going into too much detail.
_____ Content of the speech did not get persuasive.

Conclusion:
_____ Cued the audience that the speech was coming to an end
_____ Paraphrased the central idea to summarize the goal of the speech.
_____ Left audience with a memorable closing statement that relayed back to the introduction.

Delivery:
_____ Maintained appropriate amount of eye contact with audience.
_____ Did not read speech (glanced at notes periodically).
_____ Gestures and movement added enthusiasm.
_____ Speaking rate was appropriate (not too fast or slow).
_____ Avoided vocalized pauses: "uh", "um", "ah", "OK", "you know", "like", etc.
_____ Avoided distracting mannerisms and/or movement that indicate nervousness.
_____ Overall, speaker seemed prepared and ready to give the speech.

Comments

Strengths	Weaknesses

Peer Evaluator: _____
For evaluator: "This is my   1st   or   2nd   evaluation."   (Circle one for participation points)

#2B – Peer Critique Form: Informative Speech

Your Name: _____ Your Topic: _____

INSTRUCTIONS: Familiarize yourself with this critique form before speeches begin. As the speech progresses, you should check off each item covered effectively by the speaker. You must provide written comments that communicate the speaker's strengths and weaknesses. This will help them identify area to work on for the next presentation.

Introduction:
_____ Speech began with a strong attention-getter that established the topic.
_____ Strong personal credibility was established.
_____ Central idea was clearly stated.
_____ Transitioned effectively to the body.

Body:
_____ Organizational pattern made it easy to follow speaker's progression of ideas.
_____ Information given was all relevant to explain the thesis.
_____ Speaker attempted to filter key points through common experiences to engage listeners.
_____ At least one expert source was cited to support each main point.
(___) Full oral citations heard during presentation. (Use tally marks: _____)
_____ Oral citations included required information to qualify as credible.
_____ Connectives were used to help listeners make logical connections to points made.
_____ Topic narrowed to cover an appropriate amount of information for the time limits.
_____ Avoided skimming over points rapidly <u>or</u> going into too much detail.
_____ Content of the speech did not get persuasive.

Conclusion:
_____ Cued the audience that the speech was coming to an end
_____ Paraphrased the central idea to summarize the goal of the speech.
_____ Left audience with a memorable closing statement that relayed back to the introduction.

Delivery:
_____ Maintained appropriate amount of eye contact with audience.
_____ Did not read speech (glanced at notes periodically).
_____ Gestures and movement added enthusiasm.
_____ Speaking rate was appropriate (not too fast or slow).
_____ Avoided vocalized pauses: "uh", "um", "ah", "OK", "you know", "like", etc.
_____ Avoided distracting mannerisms and/or movement that indicate nervousness.
_____ Overall, speaker seemed prepared and ready to give the speech.

Comments

Strengths	Weaknesses

Peer Evaluator: _____
For evaluator: "This is my   1st   or   2nd   evaluation."   (Circle one for participation points)

#3 – Informative Symposium Speech

Presentations Begin	See syllabus
Typed Speech Draft Due	See syllabus
Grading Scale	100 points (90/100 = A, 80/89 = B, 70/79 = C, 60/69 = D)
Evaluation	See Grading Rubric
Time Limits	4 to 6 minutes

Instructions:

For this informative speech the goal is to share information about a specific topic in a way that provides your audience with new or enhanced knowledge. When a topic is too broad to be researched and presented by one speaker, as are the topics below, a small group symposium presentation works best.

Process:

A small group of 3 to 5 speakers will select a broad topic and divide it into small logical sections for research and individual speech development. In the individual speeches each group member will inform the audience about a different narrowed aspect of the broader topic. By the end of the group presentations, the audience will have learned a wealth of information about the broad topic.

Small Groups: select a topic from the choices below, (majority rules).

1. Share the biography of one prominent person in American history.
2. Provide a historical explanation of your city using a timeline.
3. Compare and Contrast how social networking websites has changed society since the early 1990s.
4. Explain the greatest changes in the job market over the past 50 years.
5. Explain the seven natural wonders of the world.
6. Explain fracking, its history, and why is it controversial?
7. Identify additives, chemicals, and fillers in McDonald's (or Wendy's) products and possible harms to human consumption.

Speech Requirements:

1. Extemporaneous Delivery (Chapter 6)
   ➢ Use vocal variety to help engage your listeners.
   ➢ Speakers must maintain eye contact with the audience.
   ➢ Avoid fillers or distracting mannerisms.
   ➢ The non-verbal message must match the verbal message (body language and vocal variety).
2. Supporting Material Citation Requirements
   ➢ In the body of the speech, each main point must be supported with at least one citation.
   ➢ This citation must be typed directly into the full speech and keyword delivery outline where it will be spoken.
   ➢ You may not cite yourself as an expert.
   ➢ Wikipedia, encyclopedias, non-expert dictionaries, or non-expert print or web sources may be used to fulfill your citation requirements.

Managing Presentation Day Anxiety:

1. Preparation: The most important strategy is to start early and leave time to rehearse, rehearse, rehearse.
2. Strategies discussed in Chapter 4 on controlling anxiety control should be reviewed and applied.

3. Some speakers do not feel the effects of anxiety until they stand at the podium and look at their audience. Do not underestimate the power of anxiety. Be prepared to counter-act it with self-imposed prophesies of success. Do not give way to the fallacy of perfection; you will make mistakes – it is okay.
4. Attire: studies show that a person's attire has a strong impact on emotions. Take care with your attire on presentation day. The audience will make first impression judgments about your credibility, competence, and trustworthiness that can be seen and felt as you present your speech; can trigger anxiety.
5. Lastly, know that your peers in the audience are rooting for your success.

On Your Presentation Day

You must submit the following documents:
1. Full typed preparation outlined speech with attached APA formatted bibliography
2. Keyword delivery outline or speaker's notes
3. Informative speech grading rubric located in Appendix – C
4. Two informative speech peer review forms located in Appendix – C

Speakers who do not submit a fully typed speech in a preparation outline format will not be allowed to present their speech.

DRAFT YOUR SYMPOSIUM SPEECH HEADING HERE

General Purpose: _____

Narrowed Topic: _____

_____

Specific Purpose: _____

_____

_____

Central Idea: _____

_____

_____

NOTES TO HELP BUILD THE BODY OF YOUR SPEECH

_____

_____

_____

_____

_____

_____

#3 – GRADING RUBRIC: Informative Symposium Speech

Name: _____ Topic: _____

	F	D	C	B	A
Introduction (20 pts.)					
Used hook & bait method to grab audience's attention	1	2	3	4	5
Provided a credibility statement	1	2	3	4	5
Central idea summarized speech	1	2	3	4	5
Transitioned to the body	1	2	3	4	5
Body (45 pts.)					
Subject Knowledge: depth of content reflects knowledge of topic	2	4	6	8	10
Provided adequate supporting material to explain each main point	2	4	6	8	10
Provided full credible "oral" citations to support all facts	2	4	6	8	10
# of full oral citations heard: _____					
# of partial oral citations heard: _____					
# of facts or statistics used without citations: _____					
Speech was audience-centered: attempted to keep listeners engaged	2	4	6	8	10
Used a variety of connectives throughout the presentation	1	2	3	4	5
Conclusion (15 pts.)					
Signaled the end of the speech	1	2	3	4	5
Summarized residual message	1	2	3	4	5
Closing statement reinforced proposition	1	2	3	4	5
Extemporaneous Delivery (20pts.)					
Used appropriate eye contact, brief reference to notes	2	4	6	8	10
Body: gestures and movement enhanced key points made	1	2	3	4	5
Voice: volume, rate, pitch, vocal variety, fillers	1	2	3	4	5

TIME (*4 to 6 minutes*): _____ **Points earned out of 100** _____

Strengths:	Areas to work on for next speech:

Penalties:
- Over/Under Time Limit: (-3 points per 60 seconds) _____
- Read 50% of speech: (-20% of points earned) _____
- Partial speech outline submitted/essay format: (-10 points) _____
- Missing APA formatted bibliography: (-10 points) _____

Total Penalties subtracted: _____ - *point's earned* _____ = _____ Grade: _____

#3A – Peer Critique Form: Informative Symposium Speech

Your Name: _____ Your Topic: _____

INSTRUCTIONS: Familiarize yourself with this critique form before speeches begin. As the speech progresses, you should check off each item covered effectively by the speaker. You must provide written comments that communicate the speaker's strengths and weaknesses. This will help them identify area to work on for the next presentation.

Introduction:
_____ Speech began with a strong attention-getter that established the topic.
_____ Strong personal credibility was established.
_____ Central idea was clearly stated.
_____ Transitioned effectively to the body.

Body:
_____ Organizational pattern made it easy to follow speaker's progression of ideas.
_____ Information given was all relevant to explain the thesis.
_____ Speaker attempted to filter key points through common experiences to engage listeners.
_____ At least one expert source was cited to support each main point.
(___) Full oral citations heard during presentation. (Use tally marks: _____)
_____ Oral citations included required information to qualify as credible.
_____ Connectives were used to help listeners make logical connections to points made.
_____ Topic narrowed to cover an appropriate amount of information for the time limits.
_____ Avoided skimming over points rapidly <u>or</u> going into too much detail.
_____ Content of the speech did not get persuasive.

Conclusion:
_____ Cued the audience that the speech was coming to an end
_____ Paraphrased the central idea to summarize the goal of the speech.
_____ Left audience with a memorable closing statement that relayed back to the introduction.

Delivery:
_____ Maintained appropriate amount of eye contact with audience.
_____ Did not read speech (glanced at notes periodically).
_____ Gestures and movement added enthusiasm.
_____ Speaking rate was appropriate (not too fast or slow).
_____ Avoided vocalized pauses: "uh", "um", "ah", "OK", "you know", "like", etc.
_____ Avoided distracting mannerisms and/or movement that indicate nervousness.
_____ Overall, speaker seemed prepared and ready to give the speech.

Comments

Strengths	Weaknesses

Peer Evaluator: _____
For evaluator: "This is my 1st or 2nd evaluation." (Circle one for participation points)

#3B – Peer Critique Form: Informative Symposium Speech

Your Name: _____ Your Topic: _____

INSTRUCTIONS: Familiarize yourself with this critique form before speeches begin. As the speech progresses, you should check off each item covered effectively by the speaker. You must provide written comments that communicate the speaker's strengths and weaknesses. This will help them identify area to work on for the next presentation.

Introduction:
_____ Speech began with a strong attention-getter that established the topic.
_____ Strong personal credibility was established.
_____ Central idea was clearly stated.
_____ Transitioned effectively to the body.

Body:
_____ Organizational pattern made it easy to follow speaker's progression of ideas.
_____ Information given was all relevant to explain the thesis.
_____ Speaker attempted to filter key points through common experiences to engage listeners.
_____ At least one expert source was cited to support each main point.
(___) Full oral citations heard during presentation. (Use tally marks: _____)
_____ Oral citations included required information to qualify as credible.
_____ Connectives were used to help listeners make logical connections to points made.
_____ Topic narrowed to cover an appropriate amount of information for the time limits.
_____ Avoided skimming over points rapidly <u>or</u> going into too much detail.
_____ Content of the speech did not get persuasive.

Conclusion:
_____ Cued the audience that the speech was coming to an end
_____ Paraphrased the central idea to summarize the goal of the speech.
_____ Left audience with a memorable closing statement that relayed back to the introduction.

Delivery:
_____ Maintained appropriate amount of eye contact with audience.
_____ Did not read speech (glanced at notes periodically).
_____ Gestures and movement added enthusiasm.
_____ Speaking rate was appropriate (not too fast or slow).
_____ Avoided vocalized pauses: "uh", "um", "ah", "OK", "you know", "like", etc.
_____ Avoided distracting mannerisms and/or movement that indicate nervousness.
_____ Overall, speaker seemed prepared and ready to give the speech.

Comments

Strengths	Weaknesses

Peer Evaluator: _____
For evaluator: "This is my   1st   or   2nd   evaluation."   (Circle one for participation points)

#4 – Informative Process *"Demonstration"* Speech

Presentations Begin	See syllabus
Typed Speech Draft Due	See syllabus
Grading Scale	100 points (90/100 = A, 80/89 = B, 70/79 = C, 60/69 = D)
Evaluation	See Grading Rubric
Time Limits	5 to 7 minutes

Instructions:

For this speech, the goal is to teach the audience how to complete a task that is accomplished by demonstrating it through a series of steps. A demonstration speech is an in informative speech that is categorized as "speeches about a process." Be sure to select a topic that meets this general purpose of the assignment. Topic examples can be: "How to study for a test," or "How to back a chocolate cake from scratch." To identify a topic, think of processes that you have mastered to teach your audience. Another option use Google to search for demonstration topic examples. Topic should be college level. Process speeches that teach the audience how to make a peanut butter and jelly sandwich does not constitute a college level presentation.

Visual aids are important tools to have for a process speech. However, they require you to handle them quite a bit while speaking to the audience. This can be tricky as you can spend too much time fumbling with an object wasting valuable time. To avoid this disaster, you must practice your speech with the visual aids to ensure you stay within your time limits. When demonstrating how to prepare a food item, it is customary to provide samples for the audience; bring serving utensils or napkins.

Guideline for Using Visual Aids

1. Do not bring animals or illegal products into the building.
2. All visual aids must be setup on a staging table prior to the start of presentations; arrive early to do this.
3. PowerPoint or visual aids that require the use of a computer must be tested prior to the start of class. Unexpected technological glitches can destroy a presentation.
4. Must be big enough for all audience members to see; even those in the far corners of the room.
5. Must not be passed around during your speech; distracting.
6. The speaker must not talk to the visual aid; remember that your audience must be engaged through eye contact.
7. "How to" video clips from an outside source may not be used to show how a process is done; however, you may record yourself doing the process (without sound) in a step-by-step manor to use as a visual while you explain the process. This normally occurs when the process is too large or small to for classroom use.
8. PowerPoint slides should only be visible when you are discussing its content. Use a blank slide to between content slides.

Speech Requirements:

1. Extemporaneous Delivery (Chapter 6)
   - ➢ Use vocal variety to help engage your listeners.
   - ➢ Speakers must maintain eye contact with the audience.
   - ➢ Avoid fillers or distracting mannerisms.
   - ➢ The non-verbal message must match the verbal message (body language and vocal variety).
2. Supporting Material Citation Requirements
   - ➢ In the body of the speech, each main point must be supported with at least one citation.
   - ➢ This citation must be typed directly into the full speech and keyword delivery outline where it will be spoken.

> ➤ You may not cite yourself as an expert.
> ➤ Wikipedia, encyclopedias, non-expert dictionaries, or non-expert print or web sources may be used to fulfill your citation requirements.

Managing Presentation Day Anxiety:

1. Preparation: The most important strategy is to start early and leave time to rehearse, rehearse, rehearse.
2. Strategies discussed in Chapter 4 on controlling anxiety control should be reviewed and applied.
3. Some speakers do not feel the effects of anxiety until they stand at the podium and look at their audience. Do not underestimate the power of anxiety. Be prepared to counter-act it with self-imposed prophesies of success. Do not give way to the fallacy of perfection; you will make mistakes – it is okay.
4. Attire: studies show that a person's attire has a strong impact on emotions. Take care with your attire on presentation day. The audience will make first impression judgments about your credibility, competence, and trustworthiness that can be seen and felt as you present your speech; can trigger anxiety.
5. Lastly, know that your peers in the audience are rooting for your success.

On Your Presentation Day

You must submit the following documents:
1. Full typed preparation outlined speech with attached APA formatted bibliography
2. Keyword delivery outline or speaker's notes
3. Informative speech grading rubric located in Appendix – C
4. Two informative speech peer review forms located in Appendix – C

Speakers who do not submit a fully typed speech in a preparation outline format will not be allowed to present their speech.

DRAFT YOUR SPEECH HEADING HERE

General Purpose: _____

Narrowed Topic: _____

_____

Specific Purpose: _____

_____

_____

Central Idea: _____

_____

_____

Material Required:	Notes to help build the body of your speech:

#4 – GRADING RUBRIC: Informative Process *"Demonstration"* Speech

Name: _____ Topic: _____

	F	D	C	B	A
Introduction (20 pts.)					
Used hook & bait method to grab audience's attention	1	2	3	4	5
Provided a credibility statement	1	2	3	4	5
Central idea summarized speech	1	2	3	4	5
Transitioned to the body	1	2	3	4	5
Body (70 pts.)					
Subject Knowledge: depth of content reflects knowledge of topic	2	4	6	8	10
Provided adequate supporting material to explain each main point	2	4	6	8	10
Provided full credible "oral" citations to support all facts	2	4	6	8	10
# of full oral citations heard: _____					
Speech was audience-centered: attempted to keep listeners engaged	2	4	6	8	10
Used a variety of connectives throughout the presentation	2	4	6	8	10
Design of visual aids enhanced presentation and met guidelines	2	4	6	8	10
Use of visual aids enhanced presentation and met guidelines	2	4	6	8	10
Conclusion (15 pts.)					
Signaled the end of the speech	1	2	3	4	5
Summarized residual message	1	2	3	4	5
Closing statement reinforced proposition	1	2	3	4	5
Extemporaneous Delivery (20pts.)					
Used appropriate eye contact, brief reference to notes	2	4	6	8	10
Body: gestures and movement enhanced key points made	1	2	3	4	5
Voice: volume, rate, pitch, vocal variety, fillers	1	2	3	4	5

TIME (*6 to 8 minutes*): _____   **Points earned out of 125** _____

Strengths:	Areas to work on for next speech:

Penalties:
* Over/Under Time Limit: (-3 points per 60 seconds)   _____
* Read 50% of speech: (-20% of points earned)   _____
* Partial speech outline submitted/essay format: (-10 points)   _____
* Missing APA formatted bibliography: (-10 points)   _____

Total Penalties subtracted: _____ *- point's earned* _____ = _____   Grade: _____

#4A – Peer Critique Form: Informative Process *"Demonstration"* Speech

Your Name: _____ Your Topic: _____

INSTRUCTIONS: Familiarize yourself with this critique form before speeches begin. As the speech progresses, you should check off each item covered effectively by the speaker. You must provide written comments that communicate the speaker's strengths and weaknesses. This will help them identify area to work on for the next presentation.

Introduction:
____ Speech began with a strong attention-getter that established the topic.
____ Strong personal credibility was established.
____ Central idea was clearly stated.
____ Transitioned effectively to the body.

Body:
____ Organizational pattern made it easy to follow speaker's progression of ideas.
____ Information given was all relevant to explain the thesis.
____ Speaker attempted to filter key points through common experiences to engage listeners.
____ At least one expert source was cited to support each main point.
____ Oral citations included required information to qualify as credible.
____ Connectives were used to help listeners make logical connections to points made.
____ Topic narrowed to cover an appropriate amount of information for the time limits.
____ Avoided skimming over points rapidly <u>or</u> going into too much detail.
____ Demonstration of the process was presented in a way that made it easy to understand (duplicate).
____ Visual aid was used appropriately to help listeners understand the process.

Conclusion:
____ Cued the audience that the speech was coming to an end
____ Paraphrased the central idea to summarize the goal of the speech.
____ Left audience with a memorable closing statement that relayed back to the introduction.

Delivery:
____ Maintained appropriate amount of eye contact with audience.
____ Did not read speech (glanced at notes periodically).
____ Gestures and movement added enthusiasm.
____ Speaking rate was appropriate (not too fast or slow).
____ Avoided vocalized pauses: "uh", "um", "ah", "OK", "you know", "like", etc.
____ Avoided distracting mannerisms and/or movement that indicate nervousness.
____ Overall, speaker seemed prepared and ready to give the speech.

Comments

Strengths	Weaknesses

Peer Evaluator: _____
For evaluator: "This is my   1st   or   2nd   evaluation."   (Circle one for participation points)

#4B – Peer Critique Form: Informative Process *"Demonstration"* Speech

Your Name: _____ Your Topic: _____

INSTRUCTIONS: Familiarize yourself with this critique form before speeches begin. As the speech progresses, you should check off each item covered effectively by the speaker. You must provide written comments that communicate the speaker's strengths and weaknesses. This will help them identify area to work on for the next presentation.

Introduction:
____ Speech began with a strong attention-getter that established the topic.
____ Strong personal credibility was established.
____ Central idea was clearly stated.
____ Transitioned effectively to the body.

Body:
____ Organizational pattern made it easy to follow speaker's progression of ideas.
____ Information given was all relevant to explain the thesis.
____ Speaker attempted to filter key points through common experiences to engage listeners.
____ At least one expert source was cited to support each main point.
____ Oral citations included required information to qualify as credible.
____ Connectives were used to help listeners make logical connections to points made.
____ Topic narrowed to cover an appropriate amount of information for the time limits.
____ Avoided skimming over points rapidly <u>or</u> going into too much detail.
____ Demonstration of the process was presented in a way that made it easy to understand (duplicate).
____ Visual aid was used appropriately

Conclusion:
____ Cued the audience that the speech was coming to an end
____ Paraphrased the central idea to summarize the goal of the speech.
____ Left audience with a memorable closing statement that relayed back to the introduction.

Delivery:
____ Maintained appropriate amount of eye contact with audience.
____ Did not read speech (glanced at notes periodically).
____ Gestures and movement added enthusiasm.
____ Speaking rate was appropriate (not too fast or slow).
____ Avoided vocalized pauses: "uh", "um", "ah", "OK", "you know", "like", etc.
____ Avoided distracting mannerisms and/or movement that indicate nervousness.
____ Overall, speaker seemed prepared and ready to give the speech.

Comments

Strengths	Weaknesses

Peer Evaluator: _____
For evaluator: "This is my 1st or 2nd evaluation." (Circle one for participation points)

#5 – Persuasive Speech

Presentations Begin	See syllabus
Typed Speech Draft Due	See syllabus
Grading Scale	150 points (135/150 = A, 120/134 = B, 105/119 = C, 90/104 = D)
Evaluation	See Grading Rubric
Time Limits	7 to 9 minutes

Instructions:

The general purpose of this speech is to persuade your listeners to accept, to some degree, your proposition; which is your view of a problem and how you suggest we solve it. Remember that your credibility plays an important role in persuading audiences; as such, you must deal with oppositional arguments in a fair and convincing way. Good persuaders do not ignore the opposition, nor do they simply attack the opposition, they engage opposition's arguments in an even-handed way.

Your Challenge:

Because the thesis of this speech supports your perception of a problem and your proposed solution to satisfy the problem, your approach must include strategic persuasive methods and strategies that strengthen your arguments. Every speech begins by setting the stage. For this type of speech you will use informative speaking to describe the problem and tell the listeners why you think it warrants immediate attention. The next step is to provide supporting evidence that proves a true problem exist as some listeners may not see it as such. Connectives are critical to use as you move through your reasoning to help the listeners understand your claims and evidence. You'll end the speech by sharing your proposed solution to the problem and once again use evidence to prove that your solution will work without causing additional problems.

Steps:

1. First, you must select a topic; good topics are those that you are most passionate about; you often find yourself engaged in debates in support of your position. To search for topics, you can also use the Opposing Viewpoints database which is composed of the most popular controversial speech and essay topics that students are using today. To locate this database, go to your library's online database and look for the Controversial Issues category. The Internet is another good option; google persuasive speech topics.
2. Develop a persuasive speech heading that meets the general purpose of this assignment; and then expand your research to identify supporting material for your arguments and supporting material that helps you understand your opposition's arguments.
3. A persuasive speech cannot be presented if no one disagrees with you." Because of this reality, you must develop and circulate an audience analysis survey to test the audience for opposition to your proposition. The targeted audience are those listeners moderately opposed, neutral, and moderately in favor of your proposition. If this group is small, less than half of your audience, you must select a different topic. For this reason, the question you ask on your survey is critical, "If you don't ask the right questions, you won't get the answers you are searching for." This quote is very true. Think critically about your survey questions. Do not simply ask the listeners if they agree or disagree, find out why! The information pulled from your survey will provide you with a strategic angle to approach your arguments.
4. After analyzing the data from your surveys it's time to build your speech:
   - Select an approach, proposition of; (fact, value, or policy)
   - Select a reasoning [argument] style; (inductive, deductive, causal, or analogical).
   - Select an appropriate outline to build your speech; (problem/solution, problem/cause/solution, refutation, causal, comparative advantage, or Monroe's motivated sequence).

Speech Requirements:

> ➤ Extemporaneous Delivery
> ➤ Use vocal variety to help engage your listeners.
> ➤ Speakers must maintain at least 50% eye contact with the audience.
> ➤ Avoid fillers or distracting mannerisms.

1.   Supporting Material Citation Requirements
> ➤ Because this speech requires evidence, you will present a lot of factual information from your research. There is not a specific amount of citations required because roughly fifty percent of the body of your speech should consist of evidence (cited sources). Every argument must have a counter-argument. This means you must speak to your opposition's views or they will stop listening.
> ➤ Citations must be typed into the full preparation outlined speech and keyword delivery outline where they will be spoken.
> ➤ You may not cite yourself as an expert.
> ➤ Wikipedia, encyclopedias, non-expert dictionaries, or non-expert print or web sources may be used to fulfill your citation requirements.

2.   If you use a visual aid, remember to adhere to the guidelines as presented in Chapter 9

Managing Presentation Day Anxiety:

1.   Preparation: The most important strategy is to start early and leave time to rehearse, rehearse, and rehearse.
2.   Strategies discussed in Chapter 4 on controlling anxiety control should be reviewed and applied.
3.   Some speakers do not feel the effects of anxiety until they stand at the podium and look at their audience. Do not underestimate the power of anxiety. Be prepared to counter-act it with self-imposed prophesies of success. Do not give way to the fallacy of perfection; you will make mistakes – it is okay.
4.   Attire: studies show that a person's attire has a strong impact on emotions. Take care with your attire on presentation day. The audience will make first impression judgments about your credibility, competence, and trustworthiness.
5.   Lastly, know that your peers in the audience are rooting for your success.

On Your Presentation Day

You must submit the following documents:
1.   Full typed preparation outlined speech with attached APA formatted bibliography
2.   Keyword delivery outline or speaker's notes; typed or note cards
3.   Informative speech grading rubric
4.   Two informative speech peer review forms
Speakers who do not submit a fully typed speech in a preparation outline format will not be allowed to present their speech.

DRAFT YOUR PERSUASIVE SPEECH HEADING HERE

General Purpose: _____

Narrowed Topic: _____

_____

Position: _____

_____

Proposition: _____

_____

#5 – GRADING RUBRIC: Persuasive

Speaker: _____ Topic: _____

5	Excellent	This component was exceptionally well done. You demonstrated high competence.
4	Good	This component was done well. You demonstrated competence.
3	Adequate	An attempt was made to fulfill this component. However, you may not have shown full competence when doing it
2	Inadequate	You did not demonstrate competence with this component. You may have either not done it, or the manner in which you did it created a slight negative element in your speech
1	Unacceptable	You displayed almost the opposite of the desired component. It seemed that you were almost totally unaware of your behavior. It created a definite negative element in your speech.

_____ **Attention Getter:** Effective use of attention getting strategy (quote, statistic, question, story, etc.) to capture listeners' attention and to introduce topic. Attention getter is relevant and meaningful and seemed to gain the desired response from audience.

_____ **Proposition Statement (problem/solution):** Speaker clearly formulated and stated the proposition; the controlling idea in one grammatically correct sentence.

_____ **Connection w/Audience:** Tied the relevance of topic to audience needs and interests. Thoughtful audience analysis reflected in argument type choice and supporting evidence.

_____ **Subject Knowledge:** Depth of content reflects knowledge and understanding of topic. Main points adequately substantiated with timely, relevant and sufficient support. Provided accurate explanation of key concepts.

_____ **Organization:** Uses effective organizational pattern in support of proposition. Main points are clearly distinguished from supporting details. Connectives are effectively used for smooth and coherent transitions.

_____ **Logical Appeal:** Presents sound arguments to support major claim. Arguments are supported with sufficient, relevant and valid evidence. Reasoning is free of fallacies. Solution is logical and reasonable.

_____ **Emotional Appeal:** Effectively and ethically appeals to audience emotions (anger, fear, compassion, etc.) to achieve the persuasive goal. Vivid and emotive language used to create imagery that engaged the audience emotionally.

_____ **Credibility:** Sources of information are clearly identified and properly cited. Establishes credibility and authority of sources presented. Balances a variety of perspectives and recognizes opposing views.

(___) **Cited Sources:** Number of full sources heard during the speech? (_____)

_____ **Eye Contact:** Consistently and effectively used eye contact to establish rapport with audience. Inconspicuous use of speaker notes and effective use of scanning to established an expanded zone of interaction.

_____ **Body Language:** Expressive, dynamic, and natural use of gestures, posture and facial expressions to reinforce and enhance meaning. Body language reflects comfort interacting with audience.

_____ **Voice:** Natural variation of vocal characteristics (rate, pitch, volume, tone) in Standard English to heighten interest and match message appropriately.

_____ **Fluency:** Appropriate pronunciation, enunciation, and articulation. Lack of noticeable vocalized fillers

Comments

Strengths	Weaknesses

Penalties:
- Over/Under Time Limit: (-2.5 points per 30 seconds) _____
- Read 50% of speech: (-20% of points earned) _____
- Partial speech outline submitted/essay format: (-10 points) _____
- Missing APA formatted bibliography: (-10 points) _____
- Misuse of Visual Aid (-5 points) _____

Total Penalties subtracted: _____ *- point's earned* _____ = _____   Grade: _____

#5A – Peer Critique Form: Persuasive

Speaker: _____ Topic: _____

Instructions: Respond "Yes" or "No" to each critique question; one questions calls for a numerical response.

_____ **Attention Getter:** Effective use of attention getting strategy (quote, statistic, question, story, etc.) to capture listeners' attention and to introduce topic. Attention getter is relevant and meaningful and seemed to gain the desired response from audience.

_____ **Proposition Statement (central idea):** Speaker clearly formulated and stated the proposition statement; the controlling idea. Topic is clearly understood and main points previewed in accordance with organizational pattern used.

_____ **Connection w/Audience:** Clearly stated the relevance of topic to audience needs and interests. Thoughtful audience analysis reflected in argument type choice and supporting evidence.

_____ **Subject Knowledge:** Depth of content reflects knowledge and understanding of topic. Main points adequately substantiated with timely, relevant and sufficient support. Provided accurate explanation of key concepts.

_____ **Organization:** Uses effective organizational pattern for speech purpose. Main points are clearly distinguished from supporting details. Signposts are effectively used for smooth and coherent transitions.

_____ **Logical Appeal:** Presents sound arguments to support major claim. Arguments are supported with sufficient, relevant and valid evidence. Reasoning is free of fallacies. Solution is logical and reasonable.

_____ **Emotional Appeal:** Effectively and ethically appeals to audience emotions (anger, fear, compassion, etc.) to achieve the persuasive goal. Vivid and emotive language effectively used to create imagery to engage audience emotionally.

_____ **Credibility:** Sources of information are clearly identified and properly cited. Establishes credibility and authority of sources presented. Balances a variety of perspectives and recognizes opposing views.

(___) **Cited Sources:** How many cited sources did you hear during the speech? (Use tally marks: _____)

_____ **Eye Contact:** Consistently and effectively used eye contact to establish rapport with audience. Inconspicuous use of speaker notes and effective use of scanning to established an expanded zone of interaction.

_____ **Body Language:** Expressive, dynamic, and natural use of gestures, posture and facial expressions to reinforce and enhance meaning. Body language reflects comfort interacting with audience.

_____ **Voice:** Natural variation of vocal characteristics (rate, pitch, volume, tone) in Standard English to heighten interest and match message appropriately.

_____ **Fluency:** Appropriate pronunciation, enunciation, and articulation. Lack of noticeable vocalized fillers

Comments

Strengths	Weaknesses

Name of Peer Evaluator: _____

For evaluator: "This is my 1st or 2nd evaluation." (Circle one for participation points)

#5B – Peer Critique Form: Persuasive

Speaker: _____ Topic: _____

Instructions: Respond "Yes" or "No" to each critique question; one questions calls for a numerical response.

_____ **Attention Getter:** Effective use of attention getting strategy (quote, statistic, question, story, etc.) to capture listeners' attention and to introduce topic. Attention getter is relevant and meaningful and seemed to gain the desired response from audience.

_____ **Proposition Statement (central idea):** Speaker clearly formulated and stated the proposition statement; the controlling idea. Topic is clearly understood and main points previewed in accordance with organizational pattern used.

_____ **Connection w/Audience:** Clearly stated the relevance of topic to audience needs and interests. Thoughtful audience analysis reflected in argument type choice and supporting evidence.

_____ **Subject Knowledge:** Depth of content reflects knowledge and understanding of topic. Main points adequately substantiated with timely, relevant and sufficient support. Provided accurate explanation of key concepts.

_____ **Organization:** Uses effective organizational pattern for speech purpose. Main points are clearly distinguished from supporting details. Signposts are effectively used for smooth and coherent transitions.

_____ **Logical Appeal:** Presents sound arguments to support major claim. Arguments are supported with sufficient, relevant and valid evidence. Reasoning is free of fallacies. Minimum of eight citations from different sources.

_____ **Emotional Appeal:** Effectively and ethically appeals to audience emotions (anger, fear, compassion, etc.) to achieve the persuasive goal. Vivid and emotive language effectively used to create imagery to engage audience emotionally.

_____ **Credibility:** Sources of information are clearly identified and properly cited. Establishes credibility and authority of sources presented. Balances a variety of perspectives and recognizes opposing views.

(___) **Cited Sources:** How many cited sources did you hear during the speech? (Use tally marks: _____)

_____ **Eye Contact:** Consistently and effectively used eye contact to establish rapport with audience. Inconspicuous use of speaker notes and effective use of scanning to established an expanded zone of interaction.

_____ **Body Language:** Expressive, dynamic, and natural use of gestures, posture and facial expressions to reinforce and enhance meaning. Body language reflects comfort interacting with audience.

_____ **Voice:** Natural variation of vocal characteristics (rate, pitch, volume, tone) in Standard English to heighten interest and match message appropriately.

_____ **Fluency:** Appropriate pronunciation, enunciation, and articulation. Lack of noticeable vocalized fillers

Comments

Strengths	Weaknesses

Name of Peer Evaluator: _____

For evaluator: "This is my   1st   or   2nd   evaluation."   (Circle one for participation points)

#5 - Persuasiveness: Class Outcomes

SPEAKER'S NAME: _____

SPEAKERS TOPIC: _____

Instructions: Using the scale survey below, draw an "X" in the box that represented your view on the topic at the beginning of the speech. If your views did not change at the conclusion of the speech, draw a circle around the "X." If your views changed at the conclusion of the speech, draw a line to the degree that represents your new view on the issue and place an "X" in the box, then circle it.

Student Initials	Strongly Opposed	Moderately Opposed	Neutral	Moderately Supportive	Strongly Supportive

#6 – Tribute Speaking Exercise

Presentations Begin	See syllabus
Typed Speech Draft Due	See syllabus
Grading Scale	50 points
Evaluation	See Grading Rubric below
Time Limits	2 to 3 minutes

Assignment Objective:

This speech exercise is designed to give you an opportunity to write and present a manuscript speech. You will write a tribute speech that highlights the essence of a person, a group of people, an institution, or an event. The subject may be historical or contemporary, famous or obscure; it may even be a self-eulogy which celebrates the life of a deceased! I encourage you to use language *imaginatively* and *experiment* with audience engagement devices to enhance clarity and vividness as discussed. The words that you select to pay homage to your honoree should inspire your audience in a way that creates a sense of admiration or joy.

In a tribute speech, "less is often more." When any speech is packed with clutter (unnecessary words or information), you block the primary message from being understood. Stay focused on explaining in detail the characteristics that makes the person, institution, or event worthy of paying honor to. You must also be careful not to create a chronological report about the life of a person or generalities of an event; this is not the general purpose of the assignment. Remember, the general purpose of a speech for special occasions is to create laughter, feelings of joy or inspirations, and camaraderie.

Instructions:

The delivery type for this speech is manuscript; you will read the speech. To begin, think of three adjectives that describe *the essence* of the person, institution, or event that you are paying homage to. You will use the same three words to develop the body of your speech. On presentation day you must have a one-page typed speech manuscript that includes the speech heading followed by the essay formatted speech: introduction, body, and conclusion. At the conclusion of your presentation, you will submit the speech manuscript for grading. It is important to practice your speech with a timer to ensure your speech falls within the time limits; speeches that go over the time limit will be cut off. Even though you are reading this speech, it is important that you read at a moderate pace to allow the audience time to decode each message. The overall goal is still to engage your listeners by using attention gaining strategies throughout the presentation to keep their attention. Pauses combined with eye contact timed to punctuate key points work are essential devices for engagement.

Speech Requirements:

1. Your one-page typed manuscript speech must include a speech heading followed by the essay formatted tribute speech.
2. It is critical that you rehearse your speech with a timer to avoid being cut off when the speech exceeds thirty seconds.

Grading Rubric:

➤ 46-50 points: An excellent tribute speech will inspire the listens to react with over-whelming emotion; the residual message will become ingrained in the listener's thoughts and be applied to their own lives.
➤ 40-46 points: An above average tribute speech will receive rigorous applause from the audience; the residual message will be understood and felt.
➤ 35-39 points: An average tribute speech will earn a polite reaction form the listeners and be quickly forgotten.
➤ 30-34 points: An under-developed tribute speech will not be presented in a clear essay format. Written more as a fragmented report, there will be no audience engagement, nor will the speech highlight the essence of the honoree.

#7 – Impromptu Speaking Exercise

Presentations Begin	See syllabus
Typed Speech Draft Due	None required
Grading Scale	Participation Points
Time Limits	1 to 3 minutes

Instructions:

Impromptu speeches involve little to no time for preparation, and are designed to help you improve critical thinking and speaking skills, "on the fly." Therefore, remembering to develop a speech heading that provides you with the central idea, summary of speech, will be helpful. Also, remembering that the introduction, body, and conclusion must always be the organizational pattern provide guidance as your draft your brief speech.

For this speech activity, you will deliver a 1-3 minute presentation on a topic selected randomly. This will occur on the day/s assigned for impromptu speaking, (see syllabus). Speakers will be selected at random whether you are in attendance or not. After selecting your random topic, you will have roughly 3 to 5 minutes to draft your speech using the back of this assignment page.

Topics will be similar to the prompts below.

> ➤ What are your three biggest accomplishments?
> ➤ What are your three biggest fears?
> ➤ What is your favorite ...?
> ➤ If you won the lottery, how would you spend your money?
> ➤ What do you think about the Chicago Cubs?
> ➤ If you were the opposite sex for a week, who would you spend that time?
> ➤ What do you think about super hero movies, games, and comic books?
> ➤ What do you think about reality television?
> ➤ If you could go back in time for a year, what era would I travel to?

#8 – (May be used as Final Exam Option 2) Informative Speech: Concept (*causal*)

Presentations Begin	See syllabus
Typed Speech Draft Due	See syllabus
Grading Scale	150 points (135/150 = A, 120/134 = B, 105/119 = C, 90/104 = D)
Evaluation	See Grading Rubric
Time Limits	7 to 9 minutes

Instructions: A causal concept speech does not look at the "causes and effects" of a topic; instead, it seeks to inform the audience through proof that a specific effect is directly related to a specific cause. Your thesis should reflect a: belief, theory, principle, attitude, or notion that you believe true.

Approach: Because your personal feeling about the thesis will be biased, you must present the audience with adequate factual and credible evidence, from research, which proves and supports your thesis. This type of speech requires lots of connectives to make it easy for the audience follow your thoughts. Connectives will also help you during the developmental process.

Example: You may have a ***theory*** that, "*People are bullies because they were bullied in the past.*" In a causal speech, you must prove this thesis true by sharing credible studies and facts from research.

Caution: This is not a persuasive speech which means you must not attempt to convince the listeners to agree with your views through persuasive strategies and methods. Persuasion is not the general purpose of this speech. Making a call to action will lower your grade.

Again, informative causal speakers merely share credible information discovered during research that enhances or provides the listeners with a new awareness of the topic.

Speech Requirements:

1. Extemporaneous Delivery (Chapter 6)
   - Use vocal variety to help engage your listeners.
   - Speakers must maintain eye contact with the audience.
   - Avoid fillers or distracting mannerisms.
2. Supporting Material Citation Requirements
   - Because this speech requires evidence, you will present a lot of factual information from your research. There is not a specific amount of citations required because roughly fifty percent of the body of your speech should consist of evidence (cited sources). The audience will not be able to make the connection between a cause and its effects if you do not present enough logical cited evidence to help them see how the variables (cause and its effect/s) are related.
   - You may not cite yourself as an expert.
   - Wikipedia, encyclopedias, non-expert dictionaries, or non-expert print or web sources may be used to fulfill your citation requirements.
   - Oral citations must be typed into the full preparation outlined speech and keyword delivery outline where they will be spoken.

Managing Presentation Day Anxiety:

1. Preparation: The most important strategy is to start early and leave time to rehearse, rehearse, rehearse.
2. Strategies discussed in Chapter 4 on controlling anxiety control should be reviewed and applied.
3. Some speakers do not feel the effects of anxiety until they stand at the podium and look at their audience. Do not underestimate the power of anxiety. Be prepared to counter-act it with self-imposed prophesies of success. Do not give way to the fallacy of perfection; you will make mistakes – it is okay.

4. Attire: studies show that a person's attire has a strong impact on emotions. Take care with your attire on presentation day. The audience will make first impression judgments about your credibility, competence, and trustworthiness that can be seen and felt as you present your speech; can trigger anxiety.
5. Lastly, know that your peers in the audience are rooting for your success.

On Your Presentation Day

You must submit the following documents:
1. Full typed preparation outlined speech with attached APA formatted bibliography
2. Keyword delivery outline or speaker's notes
3. Informative speech grading rubric #4
4. Two informative speech peer review forms (#4A & #4B)

Speakers who do not submit a fully typed speech in a preparation outline format will not be allowed to present their speech.

DRAFT YOUR INFORMATIVE CONCEPT (Causal) SPEECH HEADING HERE

General Purpose: _____

Narrowed Topic: _____

_____

Specific Purpose: _____

_____

_____

Central Idea: _____

_____

_____

NOTES TO HELP BUILD THE BODY OF YOUR SPEECH

_____

_____

_____

_____

_____

_____

_____

_____

#8 – GRADING RUBRIC: Informative Causal Speech – (*concept*)

Name: _____ Topic: _____

	F	D	C	B	A
Introduction (30 pts.)					
Used hook & bait method to grab audience's attention	2	4	6	8	10
Provided a credibility statement	1	2	3	4	5
Central idea summarized speech	2	4	6	8	10
Transitioned to the body	1	2	3	4	5
Body (70 pts.)					
Subject Knowledge: depth of content reflects knowledge of topic	2	4	6	8	10
Causal organizational pattern helped audience follow with ease	2	4	6	8	10
Filtered examples through common experiences to help listeners relate	2	4	6	8	10
Provided logical evidence that proved a causal relationship exists	2	4	6	8	10
Used a variety of connectives throughout the presentation	2	4	6	8	10
Used sufficient full credible "oral" citations to support facts	2	4	6	8	10
# of full oral citations heard: _____					
Conclusion (25 pts.)					
Signaled the end of the speech	2	4	6	8	10
Summarized residual message	2	4	6	8	10
Closing statement reinforced proposition	1	2	3	4	5
Extemporaneous Delivery (25 pts.)					
Used appropriate eye contact, brief reference to notes	2	4	6	8	10
Body movement and facial expressions enhance delivery	1	2	3	4	5
Volume, rate, pitch, and vocal variety enhanced delivery	1	2	3	4	5
Pauses used to enhance delivery and to help avoid fillers	1	2	3	4	5

TIME (*7 to 9 minutes*): _____   **Points earned out of 150** _____

Strengths	Weaknesses

Penalties:
- Over/Under Time Limit: (-2.5 points per 30 seconds)   _____
- Read 50% of speech: (-20% of points earned)   _____
- Partial speech outline submitted/essay format: (-10 points)   _____
- Missing APA formatted bibliography: (-10 points)   _____

Total Penalties subtracted: _____ - *point's earned* _____ = _____   Grade: _____

#8A – Peer Critique Form: Informative Causal Speech – (*concept*)

Your Name: _____ Your Topic: _____

INSTRUCTIONS: Familiarize yourself with this critique form before speeches begin. As the speech progresses, you should check off each item covered effectively by the speaker. You must provide written comments that communicate the speaker's strengths and weaknesses. This will help them identify area to work on for the next presentation.

Introduction:
____ Speech began with a strong attention-getter that established the topic.
____ Strong personal credibility was established.
____ Central idea was clearly stated.
____ Transitioned effectively to the body.

Body:
____ Causal organizational pattern helped audience follow with ease
____ Information given was all relevant to explain the thesis.
____ Provided logical evidence that proved a causal relationship exists
____ Used more than eight full credible "oral" citations to support facts
(___) Full oral citations heard during presentation. (Use tally marks: _____)
____ Oral citations included required information to qualify as credible.
____ Connectives were used to help listeners make logical connections to points made.
____ Topic narrowed to cover an appropriate amount of information for the time limits.
____ Content of the speech did not get persuasive.

Conclusion:
____ Cued the audience that the speech was coming to an end
____ Paraphrased the central idea to summarize the goal of the speech.
____ Left audience with a memorable closing statement that relayed back to the introduction.

Delivery:
____ Maintained appropriate amount of eye contact with audience.
____ Did not read speech (glanced at notes periodically).
____ Gestures and movement added enthusiasm.
____ Speaking rate was appropriate (not too fast or slow).
____ Avoided vocalized pauses: "uh", "um", "ah", "OK", "you know", "like", etc.
____ Avoided distracting mannerisms and/or movement that indicate nervousness.
____ Overall, speaker seemed prepared and ready to give the speech.

Comments

Strengths	Weaknesses

Peer Evaluator: _____
For evaluator: "This is my   1st   or   2nd   evaluation."   (Circle one for participation points)

#8B – Peer Critique Form: Informative Causal Speech – (*concept*)

Your Name: _____ Your Topic: _____

INSTRUCTIONS: Familiarize yourself with this critique form before speeches begin. As the speech progresses, you should check off each item covered effectively by the speaker. You must provide written comments that communicate the speaker's strengths and weaknesses. This will help them identify area to work on for the next presentation.

Introduction:
____ Speech began with a strong attention-getter that established the topic.
____ Strong personal credibility was established.
____ Central idea was clearly stated.
____ Transitioned effectively to the body.

Body:
____ Causal organizational pattern helped audience follow with ease
____ Information given was all relevant to explain the thesis.
____ Provided logical evidence that proved a causal relationship exists
____ Used more than eight full credible "oral" citations to support facts
(___) Full oral citations heard during presentation. (Use tally marks: _____)
____ Oral citations included required information to qualify as credible.
____ Connectives were used to help listeners make logical connections to points made.
____ Topic narrowed to cover an appropriate amount of information for the time limits.
____ Content of the speech did not get persuasive.

Conclusion:
____ Cued the audience that the speech was coming to an end
____ Paraphrased the central idea to summarize the goal of the speech.
____ Left audience with a memorable closing statement that relayed back to the introduction.

Delivery:
____ Maintained appropriate amount of eye contact with audience.
____ Did not read speech (glanced at notes periodically).
____ Gestures and movement added enthusiasm.
____ Speaking rate was appropriate (not too fast or slow).
____ Avoided vocalized pauses: "uh", "um", "ah", "OK", "you know", "like", etc.
____ Avoided distracting mannerisms and/or movement that indicate nervousness.
____ Overall, speaker seemed prepared and ready to give the speech.

Comments

Strengths	Weaknesses

Peer Evaluator: _____
For evaluator: "This is my 1st or 2nd evaluation." (Circle one for participation points)

#9 – Final Exam Speech (Option 1): Persuasion - *Controversial social issue*

Presentations Begin	See syllabus
Typed Speech Draft Due	See syllabus
Grading Scale	150 points (135/150 = A, 120/134 = B, 105/119 = C, 90/104 = D)
Evaluation	See Grading Rubric
Time Limits	7 to 9 minutes

Instructions: The general purpose of this speech is to persuade your listeners to accept, to some degree, your proposition; which is your view of a problem and how you suggest we solve it. Remember that your credibility plays an important role in persuading audiences; as such, you must deal with oppositional arguments in a fair and convincing way. Good persuaders do not ignore the opposition, nor do they simply attack the opposition, they engage opposition's arguments in an even-handed way.

Your Challenge: Because the thesis of this speech supports your perception of a problem and your proposed solution to satisfy the problem, your approach must include strategic persuasive methods and strategies that strengthen your arguments. Every speech begins by setting the stage. For this type of speech you will use informative speaking to describe the problem and tell the listeners why you think it warrants immediate attention. The next step is to provide supporting evidence that proves a true problem exist as some listeners may not see it as such. Connectives are critical to use as you move through your reasoning to help the listeners connect your claims and evidence. You'll end the speech by sharing your proposed solution to the problem and once again use evidence to prove that your solution will work without causing additional problems.

Steps:

1. First, you must select a topic; good topics are those that you are most passionate about; you often find yourself engaged in debates in support of your position. To search for topics, you can also use the Opposing Viewpoints database which is composed of the most popular controversial speech and essay topics that students are using today. To locate this database, go to your library's online database and look for the Controversial Issues category. The Internet is another good option; go to google.com and type this phrase, with quotation marks into the search bar, "social issues debate"

2. Develop a persuasive speech heading that meets the general purpose of this assignment; and then expand your research to identify supporting material for your arguments and supporting material that helps you understand your opposition's arguments.

3. "A persuasive speech cannot be presented if no one disagrees with you." Because of this reality, you must develop and circulate an audience analysis survey to test the audience for opposition to your proposition. The targeted audience are those listeners moderately opposed, neutral, and moderately in favor of your proposition. If this group is small, less than half of your audience, you must select a different topic. For this reason, the question you ask on your survey is critical, "If you don't ask the right questions, you won't get the answers you are searching for." This quote is very true. Think critically about your survey questions. Do not simply ask the listeners if the agree or disagree, find out why! The information pulled from your survey will provide you with a strategic angle to approach your arguments.

4. After analyzing the data from your surveys it's time to build your speech:
   - Select an approach, proposition of; (fact, value, or policy)
   - Select a reasoning [argument] style; (inductive, deductive, causal, or analogical).
   - Select an appropriate outline to build your speech; (problem/solution, problem/cause/solution, refutation, causal, comparative advantage, or Monroe's motivated sequence).

Speech Requirements:

- ➤ Extemporaneous Delivery
- ➤ Use vocal variety to help engage your listeners.
- ➤ Speakers must maintain eye contact with the audience.
- ➤ Avoid fillers or distracting mannerisms.
1. Supporting Material Citation Requirements
   - ➤ Because this speech requires evidence, you will present a lot of factual information from your research. There is not a specific amount of citations required because roughly fifty percent of the body of your speech should consist of evidence (cited sources). Every argument must have a counter-argument. This means you must speak to your opposition's views or they will stop listening.
   - ➤ Citations must be typed into the full preparation outlined speech and keyword delivery outline where they will be spoken.
   - ➤ You may not cite yourself as an expert.
   - ➤ Wikipedia, encyclopedias, non-expert dictionaries, or non-expert print or web sources may be used to fulfill your citation requirements.
2. If you use a visual aid, remember to adhere to the guidelines as presented in Chapter 9

Managing Presentation Day Anxiety:

1. Preparation: The most important strategy is to start early and leave time to rehearse, rehearse, rehearse.
2. Strategies discussed in Chapter 4 on controlling anxiety control should be reviewed and applied.
3. Some speakers do not feel the effects of anxiety until they stand at the podium and look at their audience. Do not underestimate the power of anxiety. Be prepared to counter-act it with self-imposed prophesies of success. Do not give way to the fallacy of perfection; you will make mistakes – it is okay.
4. Attire: studies show that a person's attire has a strong impact on emotions. Take care with your attire on presentation day. The audience will make first impression judgments about your credibility, competence, and trustworthiness that can be seen and felt as you present your speech; can trigger anxiety.
5. Lastly, know that your peers in the audience are rooting for your success.

On Your Presentation Day

You must submit the following documents:
1. Full typed preparation outlined speech with attached APA formatted bibliography
2. Keyword delivery outline or speaker's notes
3. Informative speech grading rubric located in Appendix – C
4. Two informative speech peer review forms located in Appendix – C

Speakers who do not submit a fully typed speech in a preparation outline format will not be allowed to present their speech.

DRAFT YOUR PERSUASIVE SPEECH HEADING HERE

General Purpose: _____

Narrowed Topic: _____

_____

Position: _____

_____

Proposition: _____

_____

#9 – Grading Rubric Final Exam Speech: Persuasion (*Controversial social issue*)

Speaker: _____ Topic: _____

5	Excellent	This component was exceptionally well done. You demonstrated high competence.
4	Good	This component was done well. You demonstrated competence.
3	Adequate	An attempt was made to fulfill this component. However, you may not have shown full competence when doing it
2	Inadequate	You did not demonstrate competence with this component. You may have either not done it, or the manner in which you did it created a slight negative element in your speech
1	Unacceptable	You displayed almost the opposite of the desired component. It seemed that you were almost totally unaware of your behavior. It created a definite negative element in your speech.

_____ **Attention Getter:** Effective use of attention getting strategy (quote, statistic, question, story, etc.) to capture listeners' attention and to introduce topic. Attention getter is relevant and meaningful and seemed to gain the desired response from audience.

_____ **Proposition Statement (central idea):** Speaker clearly formulated and stated the proposition statement; the controlling idea. Topic is clearly understood and main points previewed in accordance with organizational pattern used.

_____ **Connection w/Audience:** Clearly stated the relevance of topic to audience needs and interests. Thoughtful audience analysis reflected in argument type choice and supporting evidence.

_____ **Subject Knowledge:** Depth of content reflects knowledge and understanding of topic. Main points adequately substantiated with timely, relevant and sufficient support. Provided accurate explanation of key concepts.

_____ **Organization:** Uses effective organizational pattern for speech purpose. Main points are clearly distinguished from supporting details. Signposts are effectively used for smooth and coherent transitions.

_____ **Logical Appeal:** Presents sound arguments to support major claim. Arguments are supported with sufficient, relevant and valid evidence. Reasoning is free of fallacies. Minimum of eight citations from different sources.

_____ **Emotional Appeal:** Effectively and ethically appeals to audience emotions (anger, fear, compassion, etc.) to achieve the persuasive goal. Vivid and emotive language effectively used to create imagery to engage audience emotionally.

_____ **Credibility:** Sources of information are clearly identified and properly cited. Establishes credibility and authority of sources presented. Balances a variety of perspectives and recognizes opposing views.

_____ **Eye Contact:** Consistently and effectively used eye contact to establish rapport with audience. Inconspicuous use of speaker notes and effective use of scanning to established an expanded zone of interaction.

_____ **Body Language:** Expressive, dynamic, and natural use of gestures, posture and facial expressions to reinforce and enhance meaning. Body language reflects comfort interacting with audience.

_____ **Voice:** Natural variation of vocal characteristics (rate, pitch, volume, tone) in Standard English to heighten interest and match message appropriately.

_____ **Fluency:** Appropriate pronunciation, enunciation, and articulation. Lack of noticeable vocalized fillers

Comments

Strengths	Weaknesses

Penalties:
- Over/Under Time Limit: (-2.5 points per 30 seconds) _____
- Read 50% of speech: (-20% of points earned) _____
- Partial speech outline submitted/essay format: (-10 points) _____
- Missing APA formatted bibliography: (-10 points) _____
- Misuse of Visual Aid (-5 points) _____

Total Penalties subtracted: _____ *- point's earned* _____ = _____   Grade: _____

Appendix C: Active Learning Assignments

#1 Listening/Activity Teams

ASSIGNMENT:	Listening / Activity Teams
DUE DATE:	Ongoing

What Is a Listening Team?

Listening Teams keep students focused during lecture or video presentations. They also provide opportunities for peer learning and small group discussion. Teams sit together throughout the semester to have quick access to each other for brief discussion as prompted by instructor. Because each student participates in unique listening behaviors, it is helpful to identify at least two types of listening behaviors that you reflect how you listen. Each team should include each type of listener for effectiveness.

Form Groups of Four

Each student will take on one of the following roles.
1. Student 1, **Example Giver** (Facilitator/Tutor): Gives examples or applications of key concepts.
2. Student 2, **Questioner** (Inquisitive Student): Asks 2 clarifying questions about the material.
3. Student 3, **Devil's Advocate** (Critical Thinker): Identifies 2 areas of disagreement within the content and explains why.
4. Student 4, **Team Player** (Positive Believer): Points out two areas of agreement with lecture content and explains why.

Instructions:

1. While listening to the lecture or video, think of examples, questions, and areas of disagreement and agreement.
2. After the presentation, you will meet as a group for 15 minutes to ensure each member has a firm grasp on the concept discussed.
3. Afterwards, groups may share thoughts and ask clarifying questions to solidify their understanding of the key concepts.

Write Group Members Names Here:

#2 – Student as Teacher

DUE DATE:	See syllabus
GRADE POINTS:	30 points
EVALUATION:	Proof of knowledge, and successfully relaying that knowledge to class. 30 = Conveyed excellent knowledge of the concept/topic, and engaged class. 20 = Conveyed partial knowledge of concept/topic, did not connect well with class. 10 = Did not seem familiar with the concept/topic assigned, misrepresented the facts or read verbatim from textbook, and disregarded class interaction.
▶	Presentation lessons should be no shorter than 15 minutes, and no longer than 20-minute
▶	If team members are absent on the assigned presentation date, the members present will only be responsible for presenting their part of the concepts; the instructor will assist with the rest.

Each Listening Team will be assigned a specific section from the textbook **to study in advance**. Each team member is required to have a solid understanding of the assigned section to share with the class. This mean, read the material in advance and be prepared to share this information with the class. Do not read from the textbook during your presentation; instead, paraphrase what you've learned. Think of this presentation as a *group speech* with each team member presenting a specific part of the section.

Basic Presentation Outline and Criteria to Focus On

1. **Learning Outcomes:** What do you want the class to know after your presentation
2. **Lesson Organization:** Each team member must have an outline of key concepts methods, or skills, with examples, for the part of the section they will cover. This outline is the same keyword outline used in a speech.
3. **Supporting Material:** Provide examples from the textbook to help explain your lesson. Make sure the class follows your presentation in the textbook; announce the page/s of focus before you begin and as you move through the lesson.
4. **Student Involvement:** Develop a thought question or two whose purpose is to engage the class; encourage them to ask questions. Your goal is to make sure the class understands the concepts.
5. **Wrap up:** A concluding statement, similar to a speech conclusion, should be developed. Tell the listeners what you taught them and how it relates to previous lesson in the chapter.

#3 Critique of an Outside Speaker

DUE DATE:	See syllabus
GRADE POINTS:	100 points
EVALUATION:	See rubric on next page
▶	The essay report should be two to three typed pages, using a size.12 font, double spaced.

Instructions:

This assignment requires you to attend a speech presentation given outside of the classroom to evaluate the effectiveness or ineffectiveness of the presentation. In other words, this is a "show what you have learned assignment." To achieve this outcome, you must listen and think critically as you observe and listen to the presentation; take notes. As the speech begins, listen for the central idea and tell me exactly what the thesis and main points are. This vital information must be understood in order to conduct a full evaluation of how the speaker explained and supported the thesis. Provide excerpts from the speech as examples that show how the speaker used methods and strategies for speech writing that is also audience-centered. Your critique should be developed using an essay format. See the next page for a complete list of evaluation expectations.

Learning Objectives (goals):

- To show via a typed essay formatted critique, what you have learned about developing and delivering an audience centered speech presentations.
- To isolate each section of the speech in order to conduct an in-depth discussion how the goal of that section was met: introduction, each main point, and conclusion. Again use excerpts from the speech to provide your examples. Do not tell me what the speaker said from the beginning to the end of the speech. Evaluate the speech just as your instructor evaluates your speech presentations.
- To Identify and provide examples of other communication concepts learned in the first three chapters of your textbook.

How to Locate a Speaker:

Check with cultural, educational, and social organizations for upcoming speakers. Colleges, universities, and public libraries also host speaking events at various sites throughout the year. Also, if you find a speaker, share that event with your classmates. You must identify a speaker as soon as possible to avoid a last minute rush.

Speaker Exclusions:

You may not critique the following speeches:
- A class meeting or class lecture
- A sermon
- Group speeches or discussion groups
- Film showing, or Videotaped speakers
- Write-ups of past speeches

Submission of Essay Evaluation

Staple proof of attendance to the back of your typed essay critique.

Your Critique should cover the following:

INTRODUCTION (10 points):

1. Include the date and title of the speech, the name of the speaker along with his or her title or position.
2. What was the thesis (central idea) of the speech? Describe the audience.
3. How did the speaker grasp the attention of the listeners? Explain. Did this make you want to listen?
4. Did the speaker use a transitional statement signaling the end of the introduction and the beginning of the body? Explain.

BODY (50 points):

1. Was the general purpose of the speech informative, persuasive, or entertainment. Give examples of the kinds of supporting material used to explain or prove the main points: (statistics, graphs, video testimony, stories.). Did the speaker's main points help to achieve the overall goal of the presentation? Why or why not?

DELIVERY (20 points):

1. Describe the speaker's platform behavior. Include such details as posture, personal appearance, bodily movements, gestures, vocal characteristics and eye contact.
2. Was the speaker's delivery effective or ineffective? Why?
3. Describe the speaker's use of language. Include such details as volume, word choice, articulation, pronunciation, clarity, vividness, appropriateness, pausing, filler words, accent, and language devices.

CONCLUSION - What did you learn (20 points):

1. What was your overall reaction to the speech? What was the audience's reaction?
2. What did you learn that will help you become a better speaker?

#4 – Critique of Video Taped Speaker: Ted Talks

ASSIGNMENT:	TED TALKS Speaker - (located Online at ted.com)
DUE DATE:	**See syllabus**
GRADE POINTS:	100 points (see critique breakdown below)
	➢ Your two to three page essay formatted critique must be double spaced using a .12 font. ➢ There are over 2000 speeches in the Ted Talks database, select one that inspires you.

Instructions:

This assignment requires you to view a video-taped speech to evaluate the strengths and weaknesses of the presentation. To achieve this outcome, you must listen and think critically as you observe and listen to the presentation; take notes. As the speech begins, listen for the central idea and tell me exactly what the thesis and main points are. This vital information must be understood in order to conduct a full evaluation of how the speaker explained and supported the thesis. Provide excerpts from the speech as examples that show how the speaker used methods and strategies for speech writing that is also audience-centered. Your critique should be developed using an essay format. A complete list of evaluation expectations is listed below.

Objectives:

- To isolate each section of the speech in order to conduct an in-depth discussion how the goal of that section was met: introduction, each main point, and conclusion. Again use excerpts from the speech to provide your examples. Do not tell me what the speaker said from the beginning to the end of the speech. Evaluate the speech just as your instructor evaluates your speech presentations.
- To identify and provide examples of other communication concepts learned in the first three chapters of your textbook.

Your Critique should cover the following:

INTRODUCTION (10 points):
1. Include the title of the speech, the name of the speaker along with his or her title or position. Describe the introduction and discuss whether it made you want to listen.
2. Identify the central idea; thesis and main points.
3. How did the speaker grasp the attention of the audience? Explain.
4. Did the speaker use a transitional statement telling the audience that the introduction was ending and the body was beginning. Explain how this was achieved.

BODY (50 points):
1. What was the general purpose of the speech: informative, persuasive, or entertainment?
2. Provide excerpts from the speech to show how the speaker explained each main point. What kind of supporting material was used (facts, examples, statistics, or testimony)? Provide examples.
3. What strategies did the speaker engage the audience throughout the presentation?

DELIVERY (20 points):
1. Describe the speaker's platform behavior. Include such details as posture, personal appearance, bodily movements, gestures, vocal characteristics and eye contact.
2. Was the speaker's delivery effective or ineffective? Why?

3. Describe the speaker's use of language. Include such details as volume, word choice, articulation, pronunciation, clarity, vividness, appropriateness, pausing, filler words, accent, and language devices.

CONCLUSION - What did you learn (20 points):

1. What was your overall reaction to the speech? What was the audience's reaction?
2. What did you learn that will help you become a better speaker?

#5 – Panel Discussion

DUE DATE:	See syllabus
GRADE POINTS:	100 points
EVALUATION:	See grading rubric below.
TIME LIMITS	20 to 30 minutes

Objectives and Goals:

For this assignment, groups of four to five members will select a few topics of interest from the list below. Teams will vote on a topic for their discussion; majority wins.

The goal is to participate in a problem solving discussion that encourages full participation, and that actively works to avoid miscommunication, conflict, stage hogging, or other behaviors that prevents the group from identifying a solution to the problem. All strategies and methods studied for effective speaking and listening must be reflected in each member's communication. After the topic is agreed upon, each group member must conduct research to familiarize themselves with the topic and formulate an opinion. Bring your research with you to use as source citations during your discussion. Remember that opinions must be supported by credible evidence. All topics call for in-depth critical thinking to prepare for your groups discussion.

Topic Ideas

1. Is human cloning justified, and should it be allowed?
2. Is age an important factor in relationships?
3. Are humans too dependent on computers?
4. Are credit cards are more harmful than debit cards?
5. Is it better to date someone attractive and popular or intelligent and wise?
6. Does access to condoms in high schools lead to irresponsible, dangerous, or bad behavior?
7. Are law enforcement cameras an invasion of privacy?
8. Do you think the word "Smart" is harmful to human development?
9. Is competition good?

Small Group Panel Discussion Grading Rubric

(25)_____ Group Meeting (*participated in topic selection*).
(25)_____ GROUP GRADE
_____ Stayed on task during the discussion (*did not get off subject*).
_____ Managed conflict within group.
(50)_____ INDIVIDUAL GRADE (*knowledge, contribution, focus*)
_____ Shared knowledge of Issue
_____ Supported views with credible oral citation
_____ Did not attempt to push for conclusion prior to group's analysis of problem/solutions
_____ Listened and responded courteously to others
_____ Comments indicated student was practicing reflective thinking.
_____ Applied strategies and methods of public speaking (communication) in a way that enhanced participation instead of confuse.

#6 – Self-introduction Reflection Form

Name: _____ Section: _____ Date: _____

> When students of public speaking reflect on their presentation, they thoughtfully consider (or reconsider) the outcome of that experience. If the reflection is critical, it challenges the customary ways of understanding or explaining an experience. Critical thinking is the act of considering options through logical thought and analysis; digging deep to understand the relationship between several variables, and uncover an unidentified problem [*like a detective*]. The opportunity to reflect on your experiences helps to develop critical thinking skills and helps students develop a deeper awareness of how to learn things for themselves.

I shared responses to each question as instructed on the assignment form: ___Yes ____ No

I applied the skills from chapter one to help control my nervousness. ___ Yes ___ No

Rate your nervousness during your introduction speech. (circle one)

   (1) Not very   (2) Average amount, but controlled   (3) Extremely

After presenting my introduction speech, I can honestly say I was:

____Prepared (spent adequate time piecing together the three main points of my speech).
____Partially prepared (I could have spent more developing the main points of my speech)
____Shocked! (*"I thought I could wing it because the assignment seemed simple, but I froze – I could not think."*)

Explain your answer: _____

_____

_____

_____

I stayed within my time limit of 1 to 2 minutes: ____Yes ____No

What section/s of this first speech experience was most challenged? Why?

_____

_____

_____

_____

_____

#7 – Informative Speech Reflection Form:all categories

Name: _____ Topic: _____

Rate your nervousness during informative speech. (circle one)

   (1) Not very   (2) Average amount, but controlled   (3) Extremely

Explain the difference between how you rated your anxiety level during your introduction speech and this one. _____

_____

What did I do well? _____

_____

_____

What could I have done better? _____

_____

_____

_____

_____

What section/s of the speech or delivery am I most challenged? Why? _____

_____

_____

_____

_____

How did the audience respond during your delivery? (Be specific – describe how the audience responded during each part of the presentation. Which section seemed to capture their attention most?)

_____

_____

_____

_____

_____

Personal Reflection on Two Peer Feedback: (Please be open to constructive peer feedback. Remember, you are seeking to engage your listeners; your peers are your listeners)

_____

_____

_____

_____

_____

_____

Reflection on Instructor Feedback:

_____

_____

_____

_____

_____

_____

_____

_____

_____

_____

_____

_____

_____

_____

#8 – Persuasive Workshop

Name: _____ **Group Members:** _____

INSTRUCTIONS: Answer the following questions before moving into your groups. Share your answers with your group for evaluation purposes. Questions that must be considered by group members: Is the statement or choice clear and appropriate for the desired goal in that section? If any group member answers, "No," then a replacement (statement) must be discussed. During the small group critique session, the instructor will conduct brief one-on-one meetings to provide guidance and assess the effectiveness of your responses to this worksheet in support of the upcoming speech.

1. **Write your Proposition Statement:** _____

   _____

2. **What type of proposition are you proposing:** _____

   - *Fact:* Your goal is to persuade your listeners to accept a particular view of the disputed facts by providing additional facts that might not otherwise be known.
   - *Value:* Your goal is to persuade your audience to agree with your value judgments about an issue. Emotional appeal is critical.
   - *Policy:* Your goal is to persuade your audience to accept a specific course of action to solve the problem.

3. **What Argument type will you use to persuade your listeners and why?** _____

   _____

   a. **Induction Reasoning**: begins with a specific instance of the problem and shows that more instances of the problem exist before moving to a probable conclusion. "Symbol: triangle."
   b. **Deduction Reasoning**: Major and minor premise moves from a general statement, to narrowed statement, and logical conclusion. "Symbol: Upside down triangle."
   c. **Causal Reasoning**: argues that there is a clear relationship between two or more events and concludes that one cause triggered a specific effect/s.
   d. **Analogical**: A known problem exits. Compares at least two other proposals to solve problem that failed in order to prove that their solution is more effective.

4. **What Organizational Pattern Outline will you use and why?** _____
   (problem/solution, problem/cause/solution, causal, Monroe's motivated sequence, comparative advantage, or refutation)

5. What Fallacies are you most likely to commit in your persuasive arguments? _____

   _____

6. What strategy can you employ to avoid this/these fallacies? _____

   _____

Persuasive Speech Workshop Notes

#9 – Library Research Worksheet

Name _____   **Section** _____

Topic _____

Find seven (7) articles in the library on the subject of your next speech. The articles should be from any database in the CCC online library. Provide the source documentation details and answer the following questions about each article. ***Respond using complete sentences.***

1. Author(s):_____

    _____

    Article Title: _____

    _____

    Publication Title: _____

    _____

    Publication Details: _____

    _____

In which database did you locate this article? _____

_____

What is the general idea of this source? _____

_____

_____

_____

_____

_____

What point does the author make? _____

_____

_____

_____

_____

_____

Evaluate the quality of the source's accuracy. _____
_____
_____
_____
_____
_____

Evaluate the quality of the source's authority. _____
_____
_____
_____
_____
_____
_____

How will this source support your project?_____
_____
_____
_____
_____
_____

2. Author(s):_____
    _____

    Article Title: _____
    _____

    Publication Title: _____
    _____

    Publication Details: _____
    _____

    In which database did you locate this article? _____
    _____

What is the general idea of this source? _____

_____

_____

_____

_____

_____

What point does the author make? _____

_____

_____

_____

_____

_____

Evaluate the quality of the source's accuracy. _____

_____

_____

_____

_____

_____

Evaluate the quality of the source's authority. _____

_____

_____

_____

_____

_____

How will this source support your project?_____

_____

_____

_____

_____

_____

3. Author(s): _____

_____

Article Title: _____

_____

Publication Title: _____

_____

Publication Details: _____

_____

In which database did you locate this article? _____

_____

What is the general idea of this source? _____

_____

_____

_____

_____

_____

What point does the author make? _____

_____

_____

_____

_____

_____

Evaluate the quality of the source's accuracy. _____

_____

_____

_____

_____

_____

Evaluate the quality of the source's authority. _____

_____

_____

_____

_____

_____

How will this source support your project?_____

_____

_____

_____

_____

_____

4. Author(s):_____

    _____

    Article Title: _____

    _____

    Publication Title: _____

    _____

    Publication Details: _____

    _____

In which database did you locate this article? _____

_____

What is the general idea of this source? _____

_____

_____

_____

_____

_____

What point does the author make? _____

_____

_____

_____

_____

_____

Evaluate the quality of the source's accuracy. _____

_____

_____

_____

_____

_____

Evaluate the quality of the source's authority. _____

_____

_____

_____

_____

_____

How will this source support your project?_____

_____

_____

_____

_____

_____

5. Author(s):_____

_____

Article Title: _____

_____

Publication Title: _____

_____

Publication Details: _____

_____

In which database did you locate this article? _____

_____

What is the general idea of this source? _____

_____

_____

_____

_____

_____

What point does the author make? _____

_____

_____

_____

_____

_____

Evaluate the quality of the source's accuracy. _____

_____

_____

_____

_____

_____

Evaluate the quality of the source's authority. _____

_____

_____

_____

_____

_____

How will this source support your project?_____

_____

_____

_____

_____

6. Author(s):_____

_____

Article Title: _____

_____

Publication Title: _____

_____

Publication Details: _____

_____

In which database did you locate this article? _____

_____

What is the general idea of this source? _____

_____

_____

_____

_____

_____

What point does the author make?_____

_____

_____

_____

_____

_____

Evaluate the quality of the source's accuracy. _____
_____
_____
_____
_____
_____

Evaluate the quality of the source's authority. _____
_____
_____
_____
_____
_____

How will this source support your project?_____
_____
_____
_____
_____
_____

7. Author(s):_____
_____

Article Title: _____
_____

Publication Title: _____
_____

Publication Details: _____
_____

In which database did you locate this article? _____
_____

What is the general idea of this source? _____

_____

_____

_____

_____

_____

What point does the author make? _____

_____

_____

_____

_____

_____

Evaluate the quality of the source's accuracy. _____

_____

_____

_____

_____

_____

Evaluate the quality of the source's authority. _____

_____

_____

_____

_____

_____

How will this source support your project?_____

_____

_____

_____

_____

_____

Photo Credits

Front Matter

© iQoncept/Shutterstock.com

Chapter 1

© Bevan Goldswain, 2014. Used under license from Shutterstock, Inc.
© Tyler Olson, 2014. Used under license from Shutterstock, Inc.
© Lan Images, 2014. Used under license from Shutterstock, Inc.
© michaeljung/Shutterstock.com
© Julenochek, 2014. Used under license from Shutterstock, Inc.
© AlenD/Shutterstock.com
© PathDoc, 2014. Used under license from Shutterstock, Inc.
© CREATISTA/Shutterstock.com
© pkchai, 2014. Used under license from Shutterstock, Inc.
© George Allen Penton, 2014. Used under license from Shutterstock, Inc.
© PathDoc, 2014. Used under license from Shutterstock, Inc.
© Dean Drobot, 2014. Used under license from Shutterstock, Inc.
© Halfpoint, 2014. Used under license from Shutterstock, Inc.
© Nik Merkulov, 2014. Used under license from Shutterstock, Inc.
© Viktor88, 2014. Used under license from Shutterstock, Inc.
© CoraMax, 2014. Used under license from Shutterstock, Inc.
© CoraMax, 2014. Used under license from Shutterstock, Inc.
Photo courtesy of the author.
© vita khorzhevska, 2014. Used under license from Shutterstock, Inc.
© michaeljung/Shutterstock.com
© glenda, 2014. Used under license from Shutterstock, Inc.
© Monkey Business Images, 2014. Used under license from Shutterstock, Inc.
© Monkey Business Images, 2014. Used under license from Shutterstock, Inc.
© JPC-PROD, 2014. Used under license from Shutterstock, Inc.
© Maslowski Marcin/Shutterstock.com
© Mega Pixel/Shutterstock.com
© Pokomeda/Shutterstock.com

Chapter 2

Chapter 3

Chapter 4

Chapter 5